OCT - - 2022

ASTONISHING TIMES

™

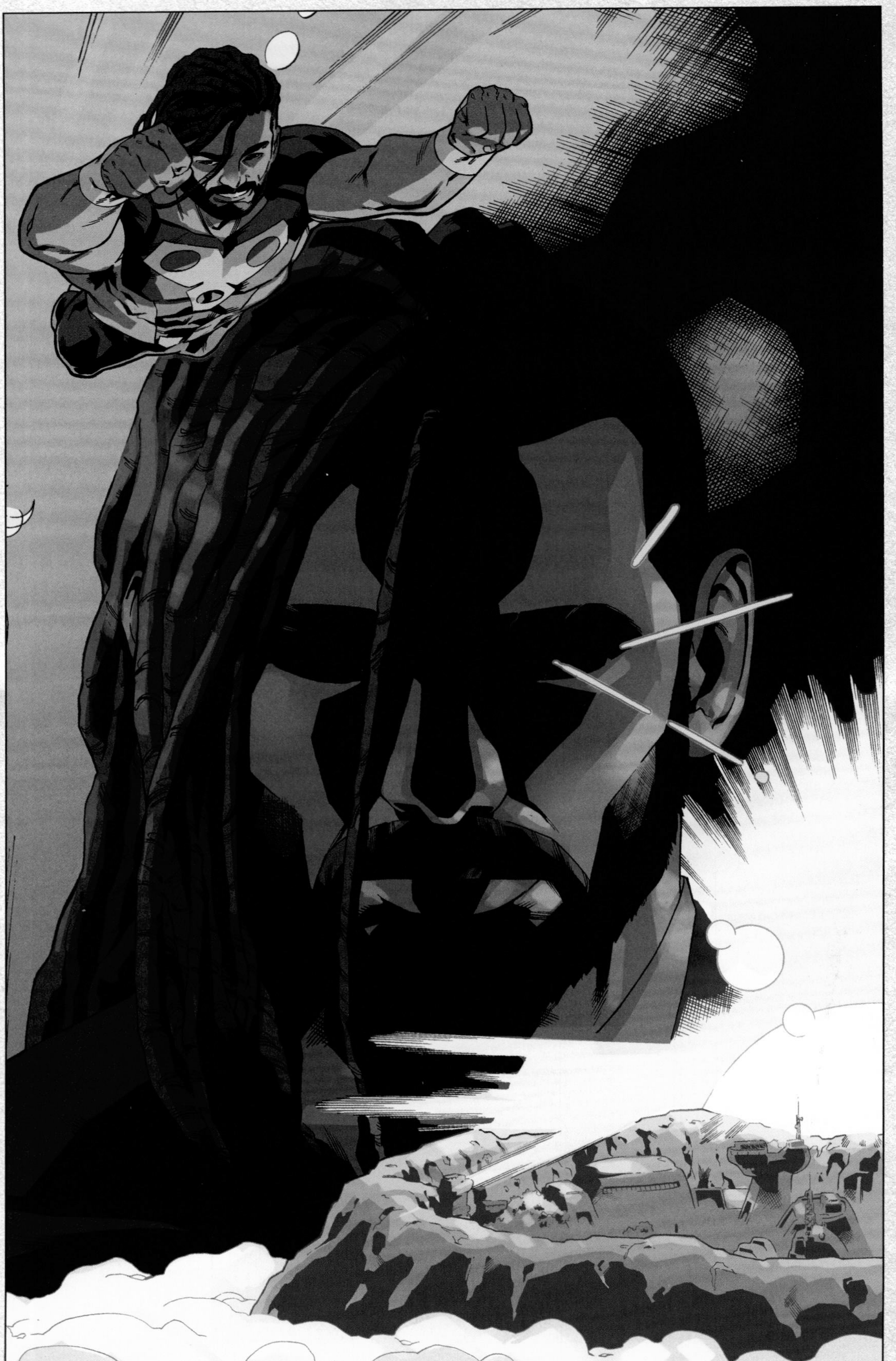

ASTONISHING TIMES ™

WRITTEN BY
**FRANK J. BARBIERE &
ARRIS QUINONES**

ART BY
RUAIRÍ COLEMAN

COLOR ART BY
LAUREN AFFE

LETTERS BY
TAYLOR ESPOSITO

ORIGINAL DESIGN BY
DYLAN TODD

COVER BY
**RUAIRÍ COLEMAN *with*
LAUREN AFFE**

DARK HORSE BOOKS

DARK HORSE TEAM

PRESIDENT AND PUBLISHER
MIKE RICHARDSON

EDITOR
DANIEL CHABON

ASSISTANT EDITORS
**CHUCK HOWITT *and*
MISHA GEHR**

DIGITAL ART TECHNICIAN
JASON RICKERD

DESIGNER
KATHLEEN BARNETT

SPECIAL THANKS TO
**DAVID STEINBERGER, CHIP
MOSHER, *and* BRYCE GOLD**

NEIL HANKERSON EXECUTIVE VICE PRESIDENT • **TOM WEDDLE** CHIEF FINANCIAL OFFICER • **DALE LAFOUNTAIN** CHIEF INFORMATION OFFICER • **TIM WIESCH** VICE PRESIDENT OF LICENSING • **MATT PARKINSON** VICE PRESIDENT OF MARKETING • **VANESSA TODD-HOLMES** VICE PRESIDENT OF PRODUCTION AND SCHEDULING • **MARK BERNARDI** VICE PRESIDENT OF BOOK TRADE AND DIGITAL SALES • **RANDY LAHRMAN** VICE PRESIDENT OF PRODUCT DEVELOPMENT • **KEN LIZZI** GENERAL COUNSEL • **DAVE MARSHALL** EDITOR IN CHIEF • **DAVEY ESTRADA** EDITORIAL DIRECTOR • **CHRIS WARNER** SENIOR BOOKS EDITOR • **CARY GRAZZINI** DIRECTOR OF SPECIALTY PROJECTS • **LIA RIBACCHI** ART DIRECTOR • **MATT DRYER** DIRECTOR OF DIGITAL ART AND PREPRESS • **MICHAEL GOMBOS** SENIOR DIRECTOR OF LICENSED PUBLICATIONS • **KARI YADRO** DIRECTOR OF CUSTOM PROGRAMS • **KARI TORSON** DIRECTOR OF INTERNATIONAL LICENSING

PUBLISHED BY DARK HORSE BOOKS
A DIVISION OF DARK HORSE COMICS LLC
10956 SE MAIN STREET
MILWAUKIE, OR 97222

FIRST EDITION: AUGUST 2022

TRADE PAPERBACK ISBN: 978-1-50673-083-7

1 3 5 7 9 10 8 6 4 2
PRINTED IN CHINA

MIX
Paper from responsible sources
FSC® C169962

COMIC SHOP LOCATOR SERVICE: COMICSHOPLOCATOR.COM

ASTONISHING TIMES™

DEDICATIONS

Dedicated to my wife Amber and
two daughters, Olivia and Ella.
With a special thanks to Ryan
and Tim Connolly.

ARRIS

For my wife Nicole and our
beautiful children.

RUAIRÍ

For everyone who
writes about comics.

FRANK

INTRODUCTION

BY GEORGE GENE GUSTINES

Y'all are in for a treat!

Astonishing Times hooked me from the first issue and kept getting better. I love superhero stories. I love true-to-the-ear dialogue and beautiful, expressive art. I love that Noah Sanz, the main character of this story, is a journalist and living my dream job: writing full time about the heroes he's passionate about.

When Frank asked me to write this intro, I was honored and jumped at the opportunity. His suggested topic was a challenge, however: to write about my experience as a journalist and why I've been so inspired by the superhero genre.

I wish I could say my love of superheroes led to my career at the *New York Times*, but it is not quite so direct. My introduction to superheroes began with *Batman* '66 reruns in the 1970s, and soon after, I quickly discovered *Super Friends*. I often think about the Age of Geek we currently live in, but growing up in the '70s and '80s gave us a taste of things to come: the *Spider-Man and His Amazing Friends* cartoon, Shazam in animated form, and the live-action *Hulk, Spider-Man,* and *Wonder Woman* shows, just to name a few.

Discovering comics—*Justice League of America* #200 is one of my touchstones, and then there are my cherished *New Teen Titans*—is what cemented me as a fan. It led me to an amateur press association, where I tried my hand at drawing (mere doodles), writing (terrible action scenes), and commentary (I showed potential).

My career at the *Times* started in 1990, but it was basically an afterschool job. I didn't have an inkling of what I wanted to do when I grew up. But the job kept getting extended, and I learned a lot on the run. There's nothing like taking feeds from reporters in the field to teach you to type fast and get an inkling of how a story is structured. I had my first comics-related byline in 2002, and seeing my name in print was intoxicating. I learned that I enjoy spreading the word about comics to folks who are not part of our tribe. I wish I had started sooner—I missed reporting on the death of Superman and the birth of Image Comics, among other stories—but I've gotten to write about many worthy comics (800+ bylines). It is an honor and a privilege that I take seriously.

Bravo to Frank Barbiere and Arris Quinones, Ruairí Coleman, Lauren Affe, Taylor Esposito, and Dylan Todd for all they accomplished in five issues. I hope we get to revisit these characters.

To echo protagonist Noah, "We live in astonishing times. I can't wait to see where we go from here."

George Gene Gustines is a senior editor at the New York Times. *He began writing about the comic book industry in 2002 and hopes to continue for many more years. He also wants to land a comic book story with his byline on the front page.*

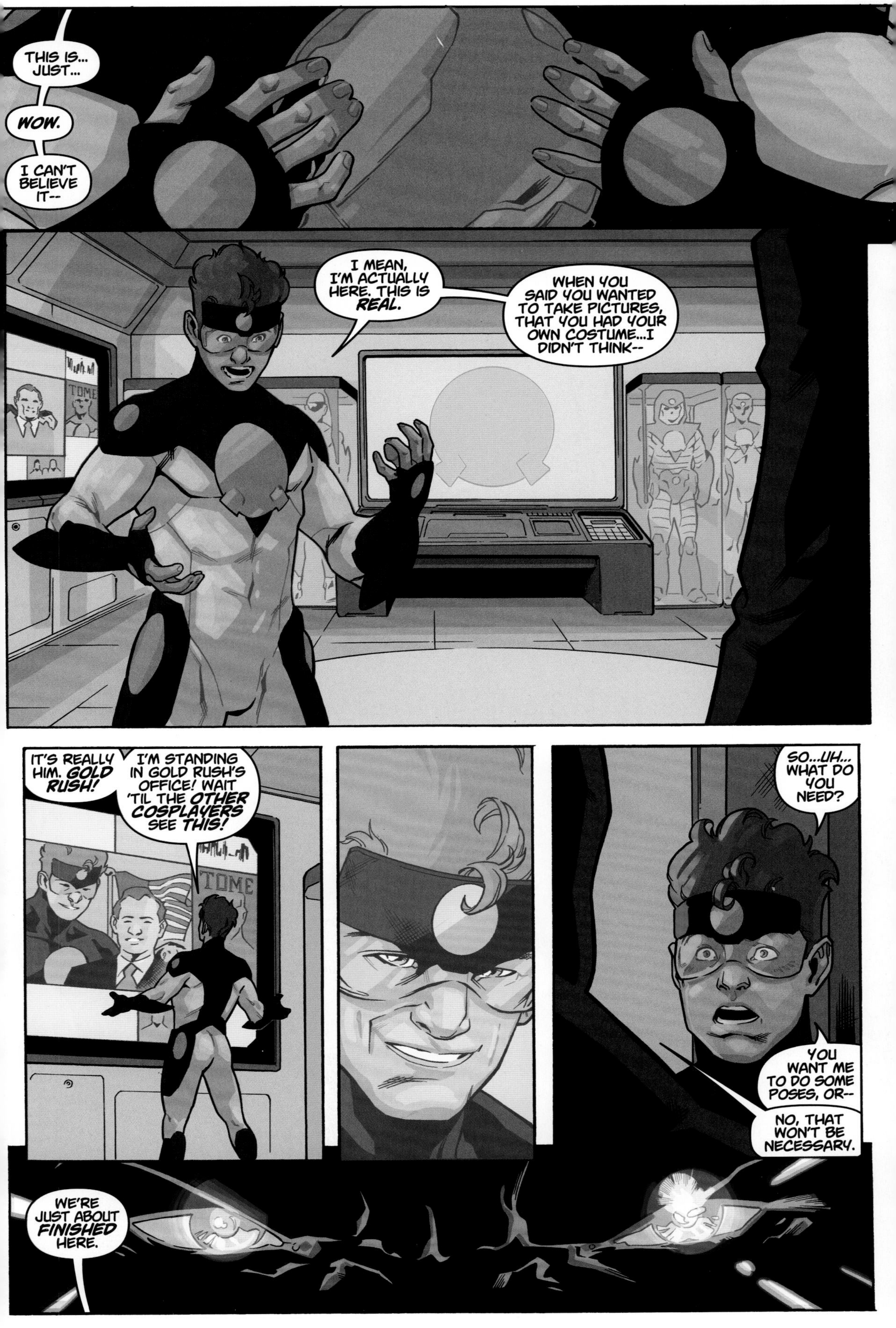
THIS IS... JUST...
WOW.
I CAN'T BELIEVE IT--
I MEAN, I'M ACTUALLY HERE. THIS IS REAL.
WHEN YOU SAID YOU WANTED TO TAKE PICTURES, THAT YOU HAD YOUR OWN COSTUME...I DIDN'T THINK--
TOME
IT'S REALLY HIM. GOLD RUSH!
I'M STANDING IN GOLD RUSH'S OFFICE! WAIT 'TIL THE OTHER COSPLAYERS SEE THIS!
TOME
SO...UH... WHAT DO YOU NEED?
YOU WANT ME TO DO SOME POSES, OR--
NO, THAT WON'T BE NECESSARY.
WE'RE JUST ABOUT FINISHED HERE.

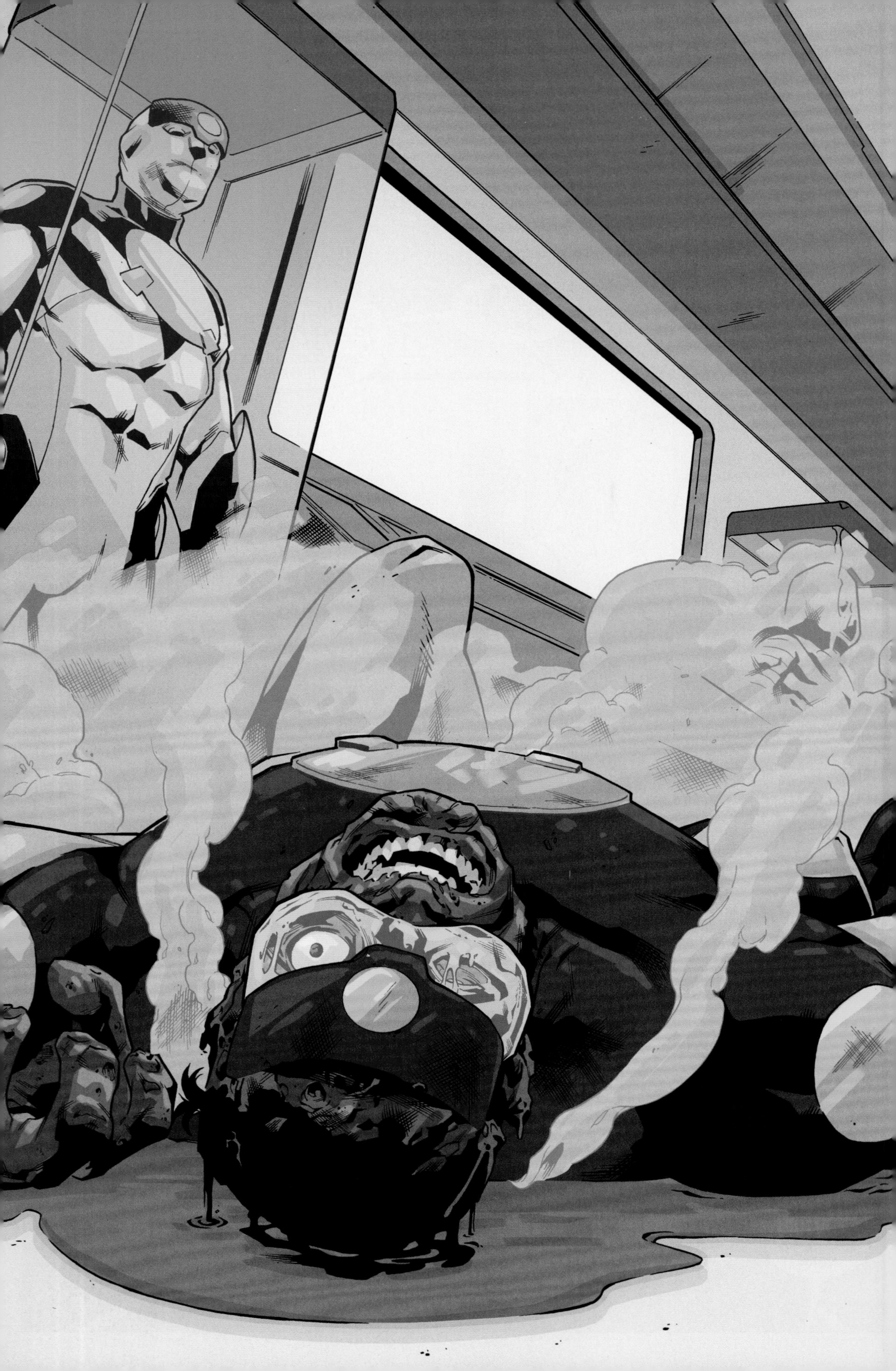

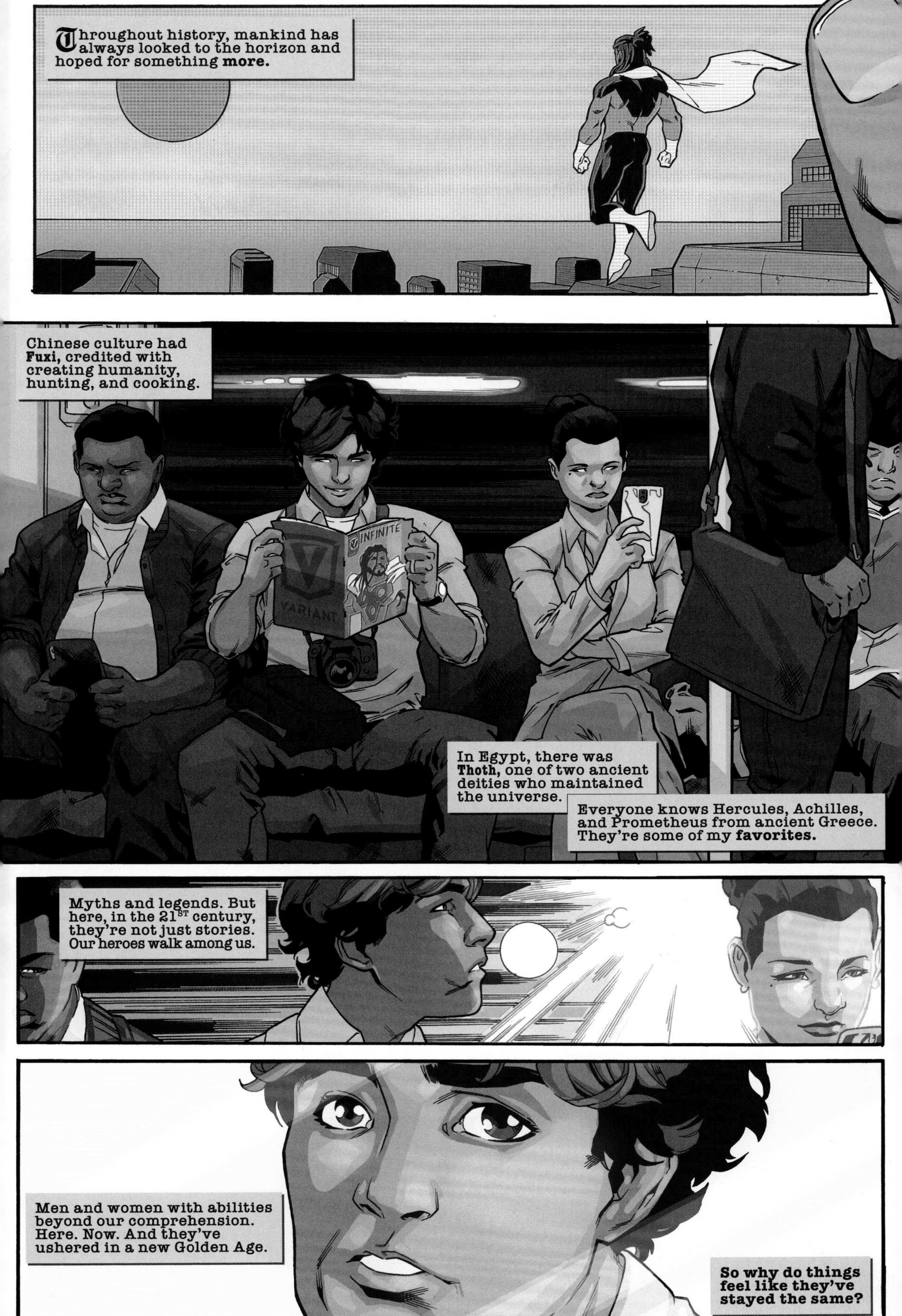
Throughout history, mankind has always looked to the horizon and hoped for something **more.**
Chinese culture had **Fuxi**, credited with creating humanity, hunting, and cooking.
VARIANT
INFINITE
In Egypt, there was **Thoth**, one of two ancient deities who maintained the universe.
Everyone knows Hercules, Achilles, and Prometheus from ancient Greece. They're some of my **favorites.**
Myths and legends. But here, in the 21ST century, they're not just stories. Our heroes walk among us.
Men and women with abilities beyond our comprehension. Here. Now. And they've ushered in a new Golden Age.
So why do things feel like they've stayed the same?

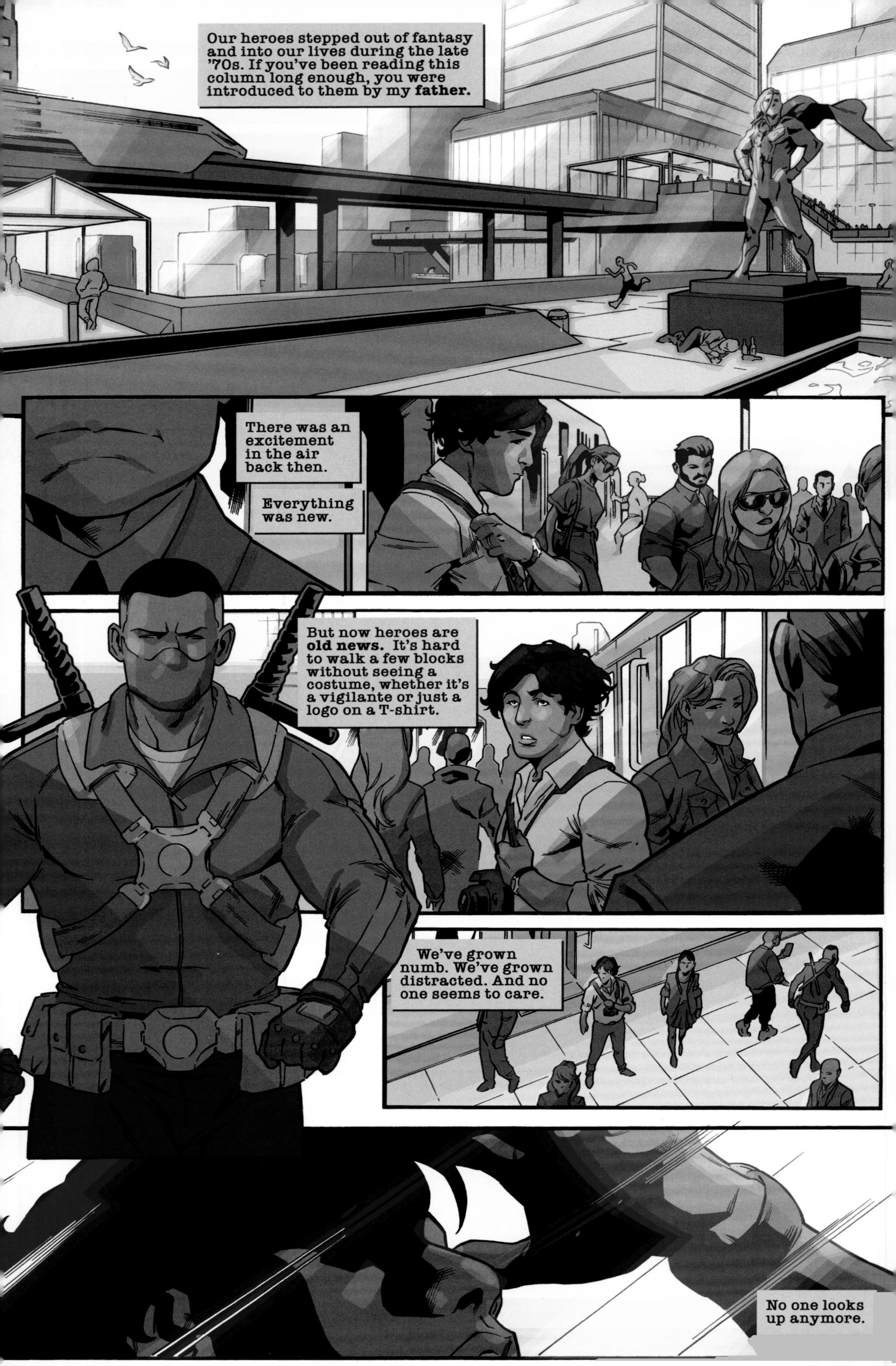
Our heroes stepped out of fantasy and into our lives during the late '70s. If you've been reading this column long enough, you were introduced to them by my **father.**
There was an excitement in the air back then.
Everything was new.
But now heroes are **old news.** It's hard to walk a few blocks without seeing a costume, whether it's a vigilante or just a logo on a T-shirt.
We've grown numb. We've grown distracted. And no one seems to care.
No one looks up anymore.

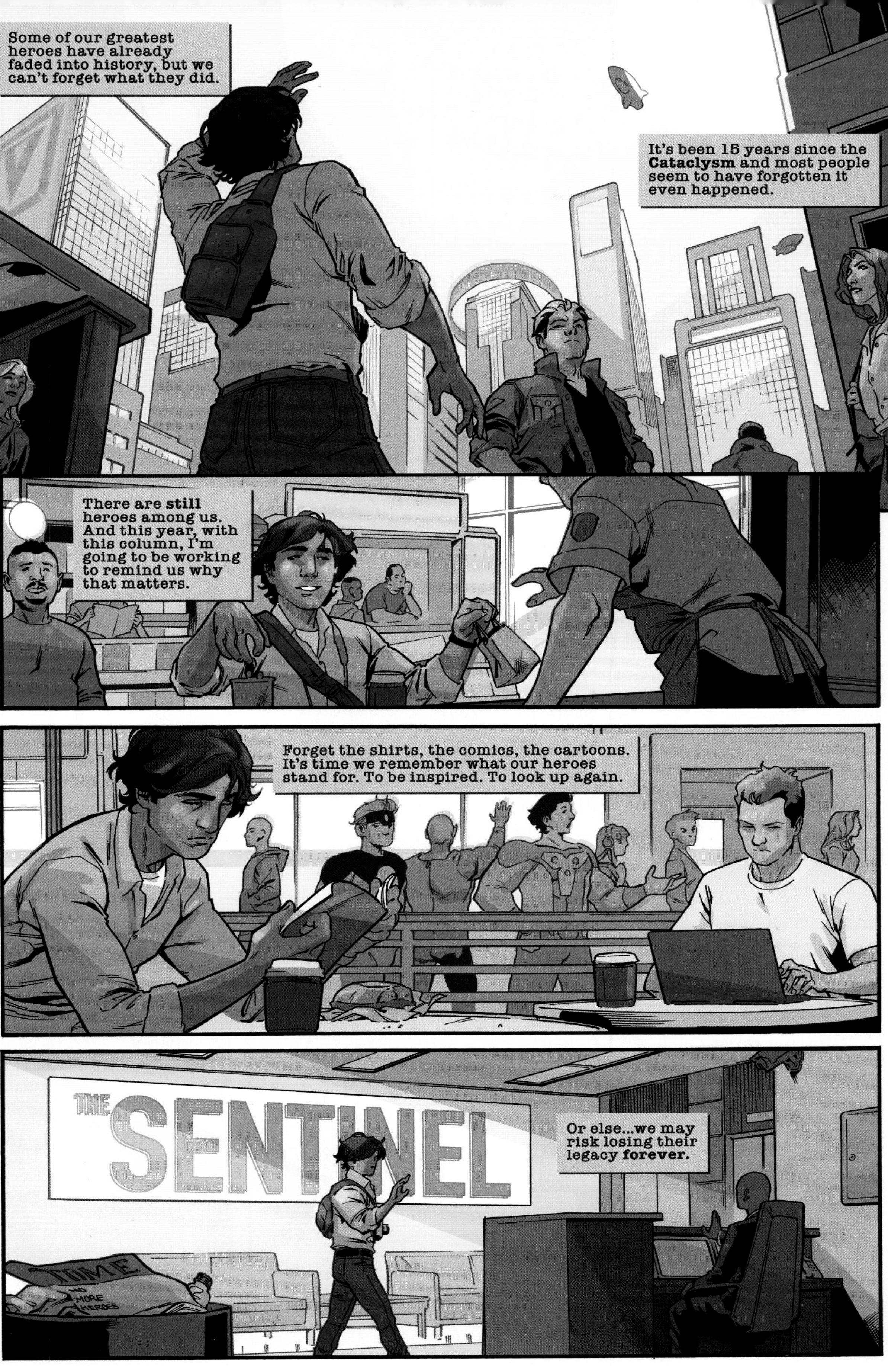
Some of our greatest heroes have already faded into history, but we can't forget what they did.
It's been 15 years since the **Cataclysm** and most people seem to have forgotten it even happened.
There are **still** heroes among us. And this year, with this column, I'm going to be working to remind us why that matters.
Forget the shirts, the comics, the cartoons. It's time we remember what our heroes stand for. To be inspired. To look up again.
THE SENTINEL
TOME
NO MORE HEROES
Or else...we may risk losing their legacy **forever.**

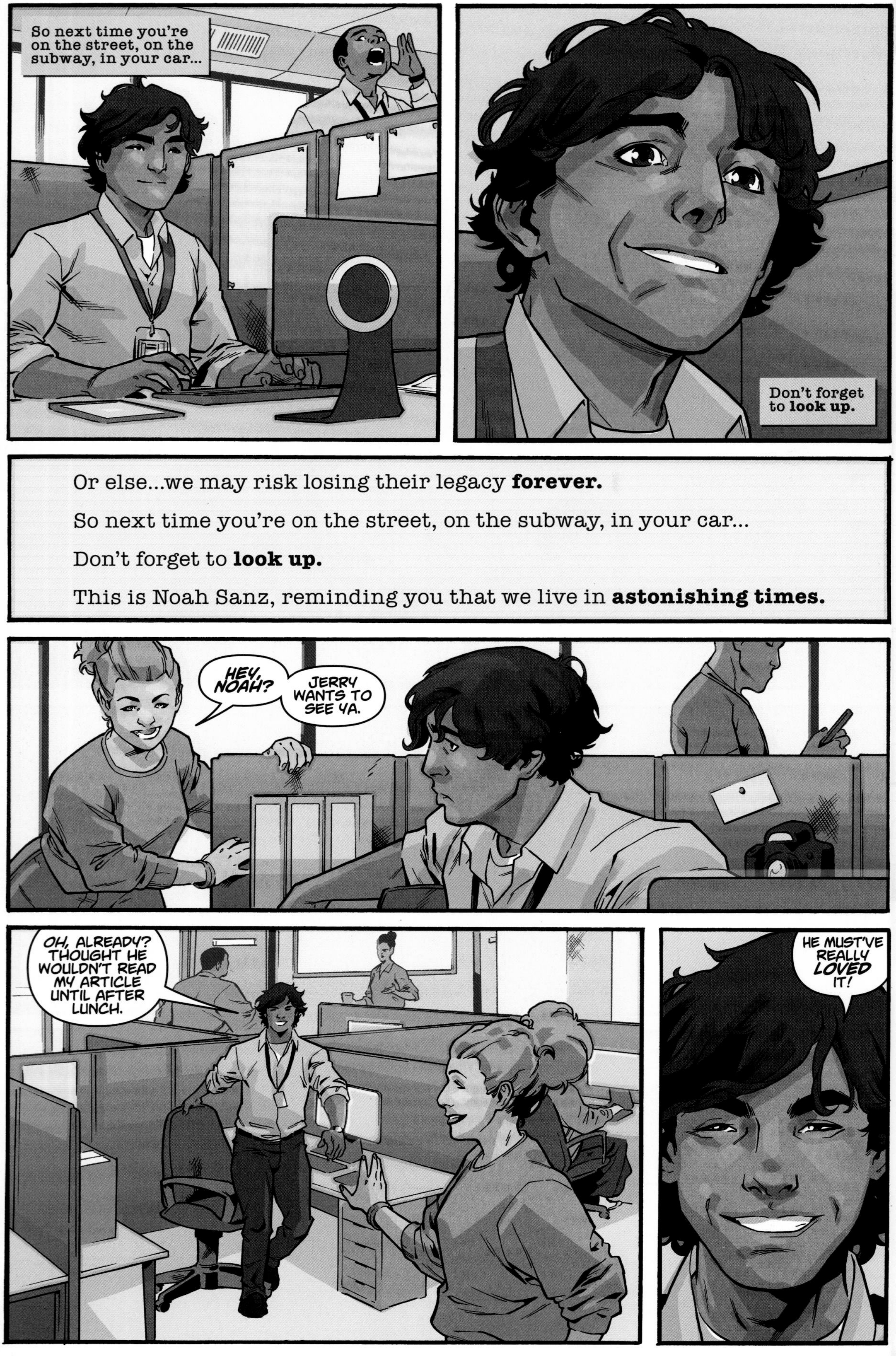

So next time you're on the street, on the subway, in your car...
Don't forget to **look up.**
Or else...we may risk losing their legacy **forever.**
So next time you're on the street, on the subway, in your car...
Don't forget to **look up.**
This is Noah Sanz, reminding you that we live in **astonishing times.**
HEY, NOAH?
JERRY WANTS TO SEE YA.
OH, ALREADY? THOUGHT HE WOULDN'T READ MY ARTICLE UNTIL AFTER LUNCH.
HE MUST'VE REALLY *LOVED* IT!

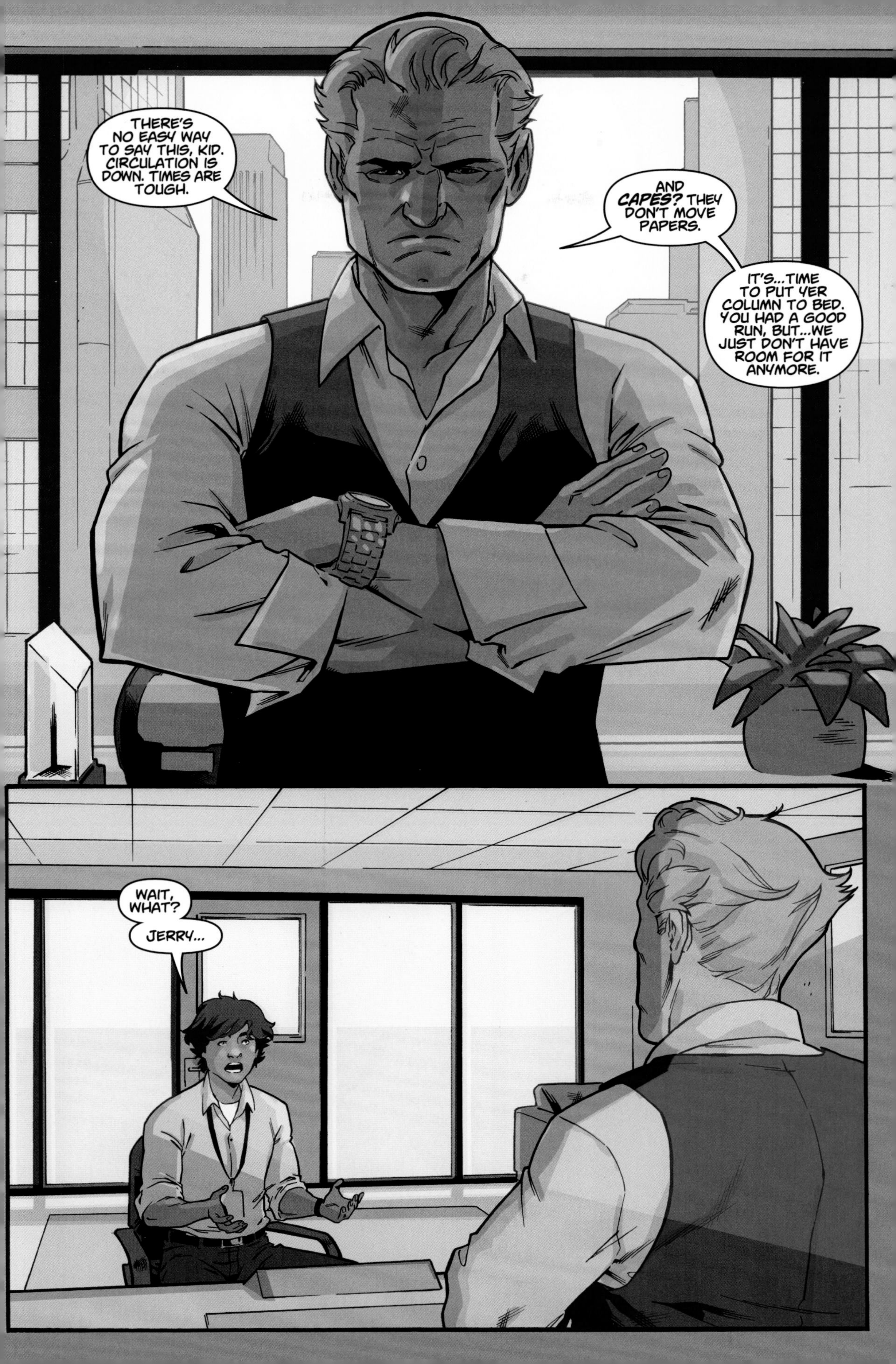
THERE'S NO EASY WAY TO SAY THIS, KID. CIRCULATION IS DOWN. TIMES ARE TOUGH.
AND CAPES? THEY DON'T MOVE PAPERS.
IT'S...TIME TO PUT YER COLUMN TO BED. YOU HAD A GOOD RUN, BUT...WE JUST DON'T HAVE ROOM FOR IT ANYMORE.
WAIT, WHAT?
JERRY...

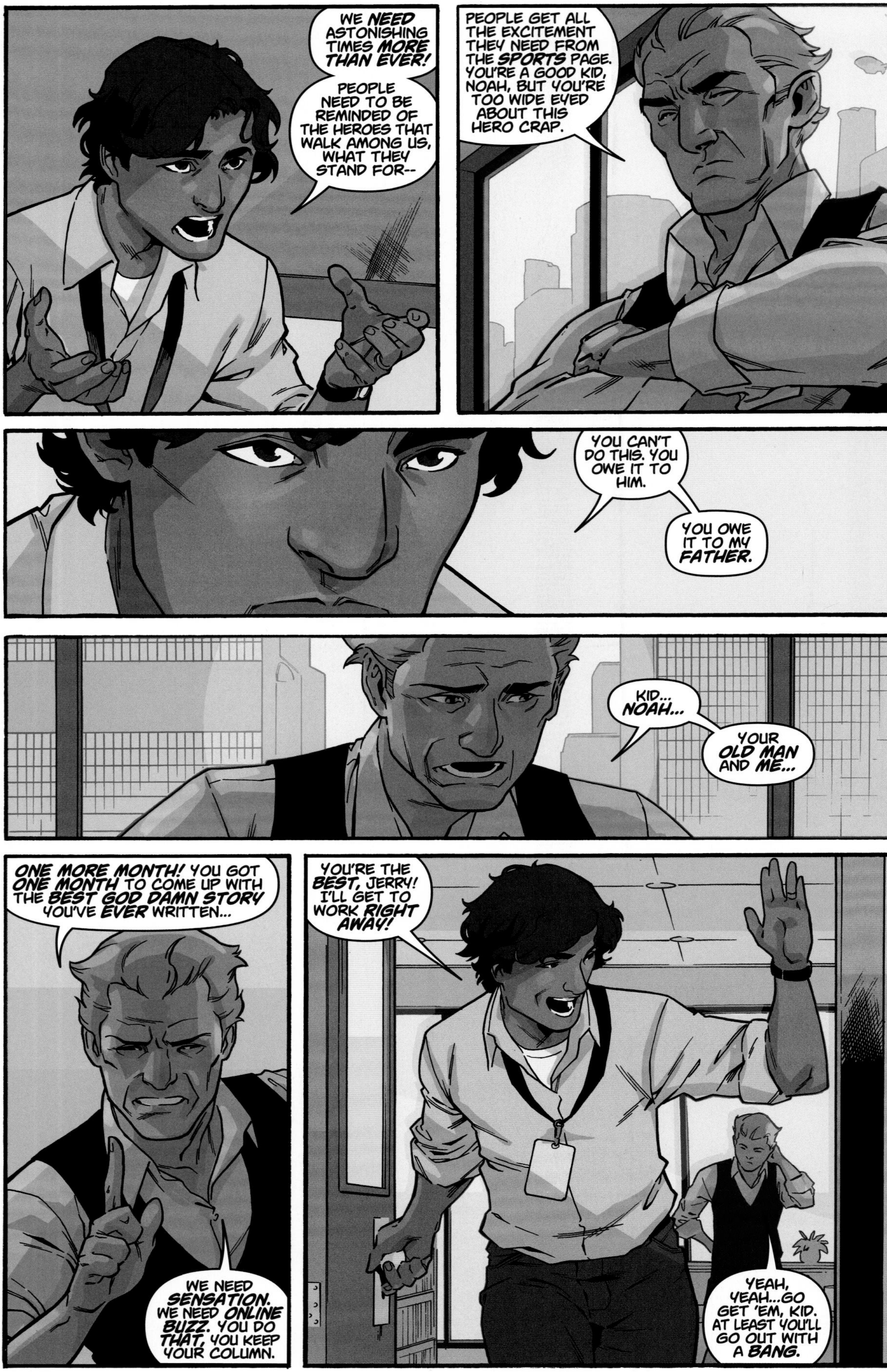

WE NEED ASTONISHING TIMES MORE THAN EVER!
PEOPLE NEED TO BE REMINDED OF THE HEROES THAT WALK AMONG US, WHAT THEY STAND FOR--
PEOPLE GET ALL THE EXCITEMENT THEY NEED FROM THE SPORTS PAGE. YOU'RE A GOOD KID, NOAH, BUT YOU'RE TOO WIDE EYED ABOUT THIS HERO CRAP.
YOU CAN'T DO THIS. YOU OWE IT TO HIM.
YOU OWE IT TO MY FATHER.
KID... NOAH...
YOUR OLD MAN AND ME...
ONE MORE MONTH! YOU GOT ONE MONTH TO COME UP WITH THE BEST GOD DAMN STORY YOU'VE EVER WRITTEN...
WE NEED SENSATION. WE NEED ONLINE BUZZ. YOU DO THAT, YOU KEEP YOUR COLUMN.
YOU'RE THE BEST, JERRY! I'LL GET TO WORK RIGHT AWAY!
YEAH, YEAH...GO GET 'EM, KID. AT LEAST YOU'LL GO OUT WITH A BANG.

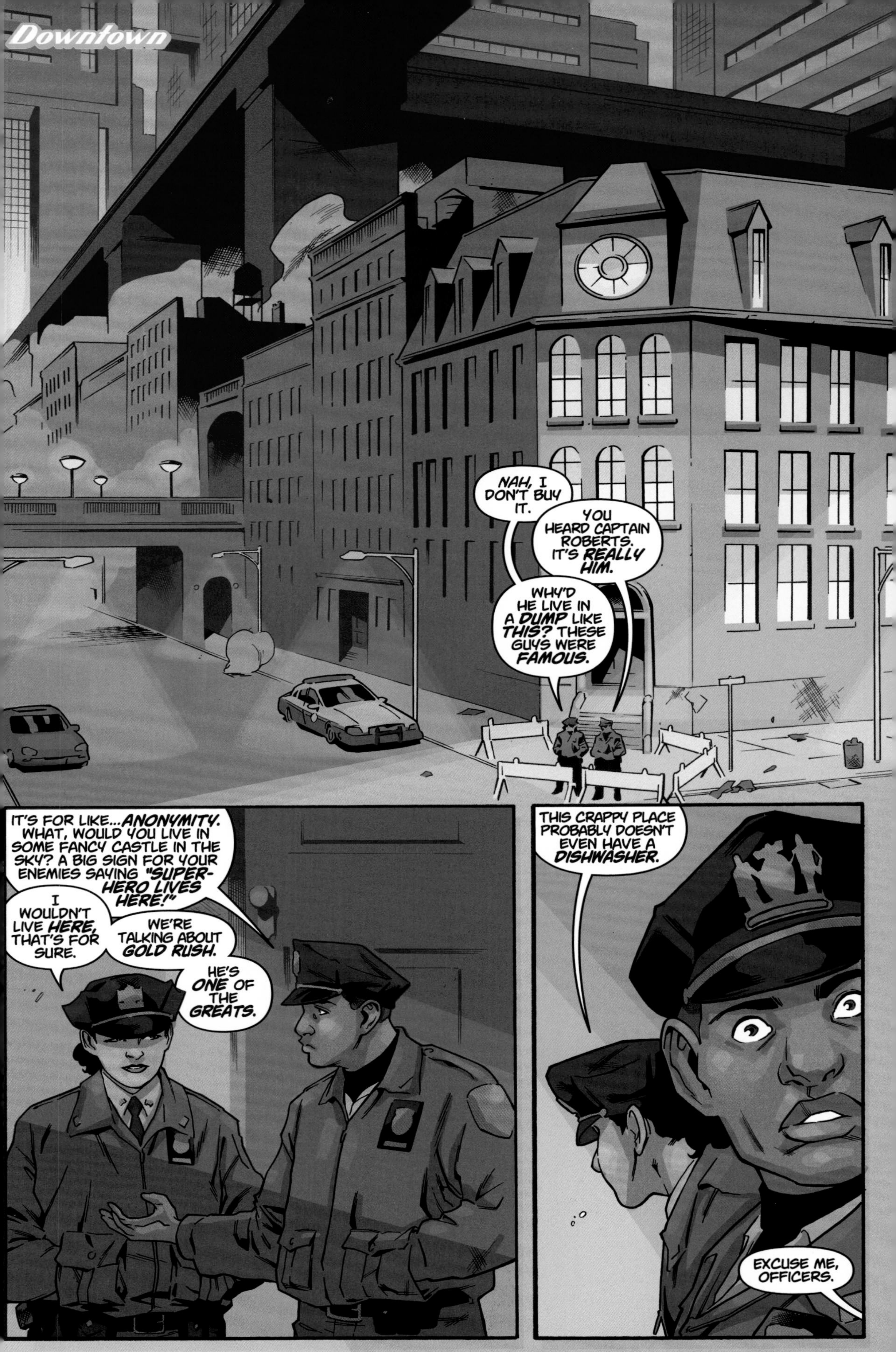
Downtown
NAH, I DON'T BUY IT.
YOU HEARD CAPTAIN ROBERTS. IT'S REALLY HIM.
WHY'D HE LIVE IN A DUMP LIKE THIS? THESE GUYS WERE FAMOUS.
IT'S FOR LIKE...ANONYMITY. WHAT, WOULD YOU LIVE IN SOME FANCY CASTLE IN THE SKY? A BIG SIGN FOR YOUR ENEMIES SAYING "SUPER-HERO LIVES HERE!"
I WOULDN'T LIVE HERE, THAT'S FOR SURE.
WE'RE TALKING ABOUT GOLD RUSH.
HE'S ONE OF THE GREATS.
THIS CRAPPY PLACE PROBABLY DOESN'T EVEN HAVE A DISHWASHER.
EXCUSE ME, OFFICERS.

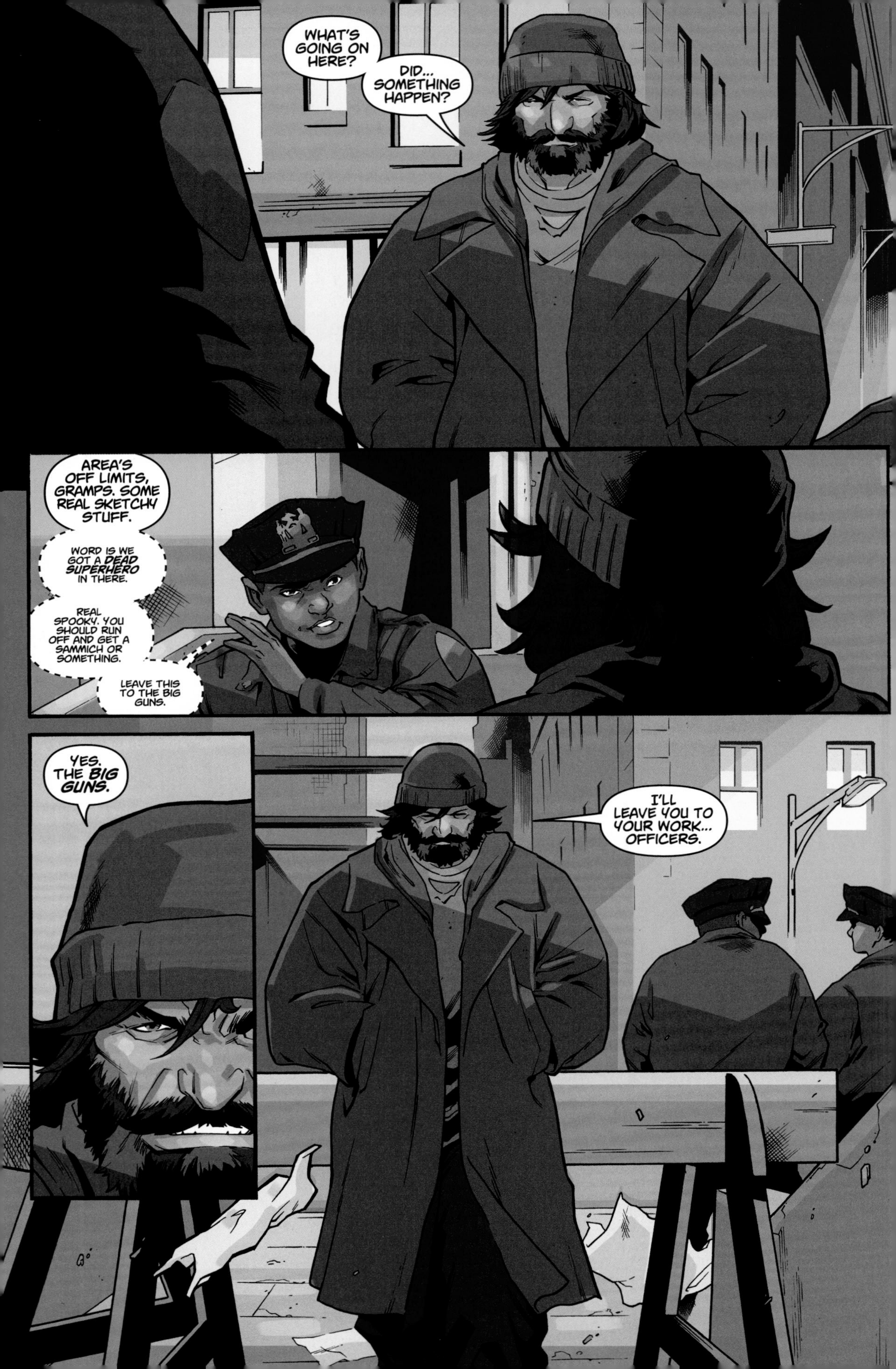
WHAT'S GOING ON HERE?
DID... SOMETHING HAPPEN?
AREA'S OFF LIMITS, GRAMPS. SOME REAL SKETCHY STUFF.
WORD IS WE GOT A *DEAD SUPERHERO* IN THERE.
REAL SPOOKY. YOU SHOULD RUN OFF AND GET A SAMMICH OR SOMETHING.
LEAVE THIS TO THE BIG GUNS.
YES. THE *BIG GUNS.*
I'LL LEAVE YOU TO YOUR WORK... OFFICERS.

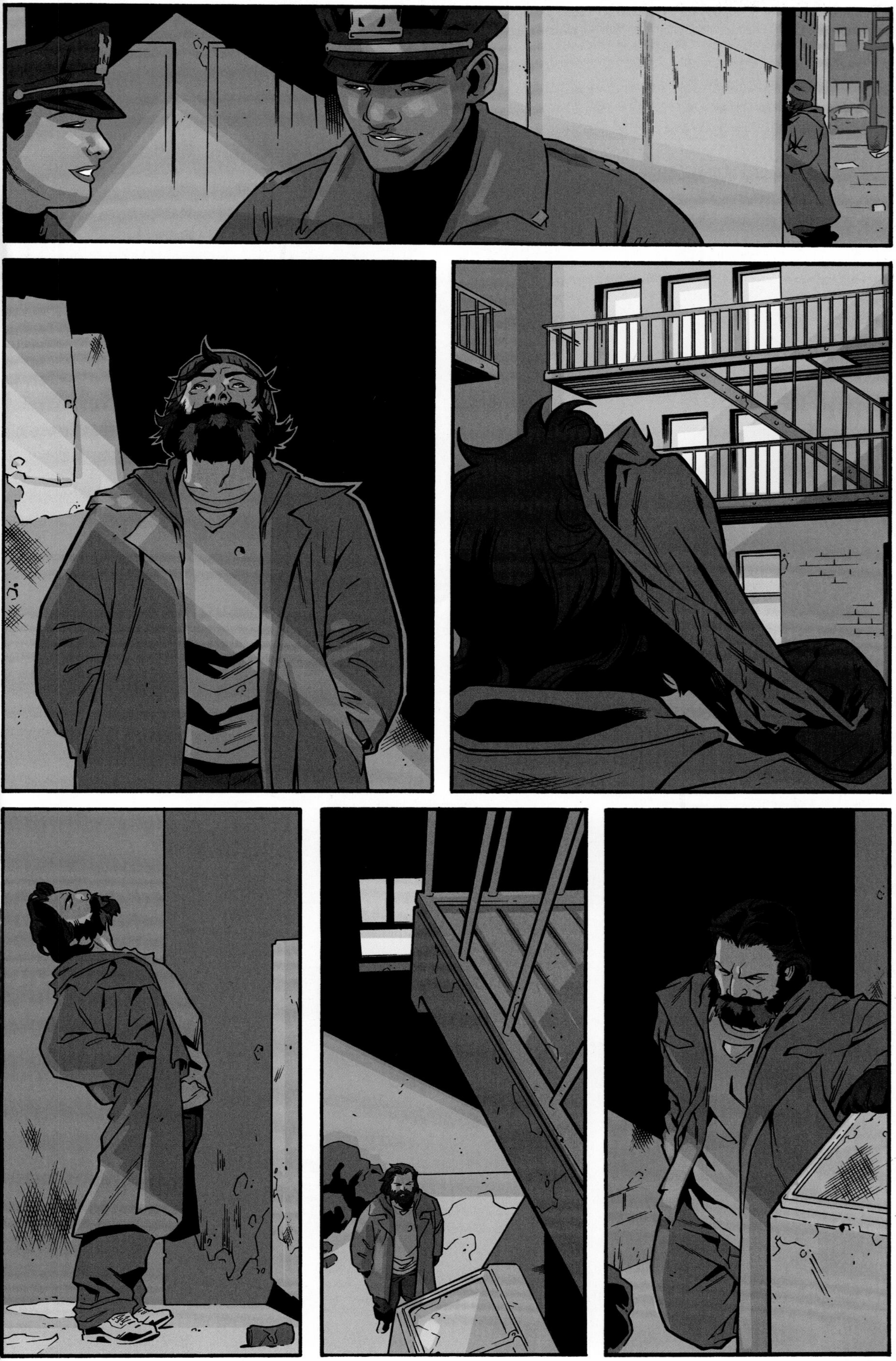

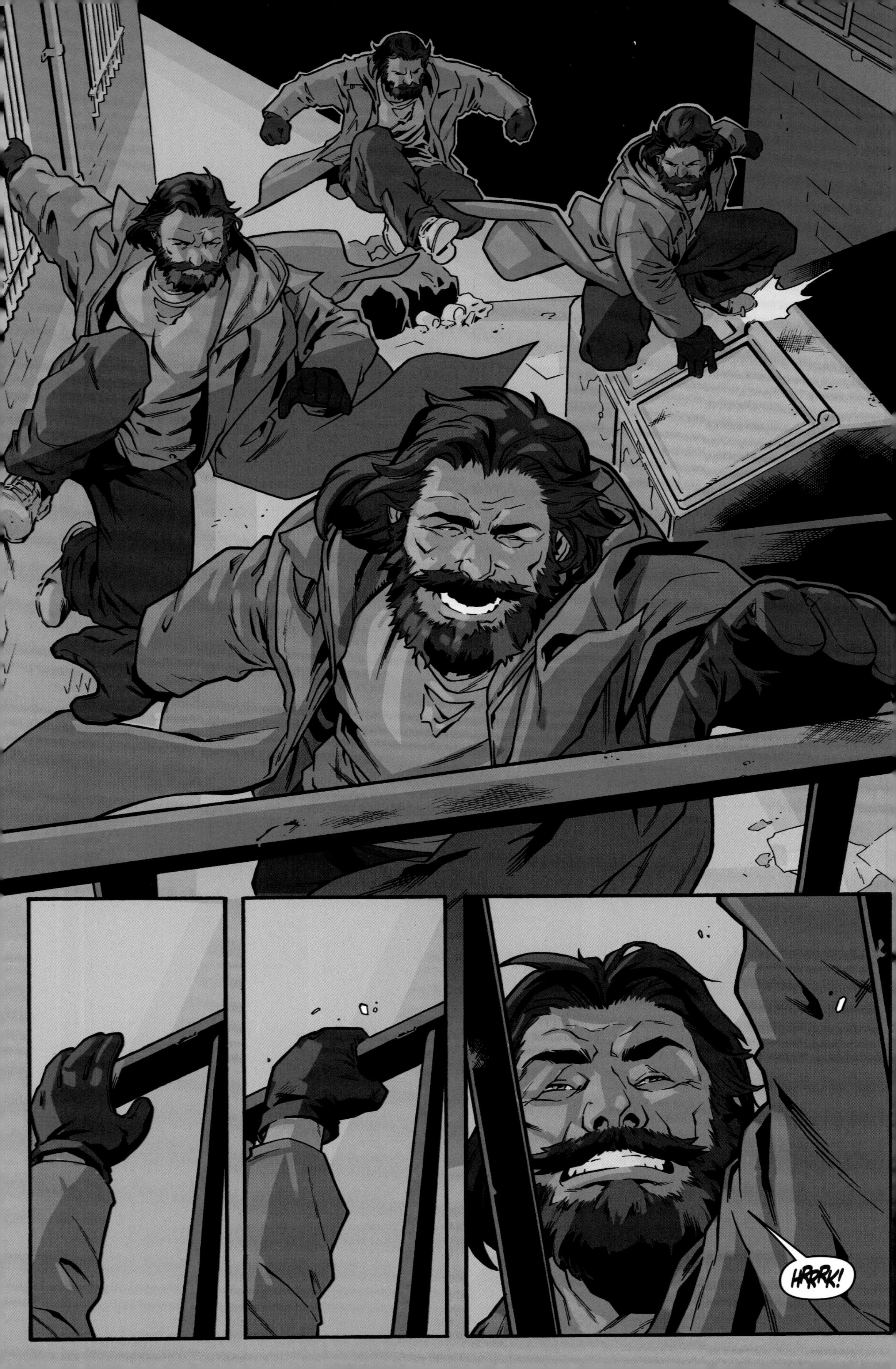
HRRRK!

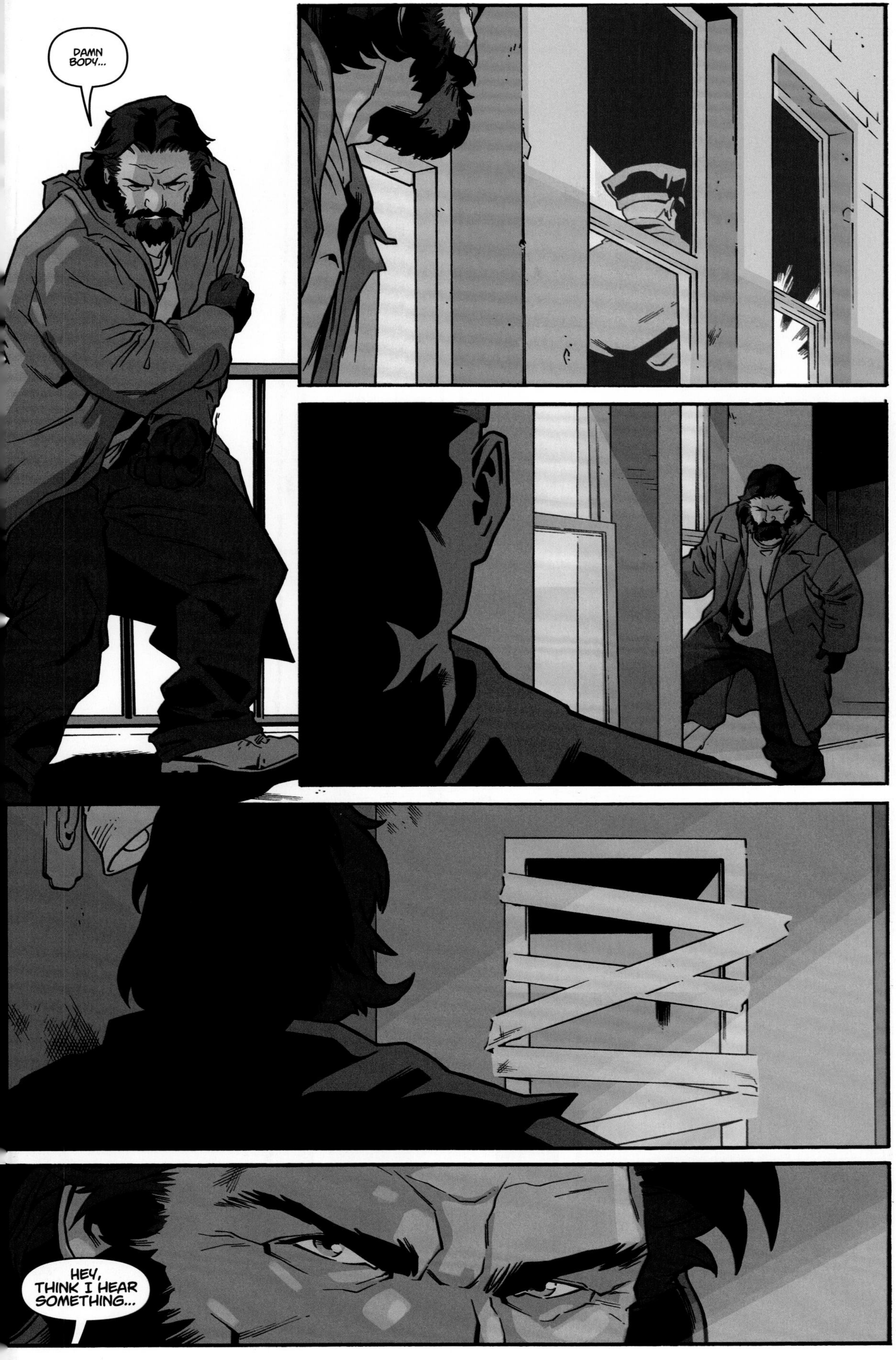
DAMN BODY...
HEY, THINK I HEAR SOMETHING...

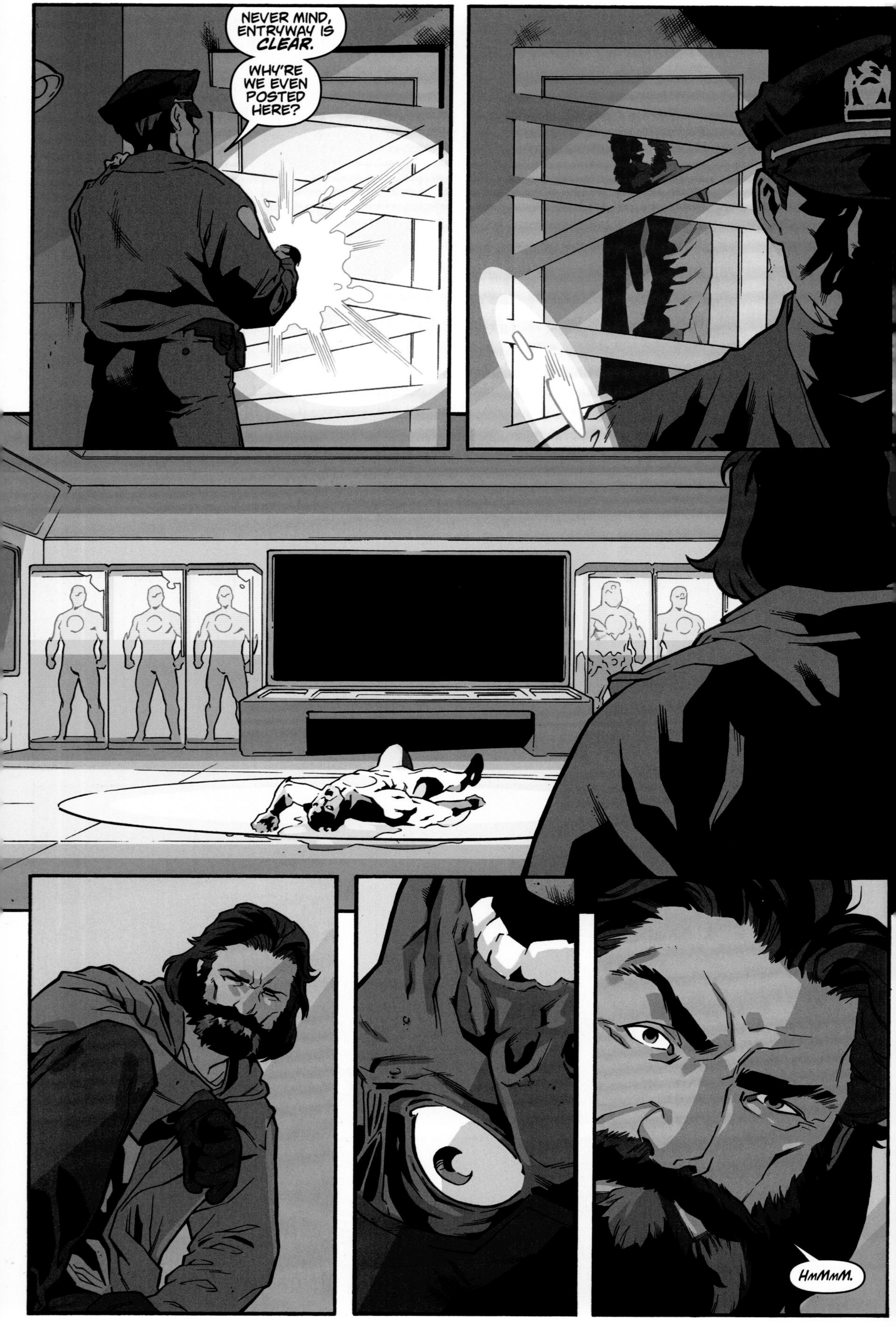
NEVER MIND, ENTRYWAY IS CLEAR.
WHY'RE WE EVEN POSTED HERE?
HmMmM.

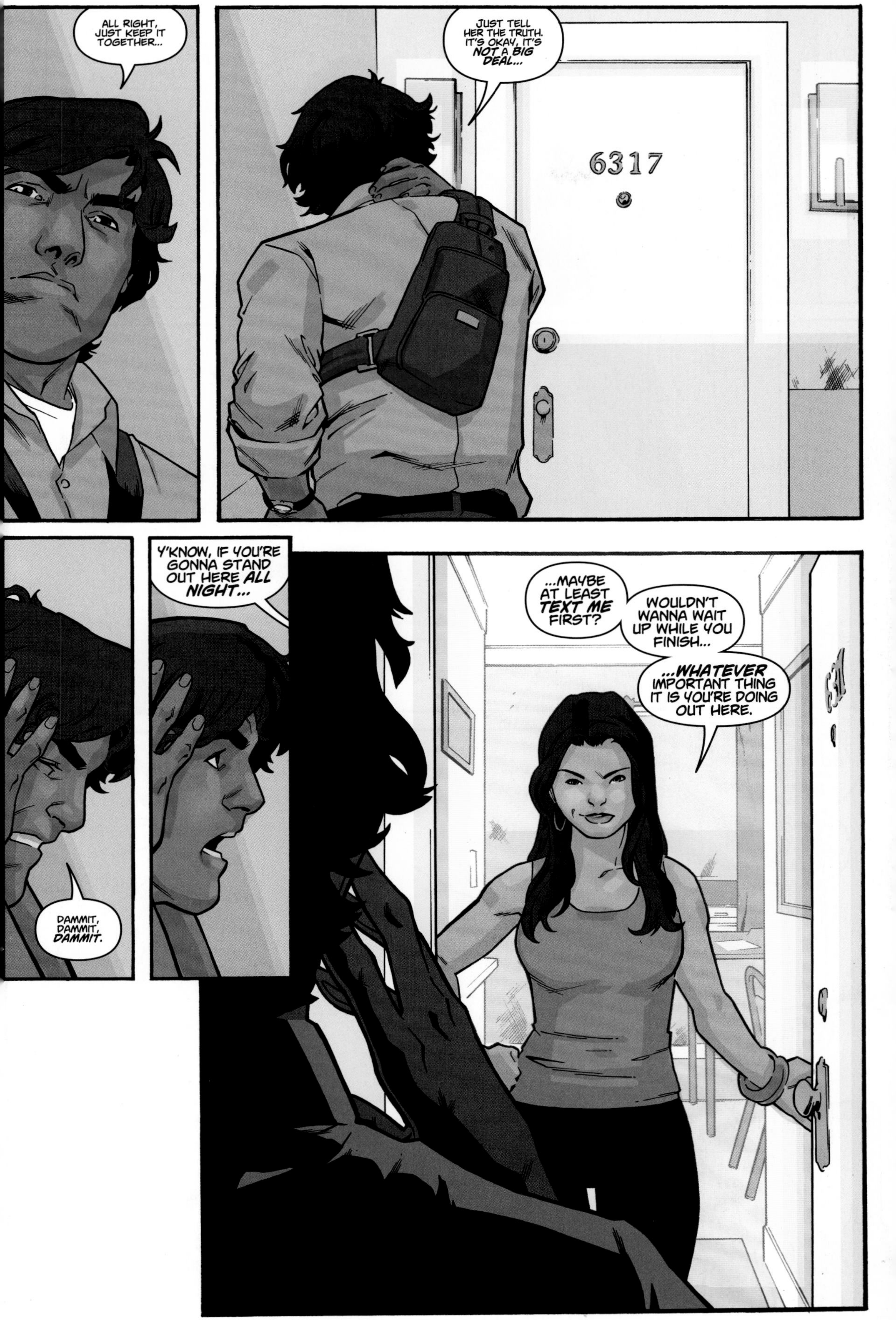
ALL RIGHT, JUST KEEP IT TOGETHER...
JUST TELL HER THE TRUTH. IT'S OKAY, IT'S NOT A BIG DEAL...
6317
DAMMIT, DAMMIT, DAMMIT.
Y'KNOW, IF YOU'RE GONNA STAND OUT HERE ALL NIGHT...
...MAYBE AT LEAST TEXT ME FIRST?
WOULDN'T WANNA WAIT UP WHILE YOU FINISH...
...WHATEVER IMPORTANT THING IT IS YOU'RE DOING OUT HERE.

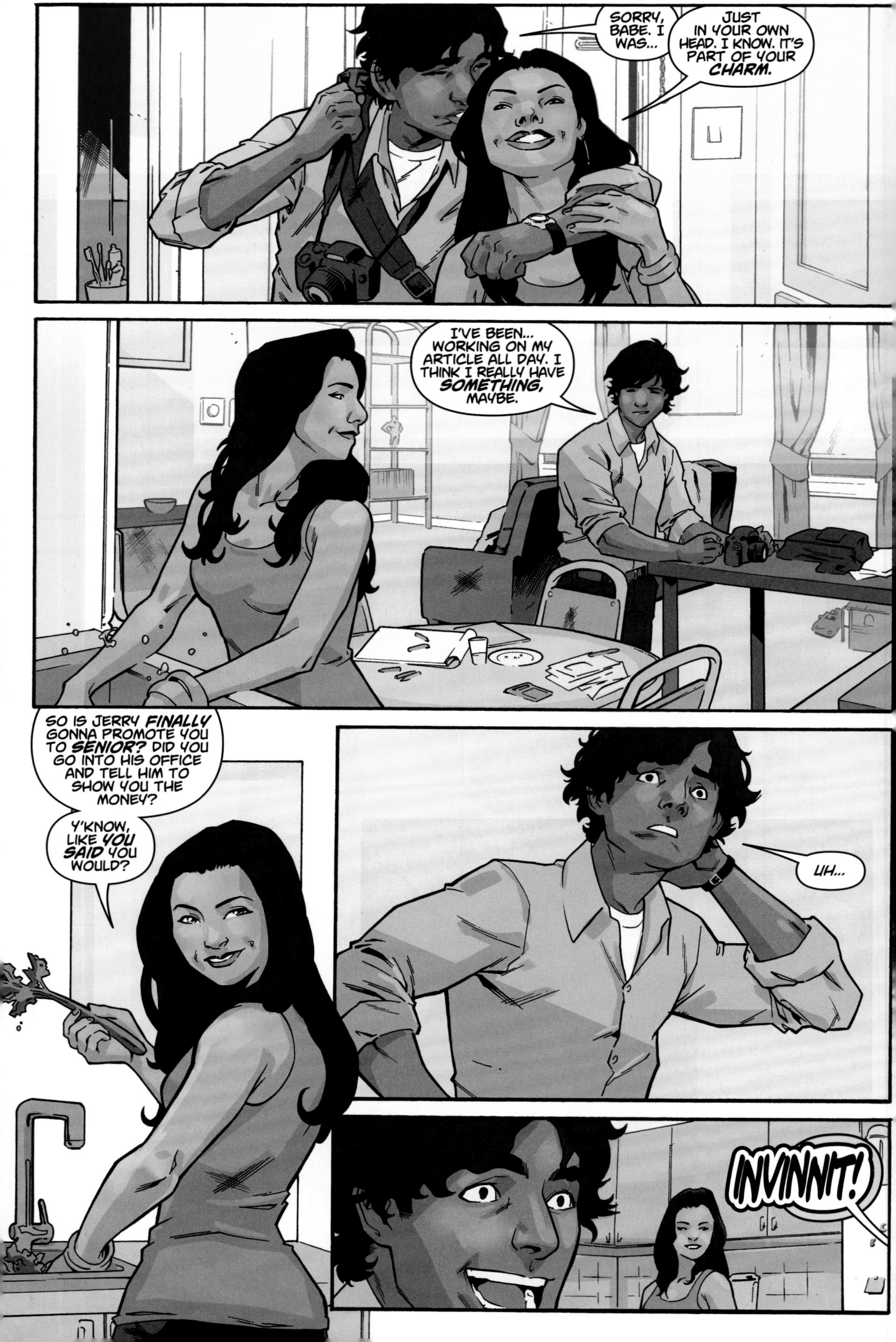
SORRY, BABE. I WAS...
JUST IN YOUR OWN HEAD. I KNOW. IT'S PART OF YOUR CHARM.
I'VE BEEN... WORKING ON MY ARTICLE ALL DAY. I THINK I REALLY HAVE SOMETHING, MAYBE.
SO IS JERRY FINALLY GONNA PROMOTE YOU TO SENIOR? DID YOU GO INTO HIS OFFICE AND TELL HIM TO SHOW YOU THE MONEY?
Y'KNOW, LIKE YOU SAID YOU WOULD?
UH...
INVINNIT!

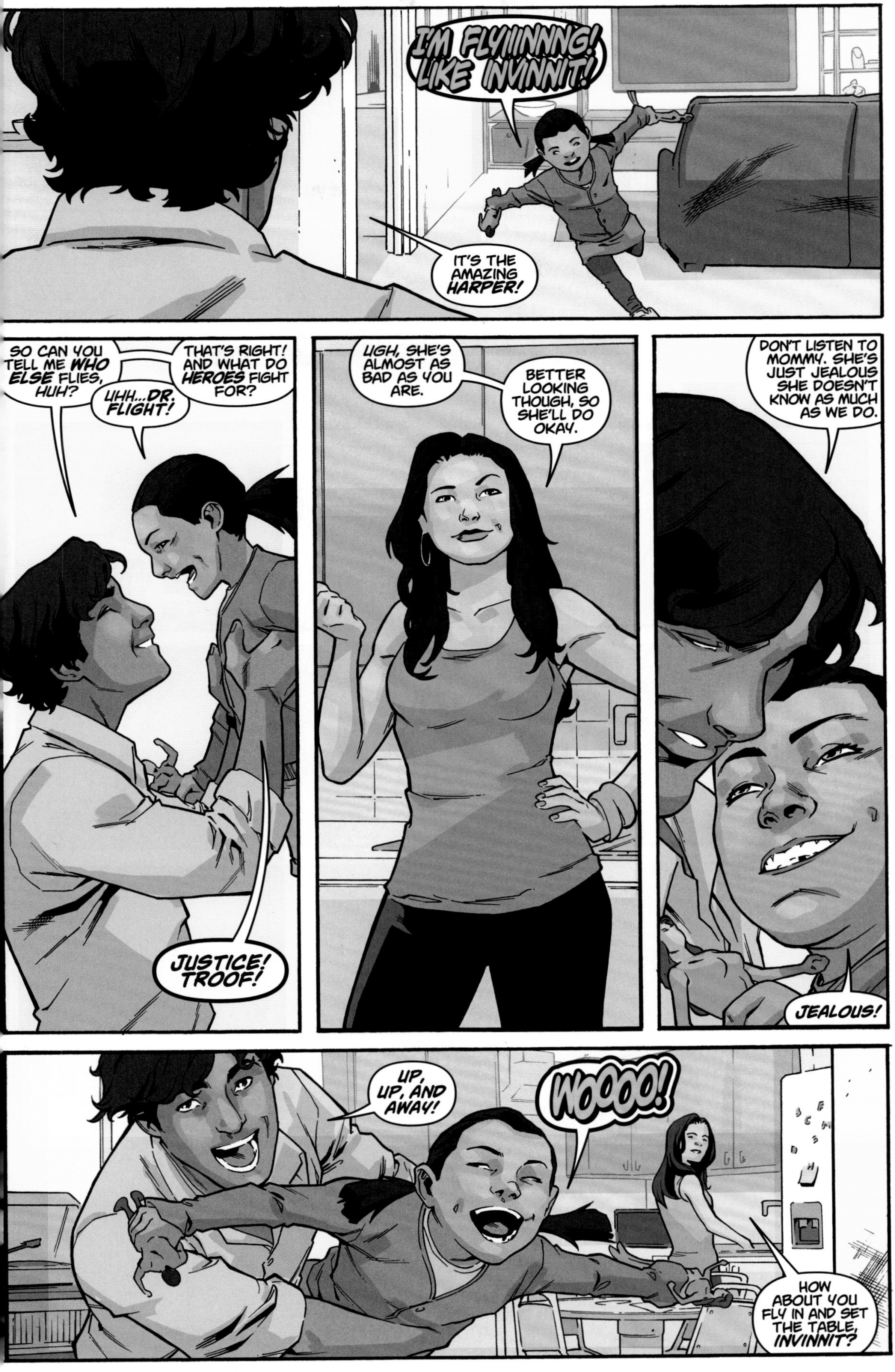
I'M FLYIIINNG! LIKE INVINNIT!
IT'S THE AMAZING HARPER!
SO CAN YOU TELL ME WHO ELSE FLIES, HUH?
UHH... DR. FLIGHT!
THAT'S RIGHT! AND WHAT DO HEROES FIGHT FOR?
JUSTICE! TROOF!
UGH, SHE'S ALMOST AS BAD AS YOU ARE.
BETTER LOOKING THOUGH, SO SHE'LL DO OKAY.
DON'T LISTEN TO MOMMY. SHE'S JUST JEALOUS SHE DOESN'T KNOW AS MUCH AS WE DO.
JEALOUS!
UP, UP, AND AWAY!
WOOOO!
HOW ABOUT YOU FLY IN AND SET THE TABLE, INVINNIT?

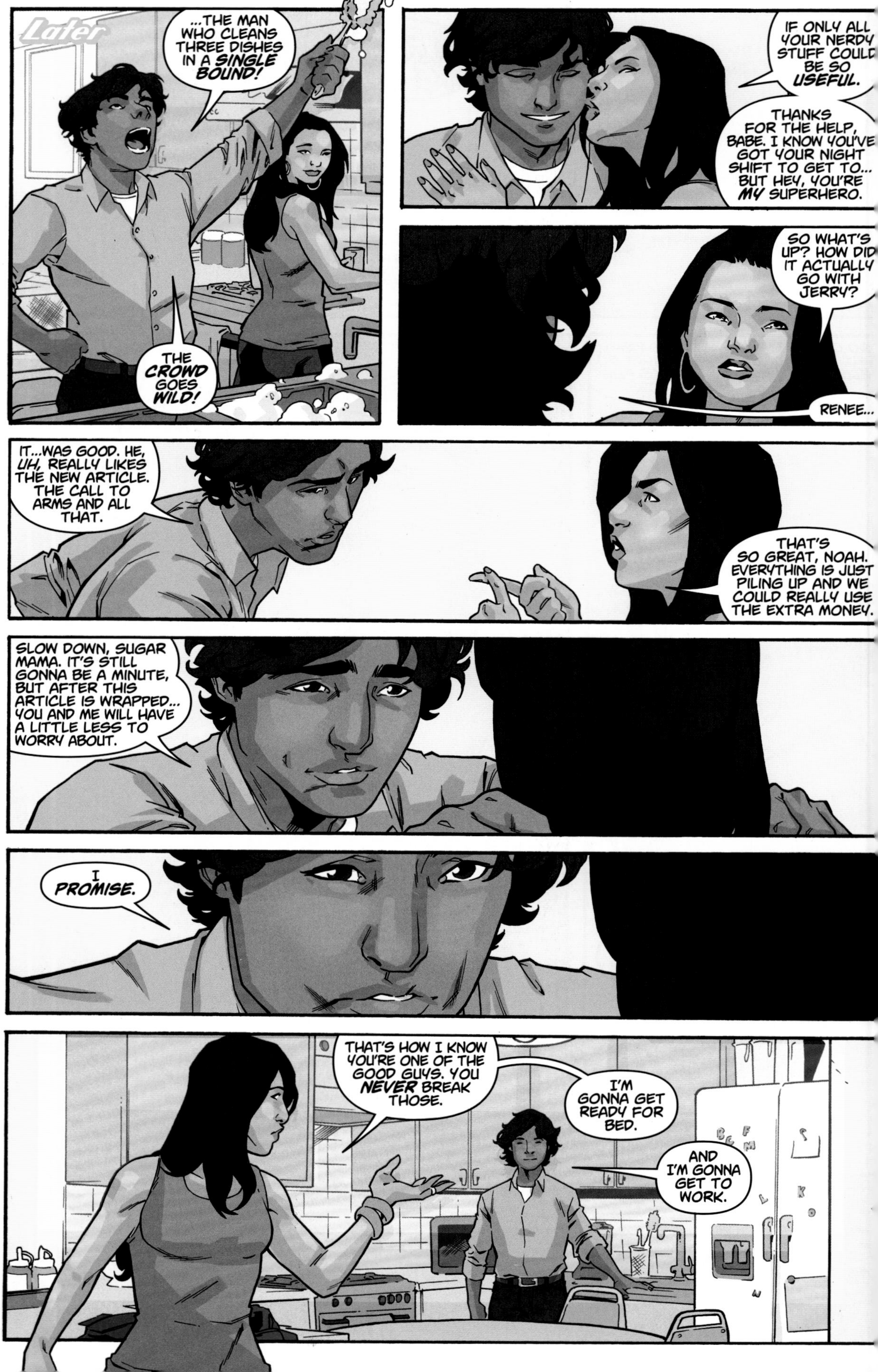
Later
...THE MAN WHO CLEANS THREE DISHES IN A SINGLE BOUND!
THE CROWD GOES WILD!
IF ONLY ALL YOUR NERDY STUFF COULD BE SO USEFUL.
THANKS FOR THE HELP, BABE. I KNOW YOU'VE GOT YOUR NIGHT SHIFT TO GET TO... BUT HEY, YOU'RE MY SUPERHERO.
SO WHAT'S UP? HOW DID IT ACTUALLY GO WITH JERRY?
RENEE...
IT...WAS GOOD. HE, UH, REALLY LIKES THE NEW ARTICLE. THE CALL TO ARMS AND ALL THAT.
THAT'S SO GREAT, NOAH. EVERYTHING IS JUST PILING UP AND WE COULD REALLY USE THE EXTRA MONEY.
SLOW DOWN, SUGAR MAMA. IT'S STILL GONNA BE A MINUTE, BUT AFTER THIS ARTICLE IS WRAPPED... YOU AND ME WILL HAVE A LITTLE LESS TO WORRY ABOUT.
I PROMISE.
THAT'S HOW I KNOW YOU'RE ONE OF THE GOOD GUYS. YOU NEVER BREAK THOSE.
I'M GONNA GET READY FOR BED.
AND I'M GONNA GET TO WORK.

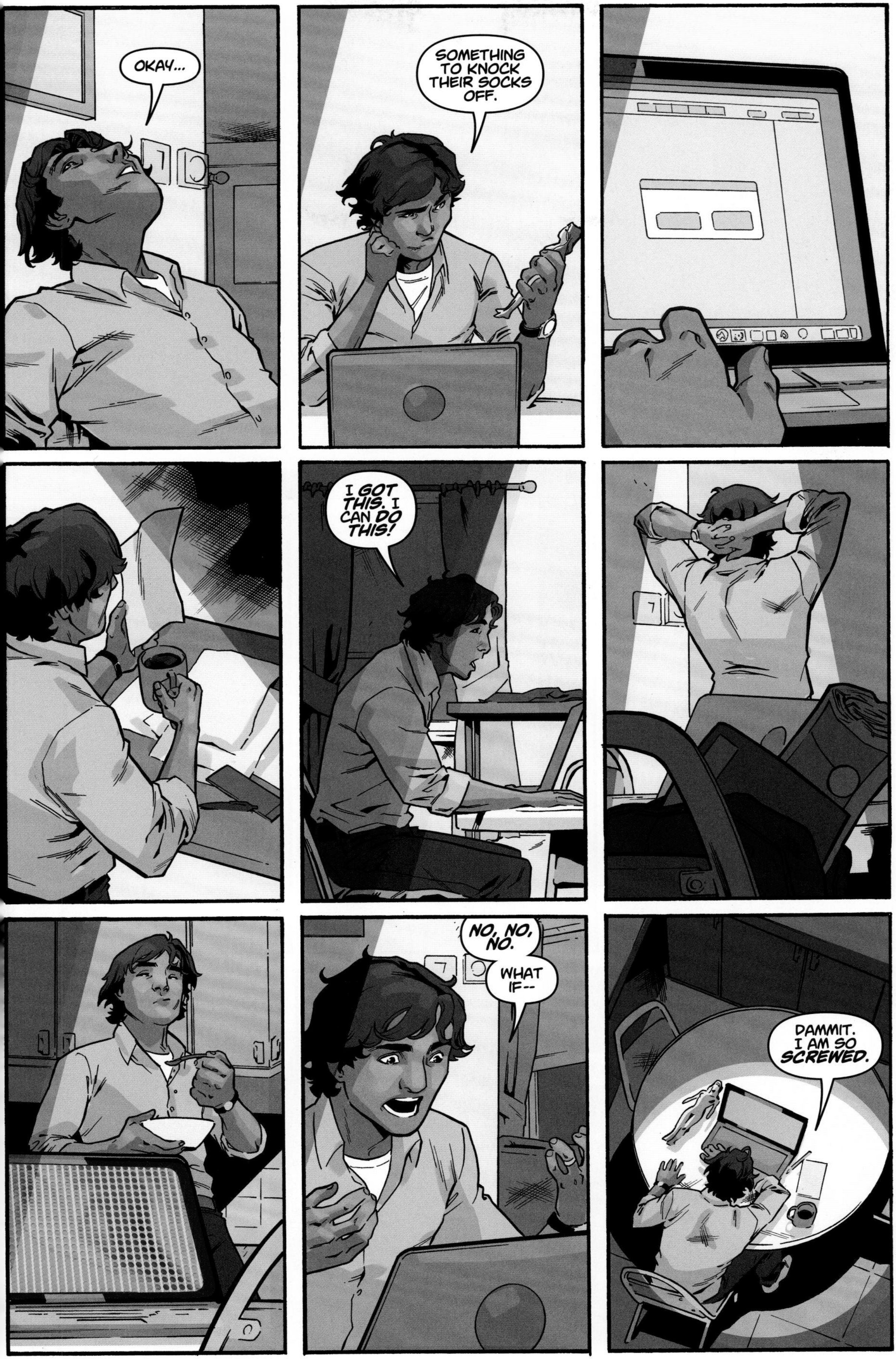
OKAY...
SOMETHING TO KNOCK THEIR SOCKS OFF.
I GOT THIS. I CAN DO THIS!
NO, NO, NO.
WHAT IF--
DAMMIT. I AM SO SCREWED.

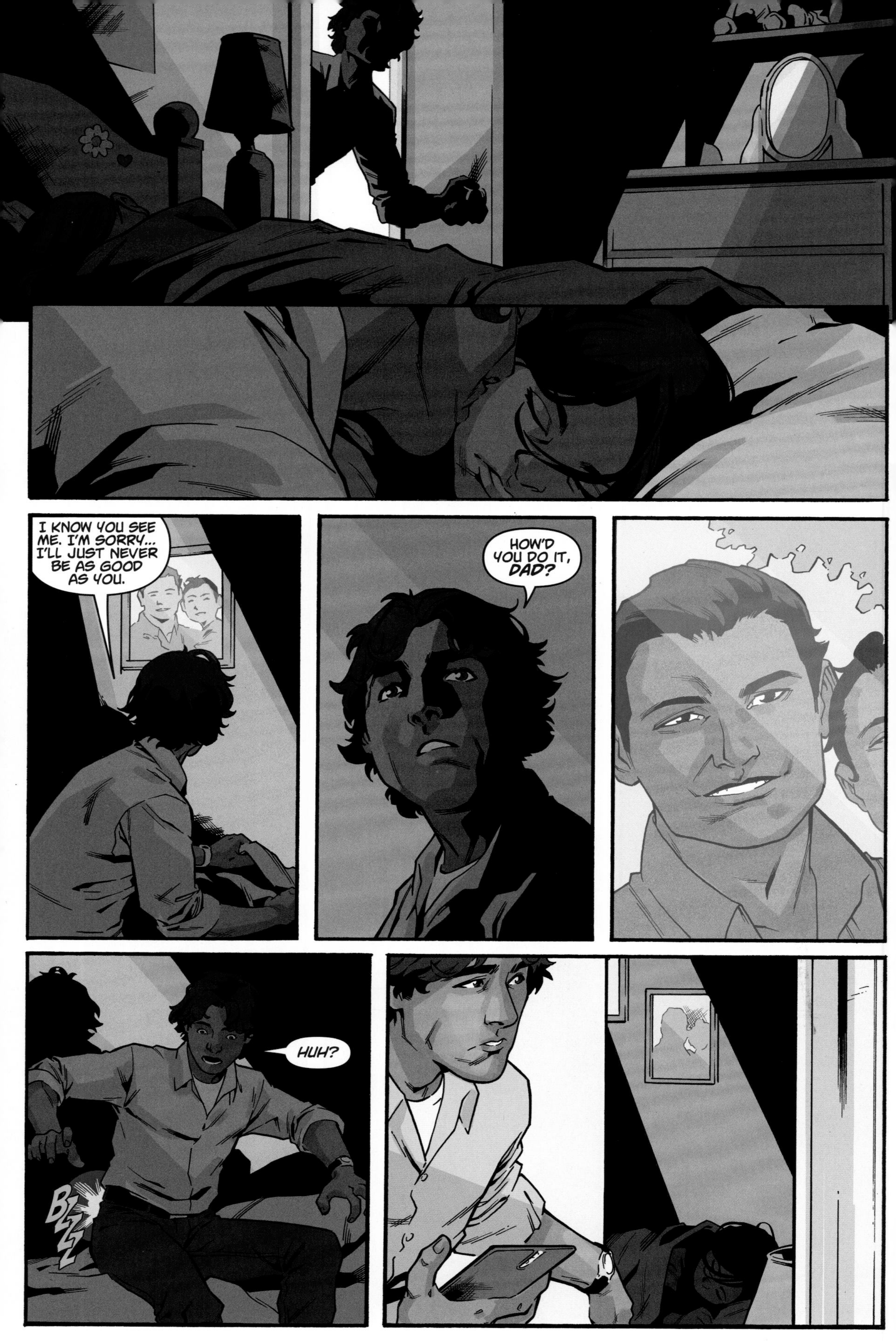
I KNOW YOU SEE ME. I'M SORRY... I'LL JUST NEVER BE AS GOOD AS YOU.
HOW'D YOU DO IT, DAD?
HUH?
BZZZ

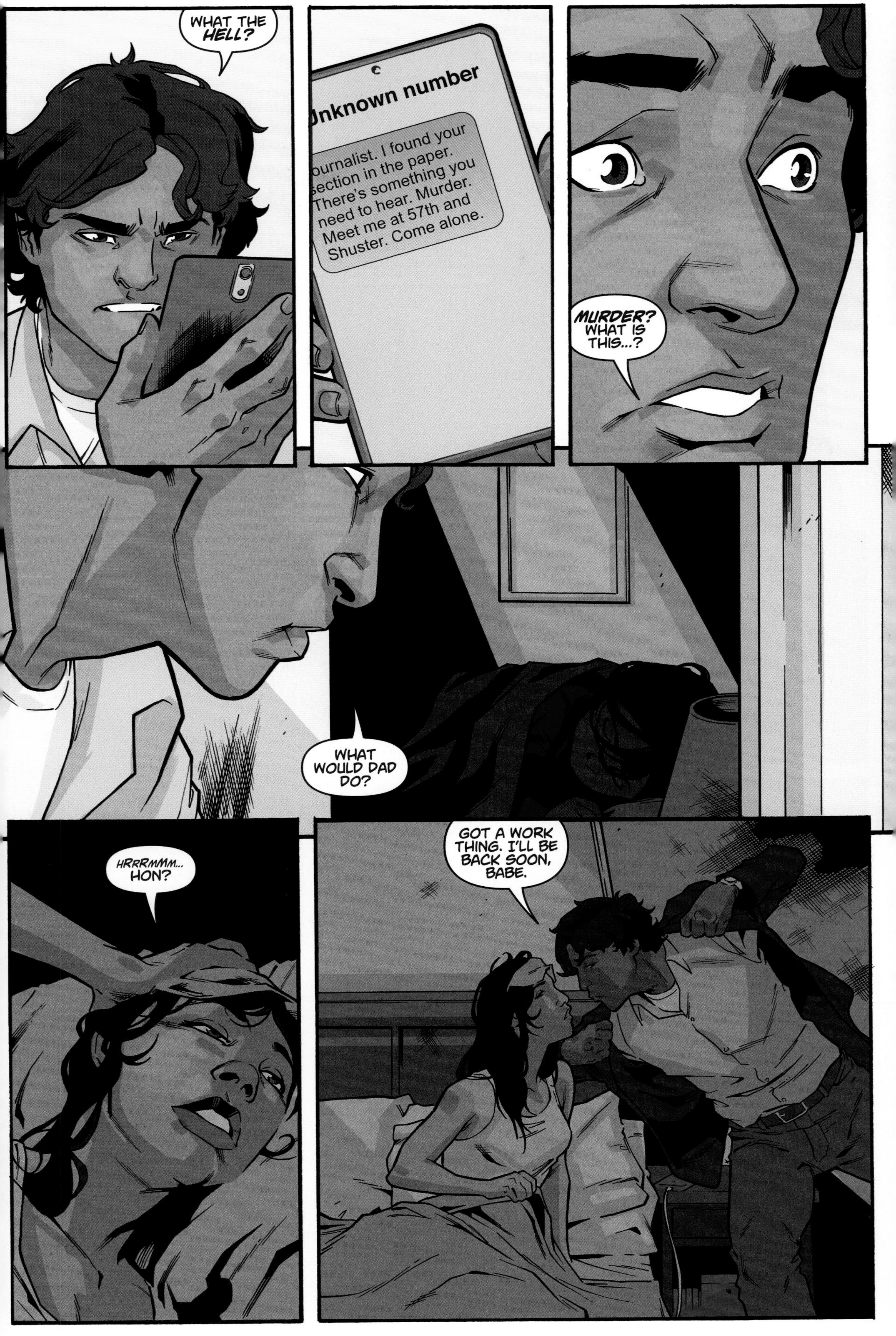
WHAT THE HELL?
Unknown number
ournalist. I found your section in the paper. There's something you need to hear. Murder. Meet me at 57th and Shuster. Come alone.
MURDER? WHAT IS THIS...?
WHAT WOULD DAD DO?
HRRRMMM... HON?
GOT A WORK THING. I'LL BE BACK SOON, BABE.

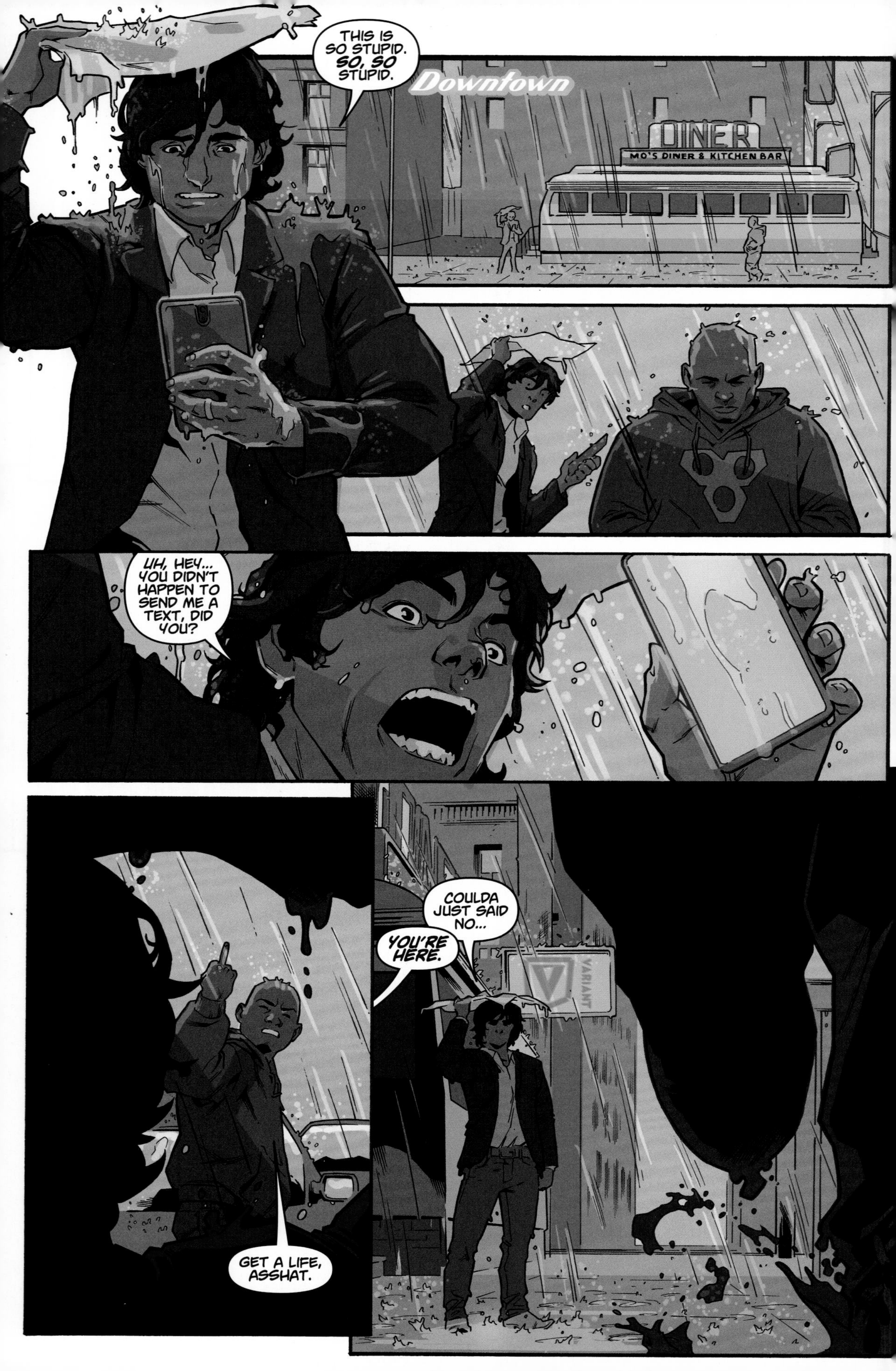
THIS IS SO STUPID. SO, SO STUPID.
Downtown
DINER
MO'S DINER & KITCHEN BAR
UH, HEY... YOU DIDN'T HAPPEN TO SEND ME A TEXT, DID YOU?
GET A LIFE, ASSHAT.
COULDA JUST SAID NO...
YOU'RE HERE.
VARIANT

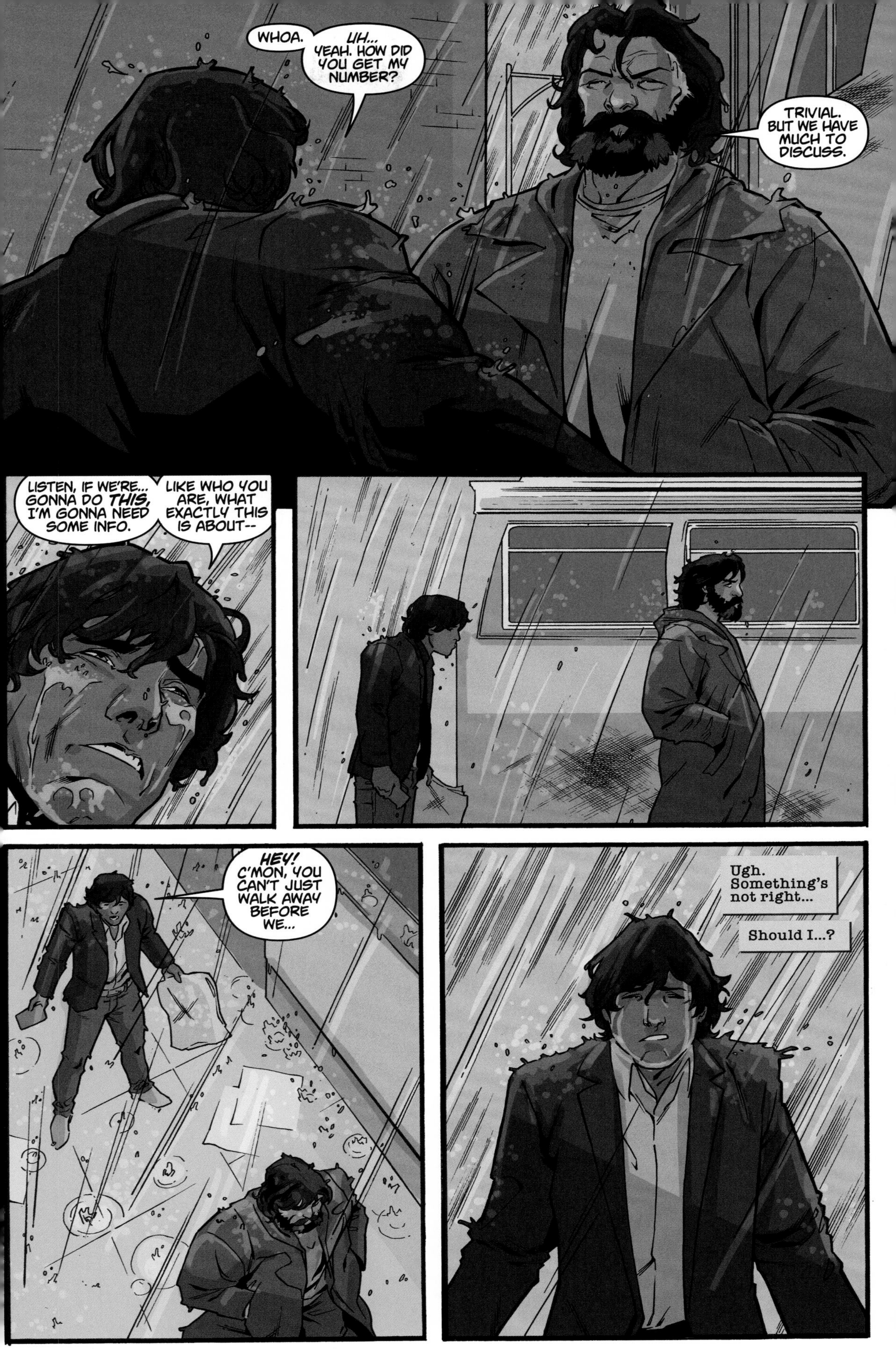
WHOA.
UH... YEAH. HOW DID YOU GET MY NUMBER?
TRIVIAL. BUT WE HAVE MUCH TO DISCUSS.
LISTEN, IF WE'RE... GONNA DO *THIS,* I'M GONNA NEED SOME INFO.
LIKE WHO YOU ARE, WHAT EXACTLY THIS IS ABOUT--
HEY! C'MON, YOU CAN'T JUST WALK AWAY BEFORE WE...
Ugh. Something's not right...
Should I...?

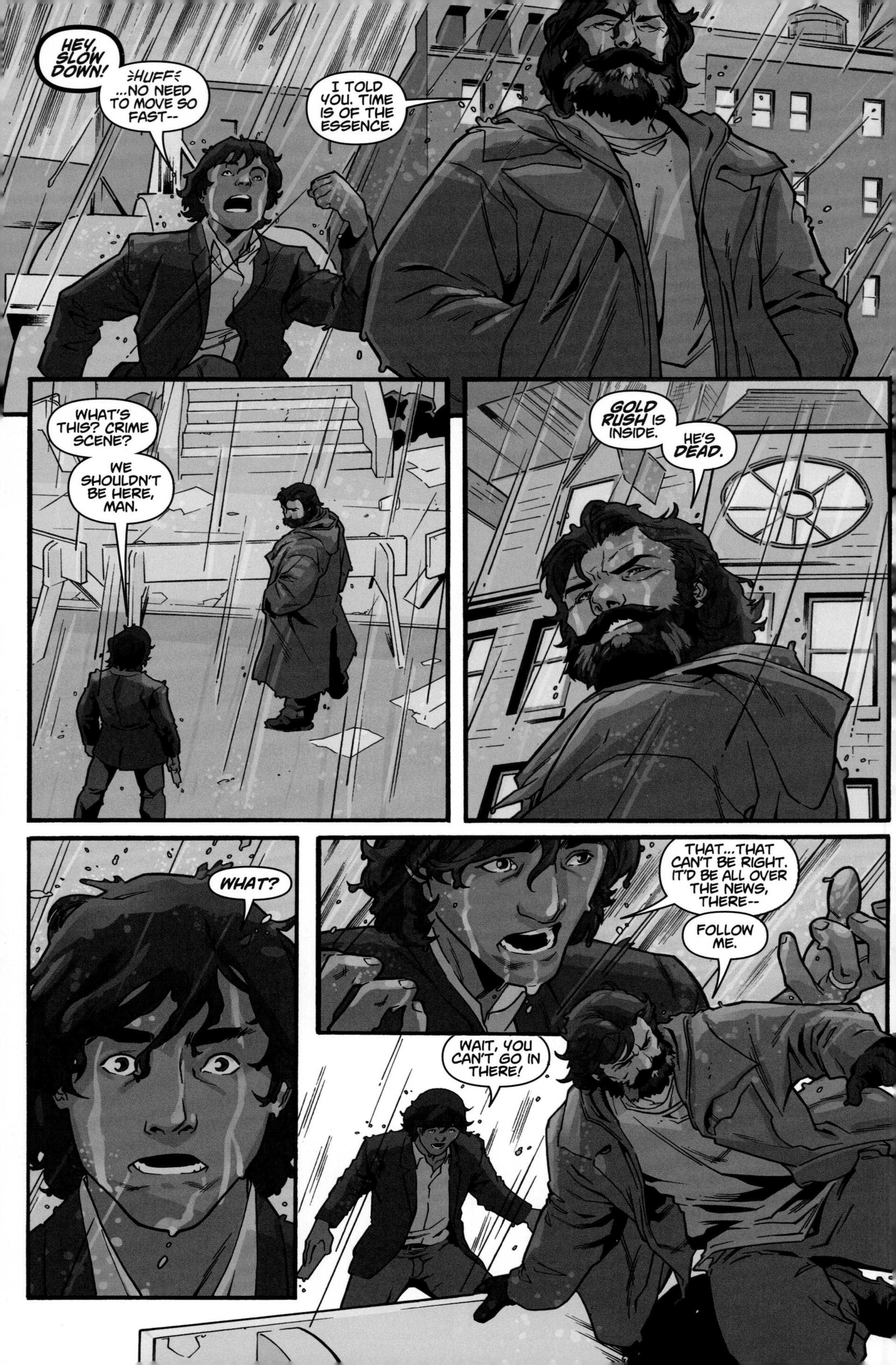
HEY, SLOW DOWN!
HUFF
...NO NEED TO MOVE SO FAST--
I TOLD YOU. TIME IS OF THE ESSENCE.
WHAT'S THIS? CRIME SCENE?
WE SHOULDN'T BE HERE, MAN.
GOLD RUSH IS INSIDE.
HE'S DEAD.
WHAT?
THAT...THAT CAN'T BE RIGHT. IT'D BE ALL OVER THE NEWS, THERE--
FOLLOW ME.
WAIT, YOU CAN'T GO IN THERE!

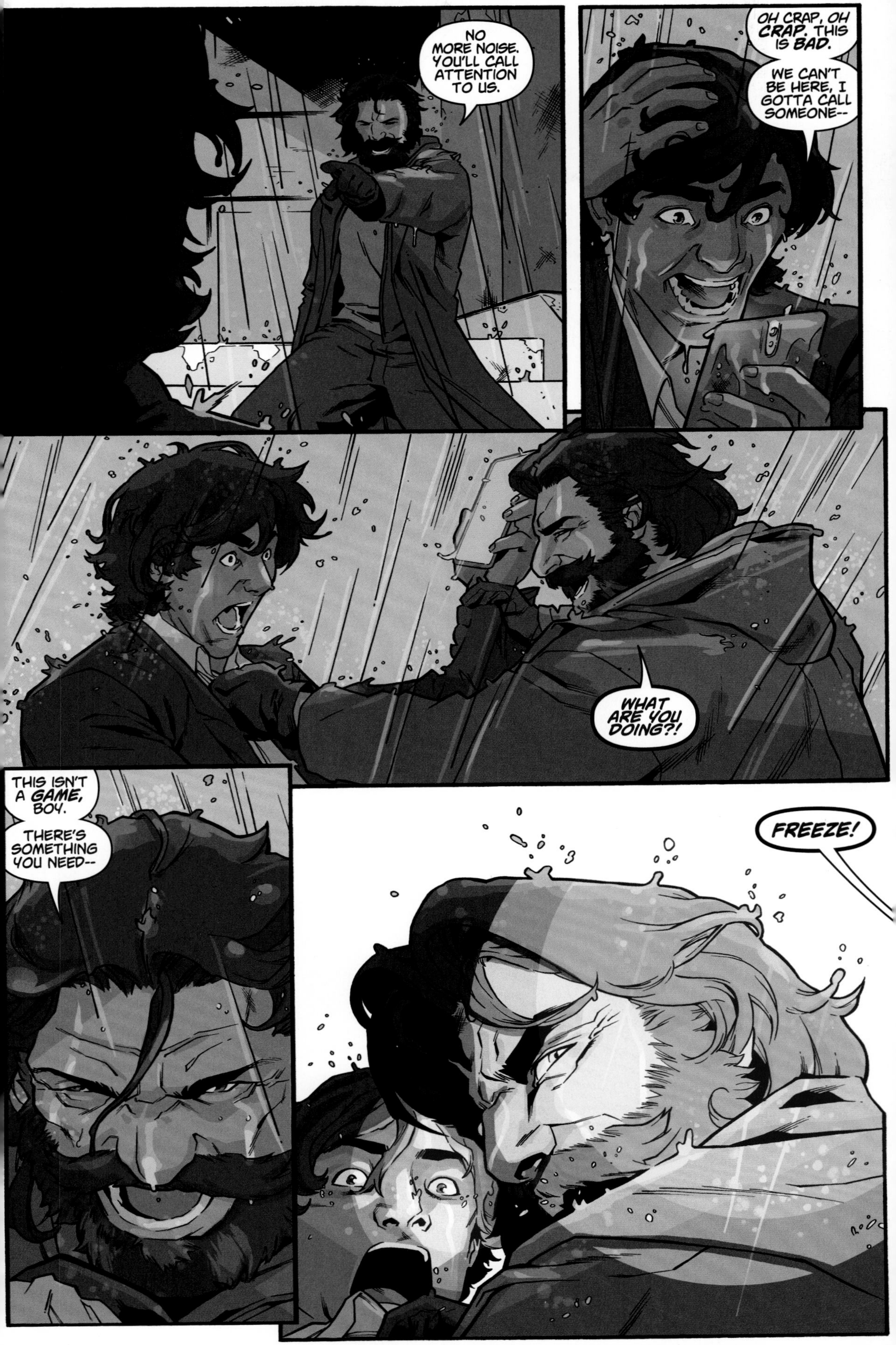
NO MORE NOISE. YOU'LL CALL ATTENTION TO US.
OH CRAP, OH CRAP. THIS IS BAD.
WE CAN'T BE HERE, I GOTTA CALL SOMEONE--
WHAT ARE YOU DOING?!
THIS ISN'T A GAME, BOY.
THERE'S SOMETHING YOU NEED--
FREEZE!

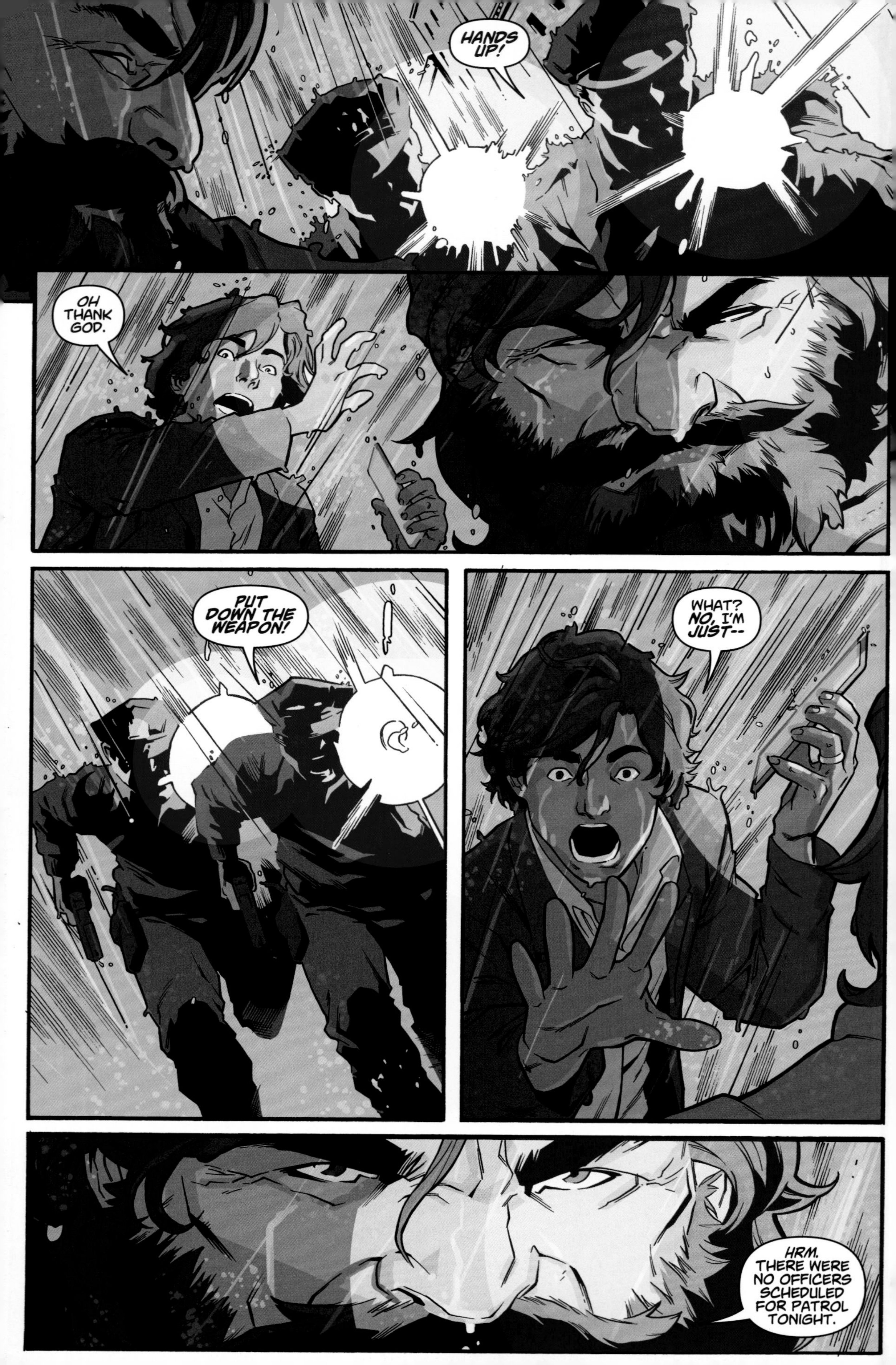
HANDS UP!
OH THANK GOD.
PUT DOWN THE WEAPON!
WHAT? NO, I'M JUST--
HRM. THERE WERE NO OFFICERS SCHEDULED FOR PATROL TONIGHT.

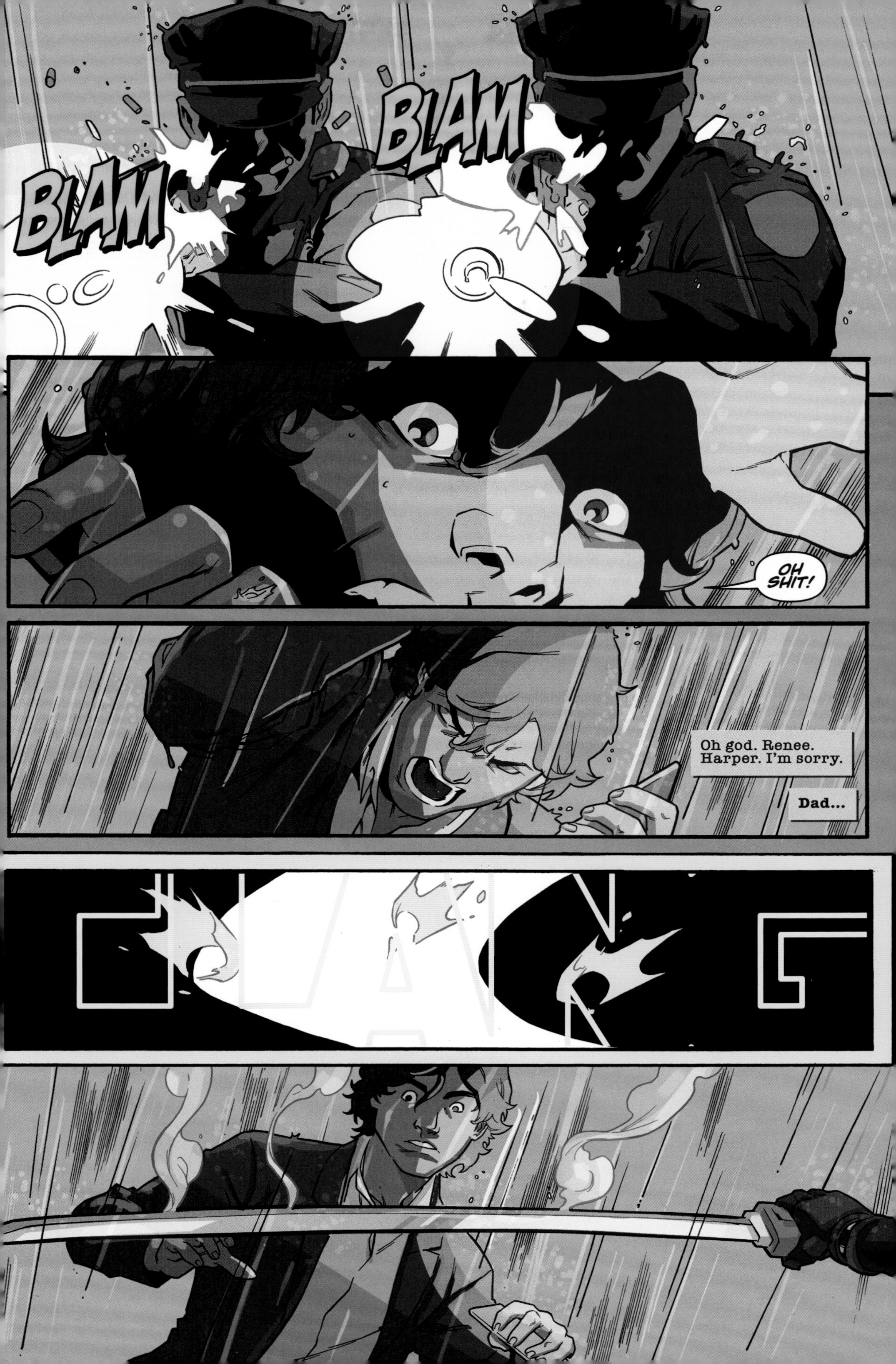
BLAM
BLAM
OH SHIT!
Oh god. Renee. Harper. I'm sorry.
Dad...
CLANG

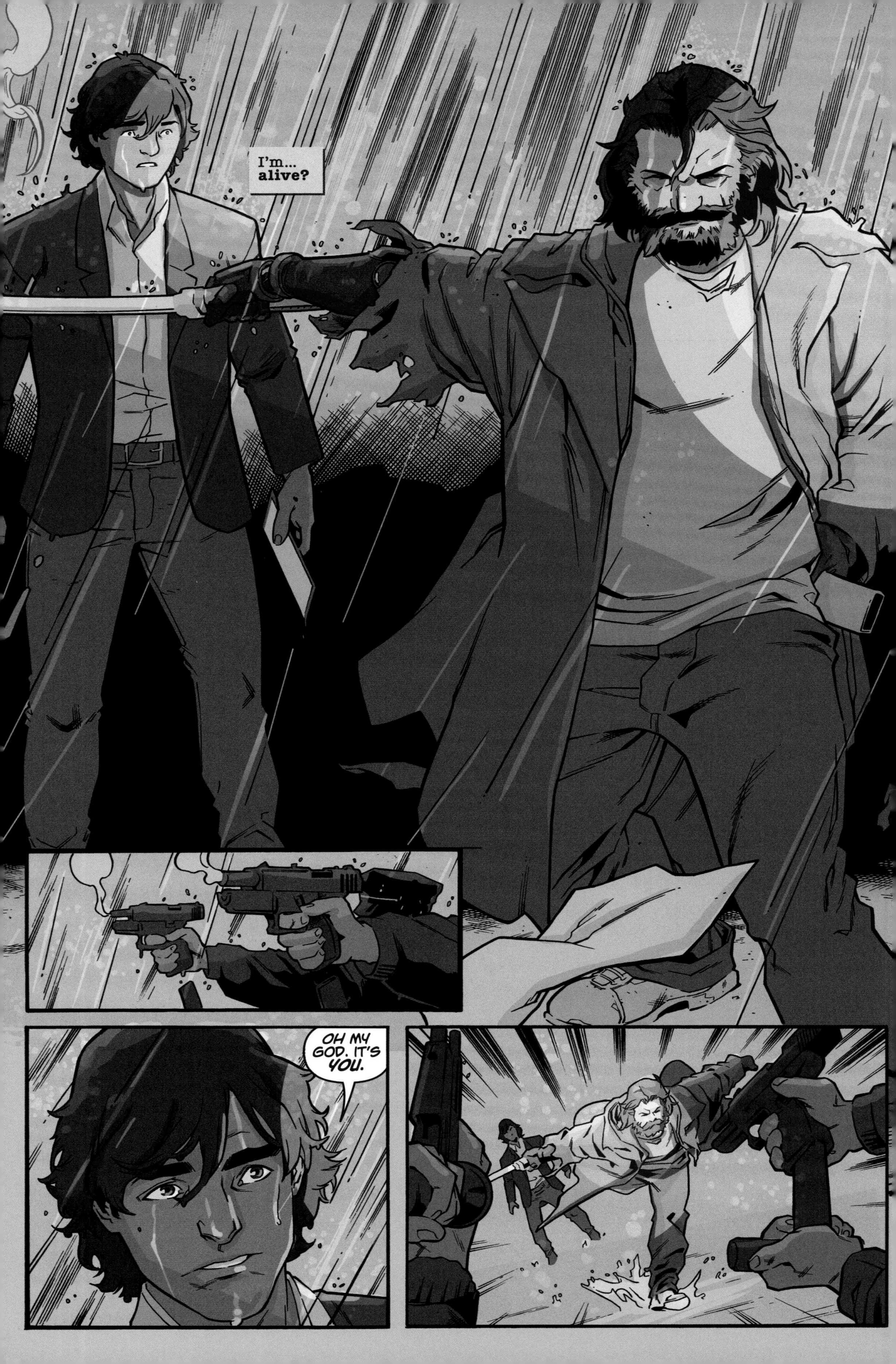
I'm...
alive?
OH MY GOD. IT'S YOU.

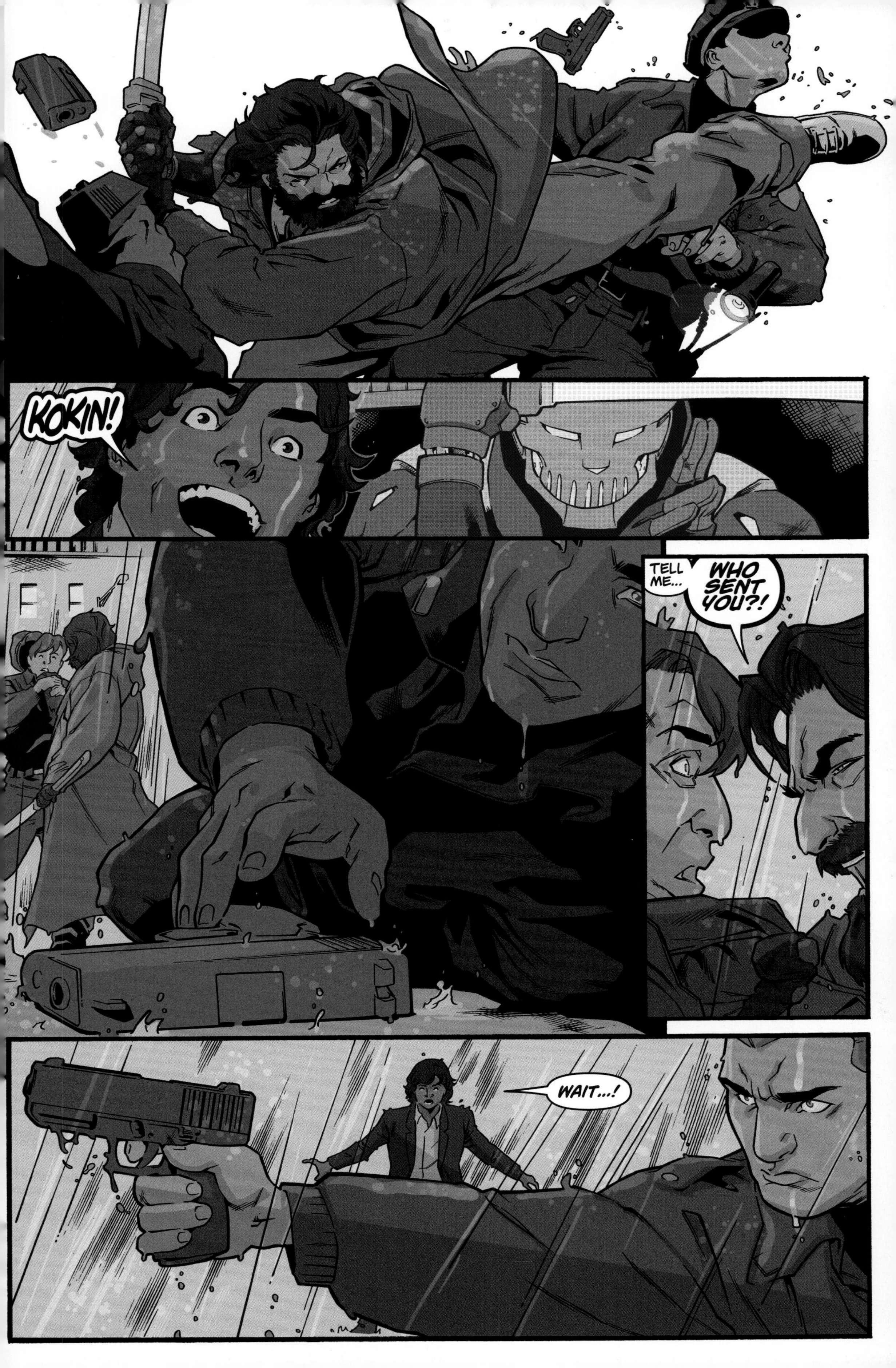
KOKIN!
TELL ME...
WHO SENT YOU?!
WAIT...!

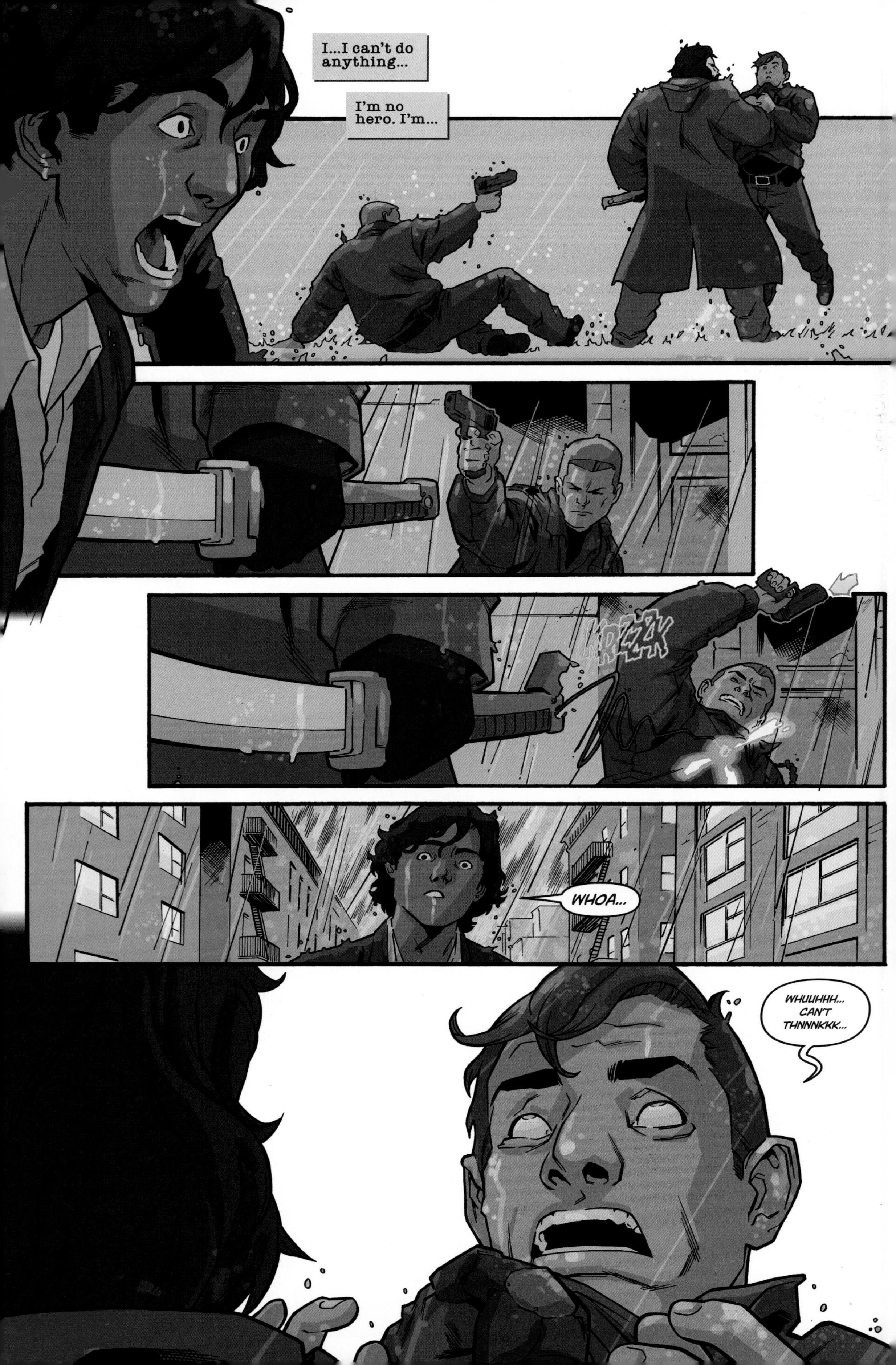
I...I can't do anything...
I'm no hero. I'm...
KRZZK
WHOA...
WHUUHHH... CAN'T THNNNKKK...

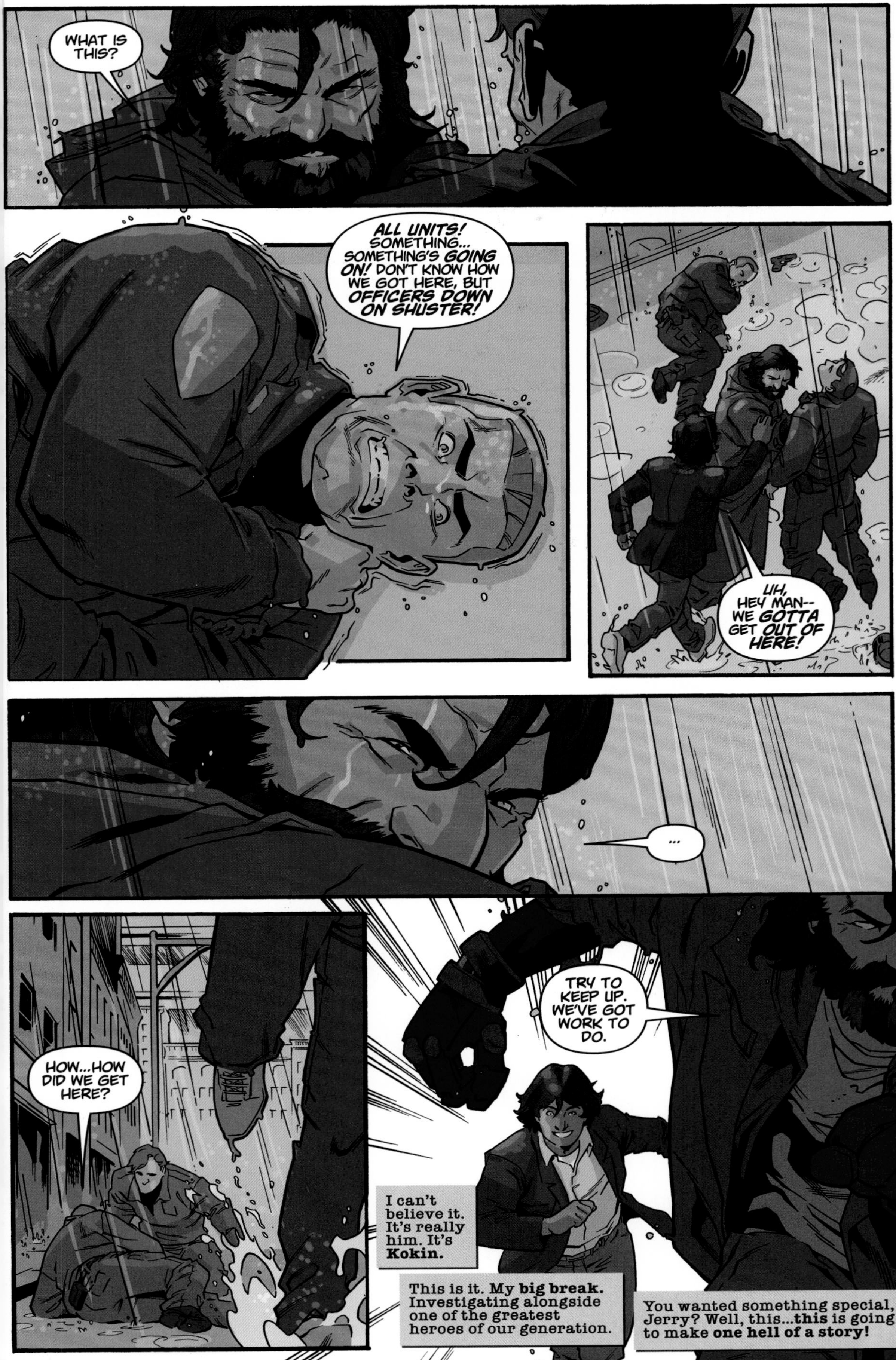
WHAT IS THIS?
ALL UNITS! SOMETHING... SOMETHING'S GOING ON! DON'T KNOW HOW WE GOT HERE, BUT OFFICERS DOWN ON SHUSTER!
UH, HEY MAN-- WE GOTTA GET OUT OF HERE!
...
HOW...HOW DID WE GET HERE?
TRY TO KEEP UP. WE'VE GOT WORK TO DO.
I can't believe it. It's really him. It's Kokin.
This is it. My big break. Investigating alongside one of the greatest heroes of our generation.
You wanted something special, Jerry? Well, this...this is going to make one hell of a story!

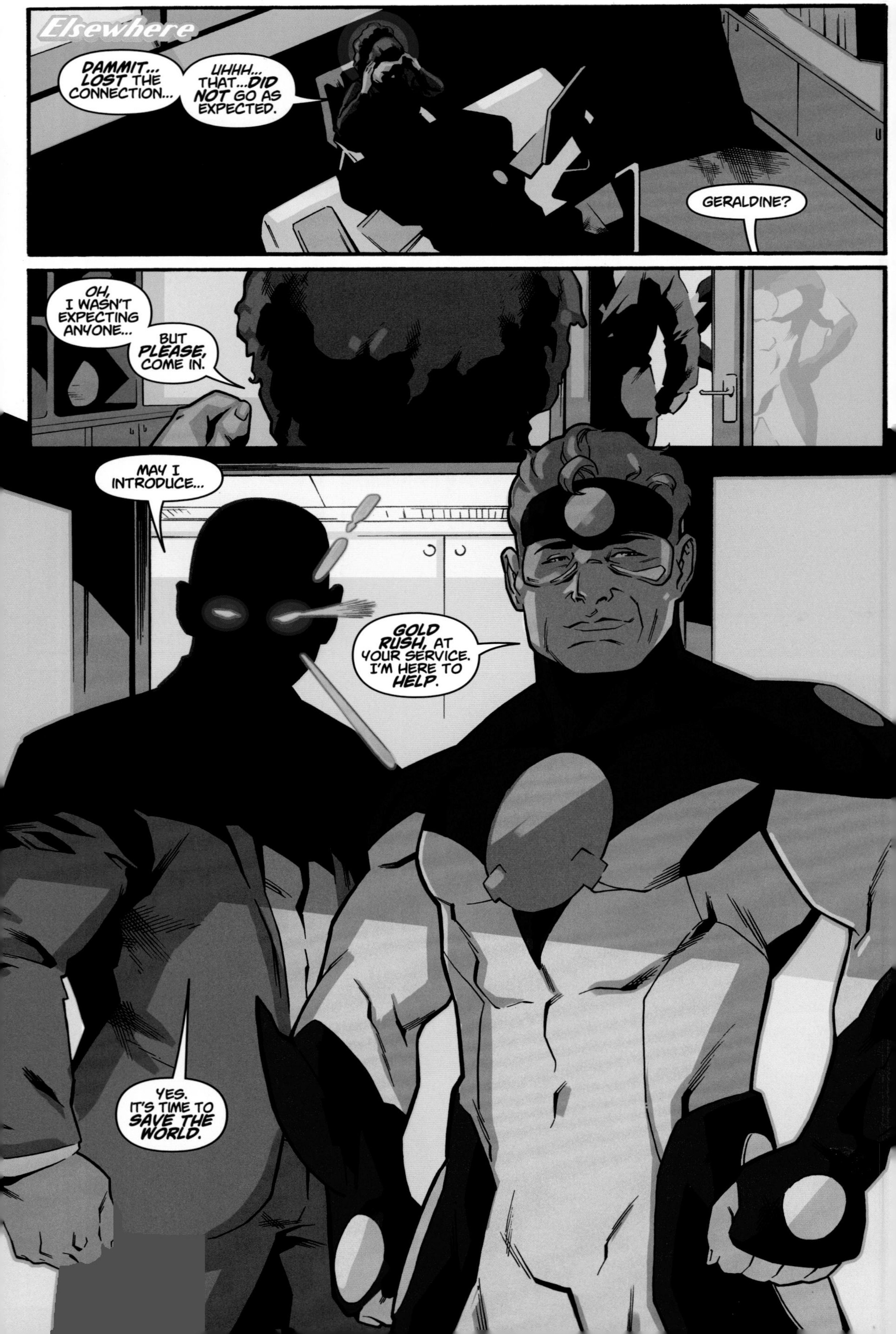
Elsewhere
DAMMIT... LOST THE CONNECTION...
UHHH... THAT...DID NOT GO AS EXPECTED.
GERALDINE?
OH, I WASN'T EXPECTING ANYONE...
BUT PLEASE, COME IN.
MAY I INTRODUCE...
GOLD RUSH, AT YOUR SERVICE. I'M HERE TO HELP.
YES. IT'S TIME TO SAVE THE WORLD.

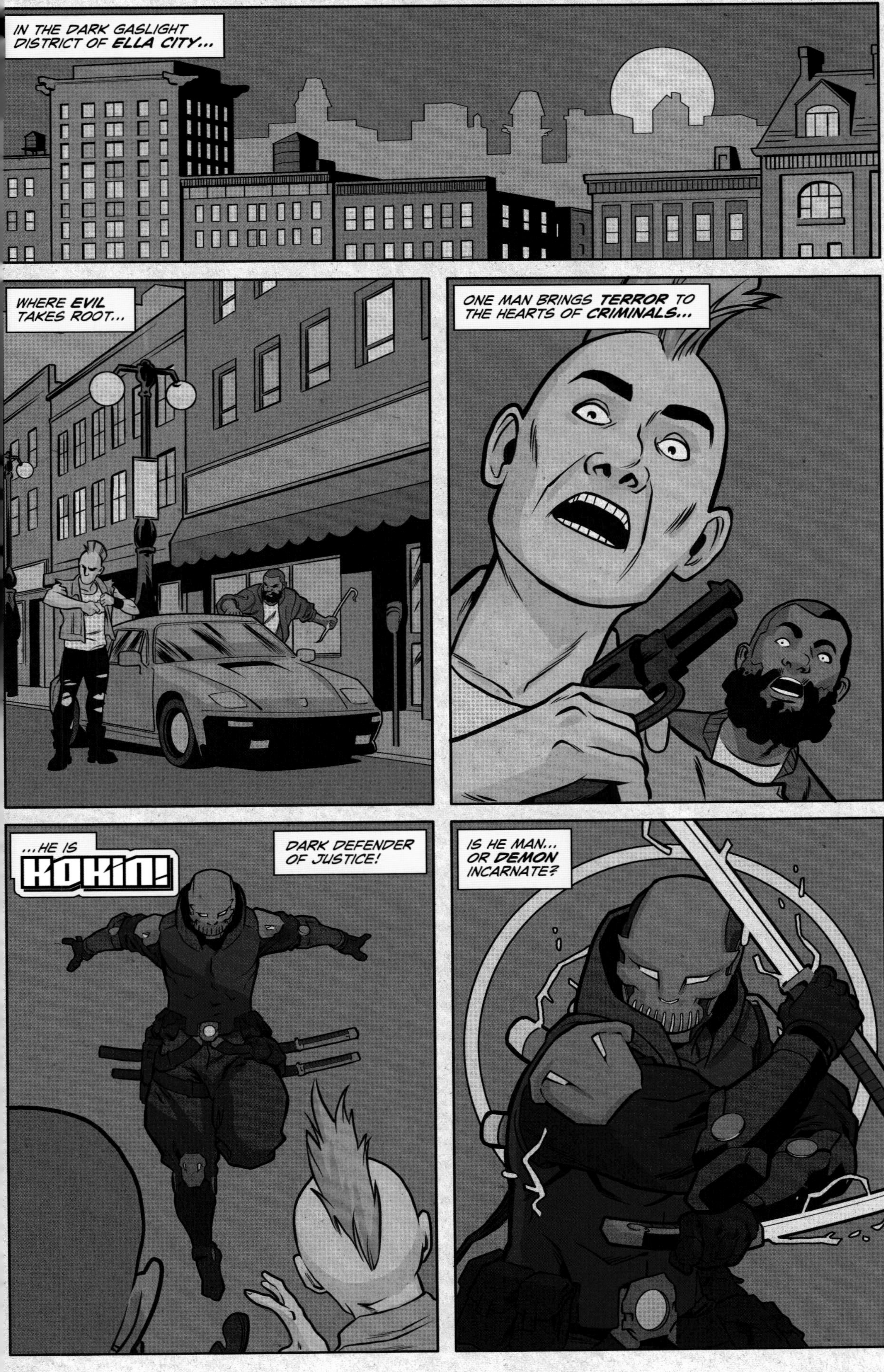
IN THE DARK GASLIGHT DISTRICT OF ELLA CITY...
WHERE EVIL TAKES ROOT...
ONE MAN BRINGS TERROR TO THE HEARTS OF CRIMINALS...
...HE IS
KOKIN!
DARK DEFENDER OF JUSTICE!
IS HE MAN... OR DEMON INCARNATE?

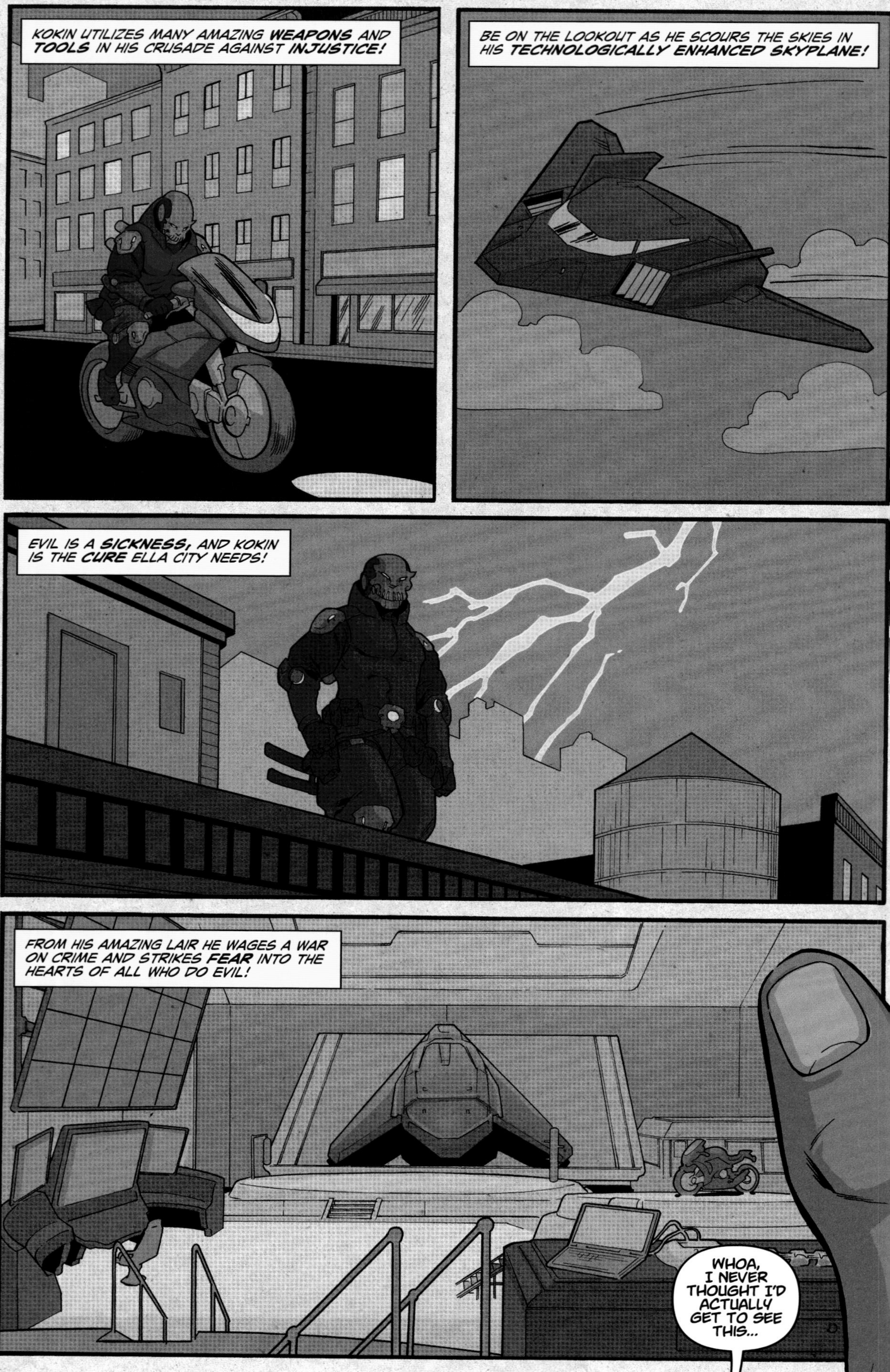
KOKIN UTILIZES MANY AMAZING **WEAPONS** AND **TOOLS** IN HIS CRUSADE AGAINST **INJUSTICE!**
BE ON THE LOOKOUT AS HE SCOURS THE SKIES IN HIS **TECHNOLOGICALLY ENHANCED SKYPLANE!**
EVIL IS A **SICKNESS,** AND KOKIN IS THE **CURE** ELLA CITY NEEDS!
FROM HIS AMAZING LAIR HE WAGES A WAR ON CRIME AND STRIKES **FEAR** INTO THE HEARTS OF ALL WHO DO EVIL!
WHOA, I NEVER THOUGHT I'D ACTUALLY GET TO SEE THIS...

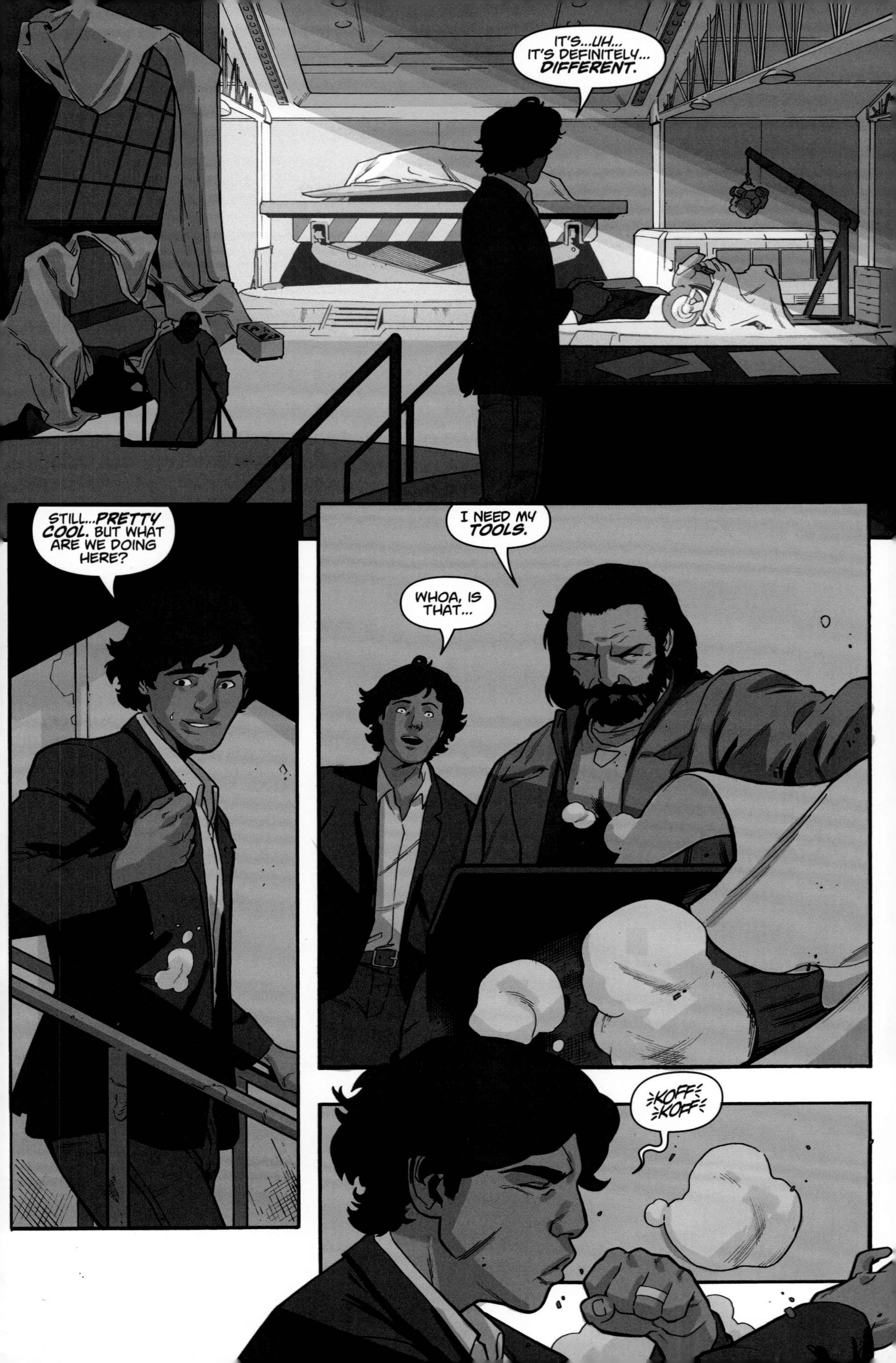
IT'S...UH... IT'S DEFINITELY... DIFFERENT.
STILL...PRETTY COOL. BUT WHAT ARE WE DOING HERE?
I NEED MY TOOLS.
WHOA, IS THAT...
KOFF KOFF

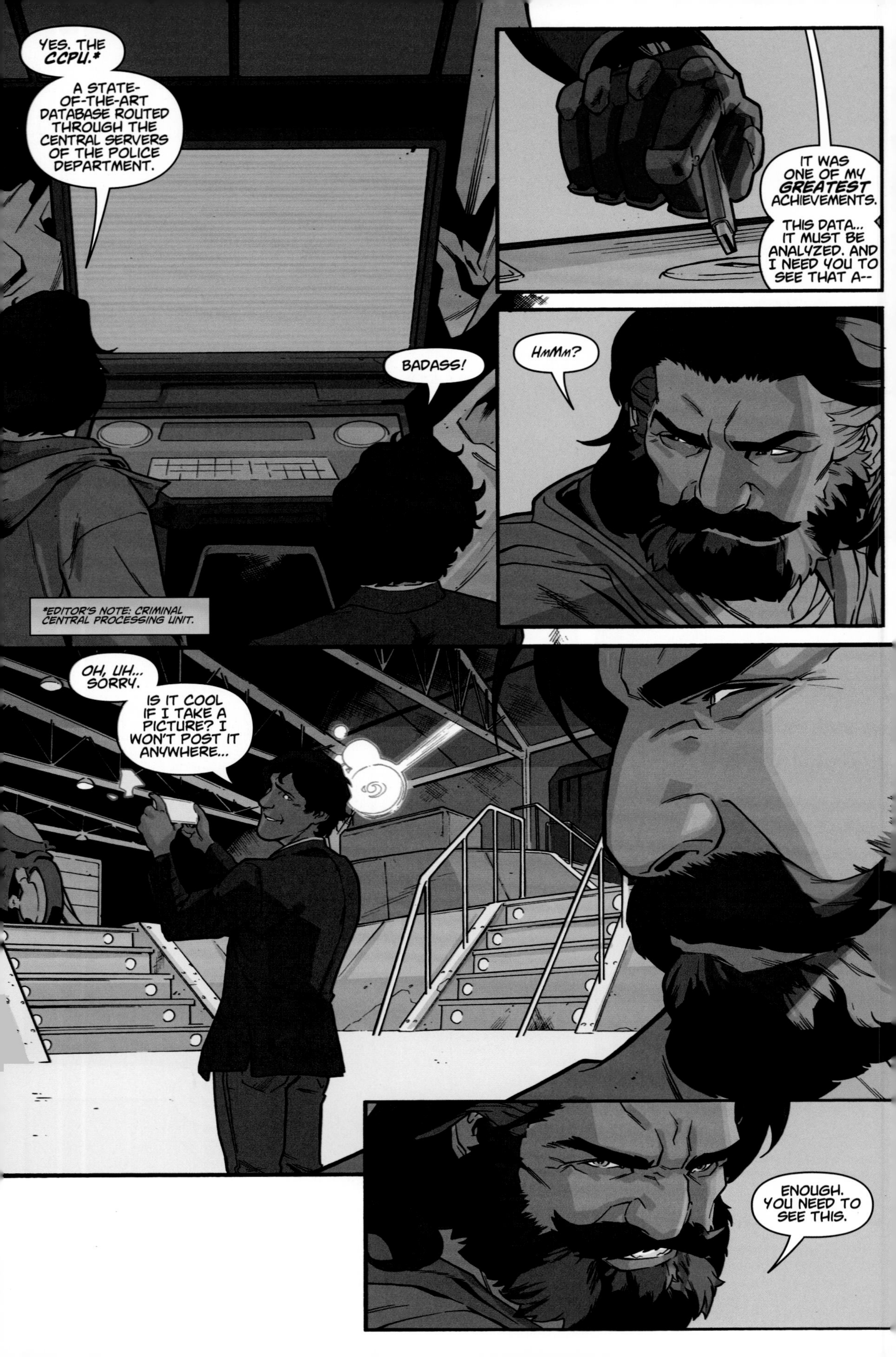
YES. THE CCPU.*
A STATE-OF-THE-ART DATABASE ROUTED THROUGH THE CENTRAL SERVERS OF THE POLICE DEPARTMENT.
BADASS!
*EDITOR'S NOTE: CRIMINAL CENTRAL PROCESSING UNIT.
IT WAS ONE OF MY GREATEST ACHIEVEMENTS.
THIS DATA... IT MUST BE ANALYZED. AND I NEED YOU TO SEE THAT A--
HMMM?
OH, UH... SORRY.
IS IT COOL IF I TAKE A PICTURE? I WON'T POST IT ANYWHERE...
ENOUGH. YOU NEED TO SEE THIS.

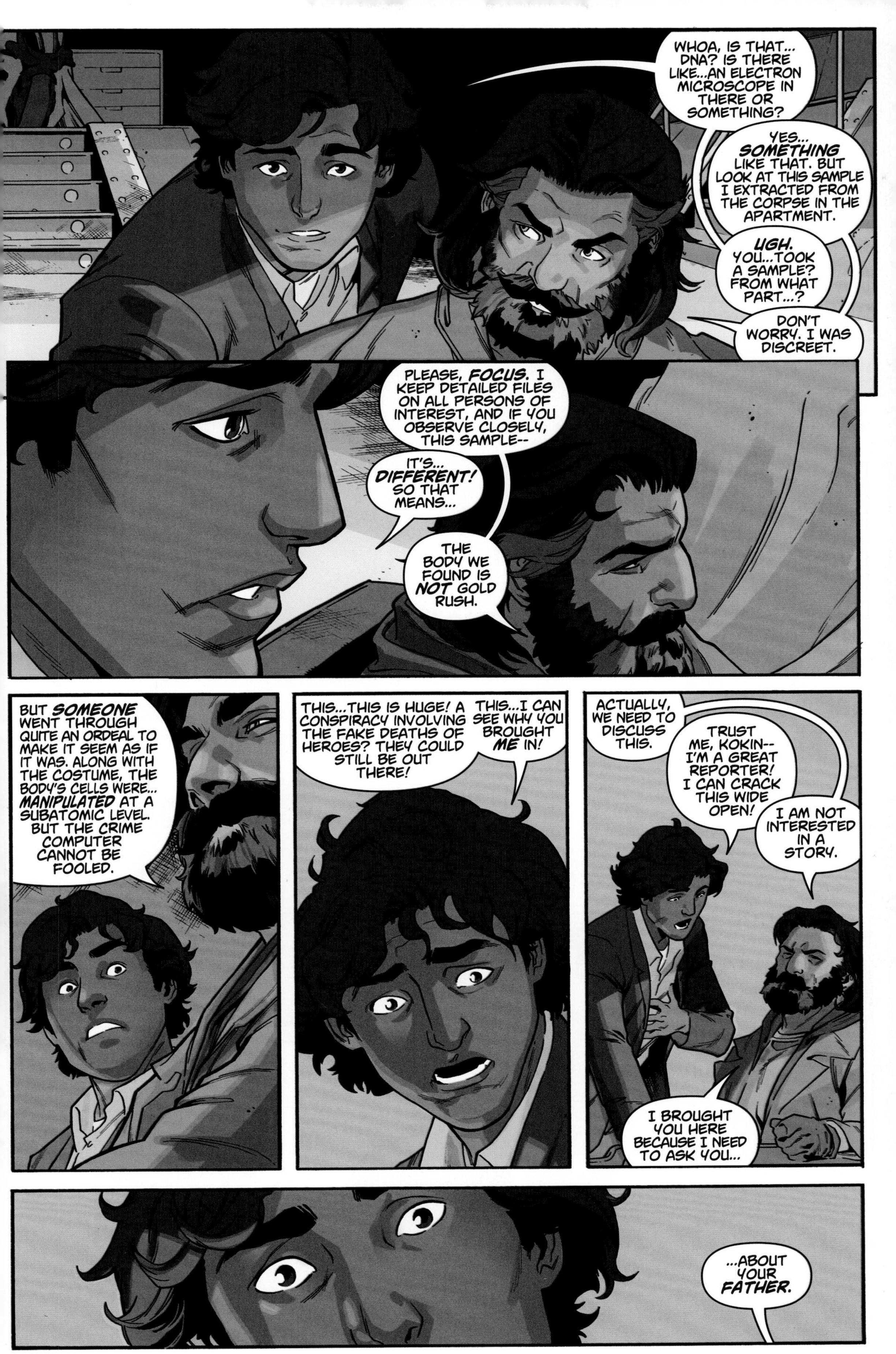
WHOA, IS THAT... DNA? IS THERE LIKE...AN ELECTRON MICROSCOPE IN THERE OR SOMETHING?
YES... SOMETHING LIKE THAT. BUT LOOK AT THIS SAMPLE I EXTRACTED FROM THE CORPSE IN THE APARTMENT.
UGH. YOU...TOOK A SAMPLE? FROM WHAT PART...?
DON'T WORRY. I WAS DISCREET.
PLEASE, FOCUS. I KEEP DETAILED FILES ON ALL PERSONS OF INTEREST, AND IF YOU OBSERVE CLOSELY, THIS SAMPLE--
IT'S... DIFFERENT! SO THAT MEANS...
THE BODY WE FOUND IS NOT GOLD RUSH.
BUT SOMEONE WENT THROUGH QUITE AN ORDEAL TO MAKE IT SEEM AS IF IT WAS. ALONG WITH THE COSTUME, THE BODY'S CELLS WERE... MANIPULATED AT A SUBATOMIC LEVEL. BUT THE CRIME COMPUTER CANNOT BE FOOLED.
THIS...THIS IS HUGE! A CONSPIRACY INVOLVING THE FAKE DEATHS OF HEROES? THEY COULD STILL BE OUT THERE!
THIS...I CAN SEE WHY YOU BROUGHT ME IN!
ACTUALLY, WE NEED TO DISCUSS THIS.
TRUST ME, KOKIN-- I'M A GREAT REPORTER! I CAN CRACK THIS WIDE OPEN!
I AM NOT INTERESTED IN A STORY.
I BROUGHT YOU HERE BECAUSE I NEED TO ASK YOU...
...ABOUT YOUR FATHER.

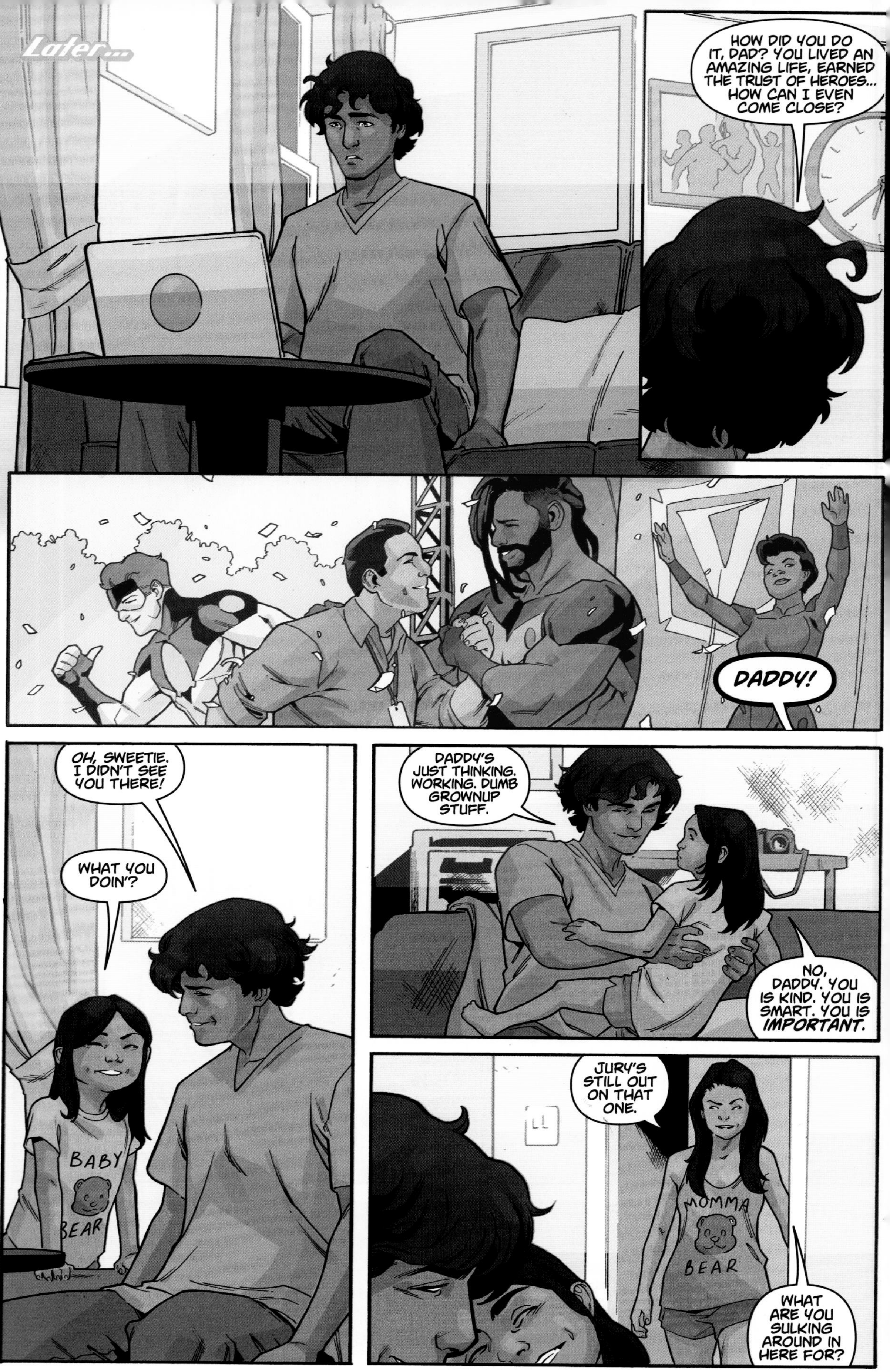
Later...
HOW DID YOU DO IT, DAD? YOU LIVED AN AMAZING LIFE, EARNED THE TRUST OF HEROES... HOW CAN I EVEN COME CLOSE?
DADDY!
OH, SWEETIE. I DIDN'T SEE YOU THERE!
WHAT YOU DOIN'?
BABY BEAR
DADDY'S JUST THINKING. WORKING. DUMB GROWNUP STUFF.
NO, DADDY. YOU IS KIND. YOU IS SMART. YOU IS IMPORTANT.
JURY'S STILL OUT ON THAT ONE.
MOMMA BEAR
WHAT ARE YOU SULKING AROUND IN HERE FOR?

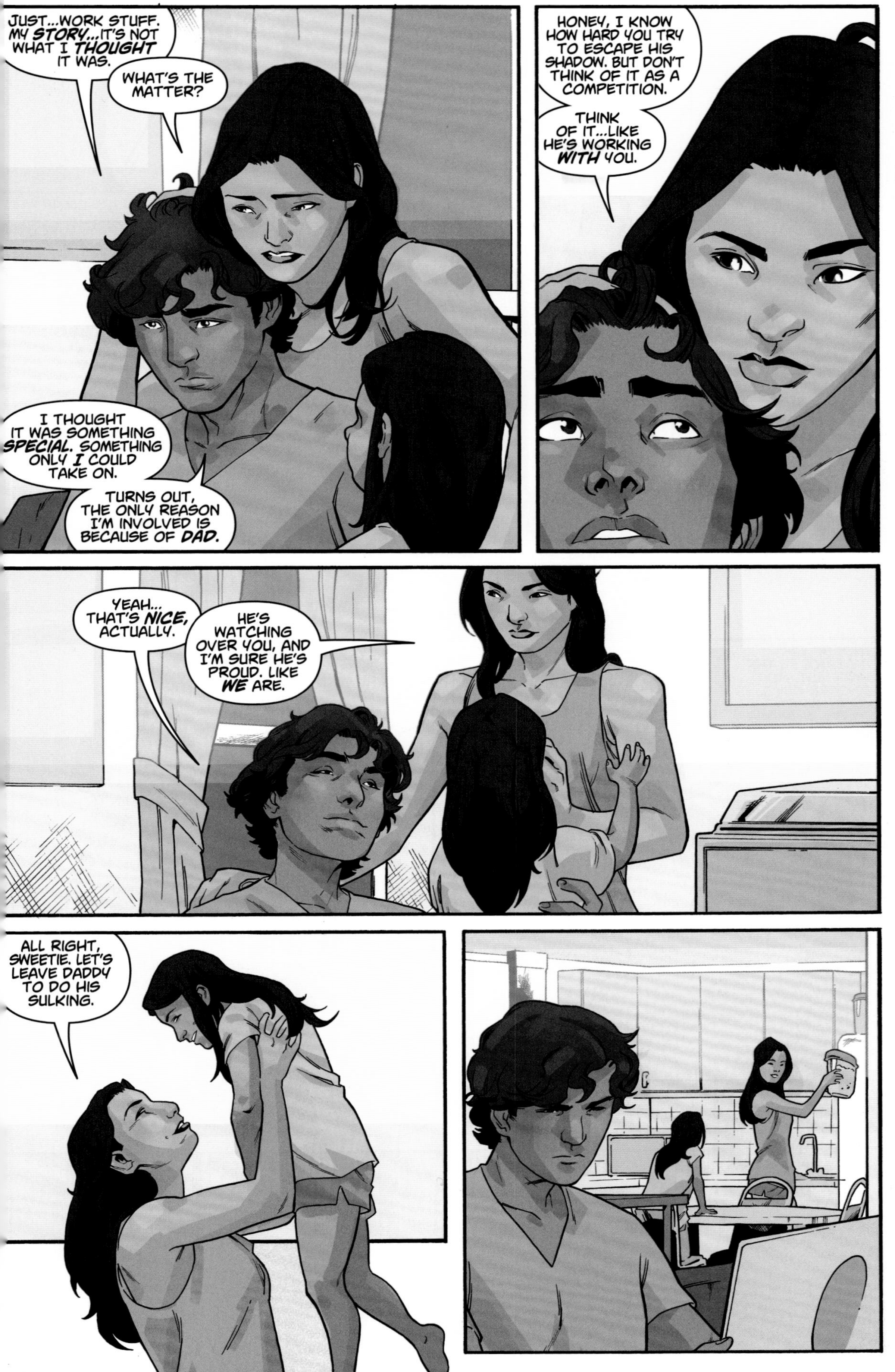
JUST...WORK STUFF. MY STORY...IT'S NOT WHAT I THOUGHT IT WAS.
WHAT'S THE MATTER?
I THOUGHT IT WAS SOMETHING SPECIAL. SOMETHING ONLY I COULD TAKE ON.
TURNS OUT, THE ONLY REASON I'M INVOLVED IS BECAUSE OF DAD.
HONEY, I KNOW HOW HARD YOU TRY TO ESCAPE HIS SHADOW. BUT DON'T THINK OF IT AS A COMPETITION.
THINK OF IT...LIKE HE'S WORKING WITH YOU.
HE'S WATCHING OVER YOU, AND I'M SURE HE'S PROUD. LIKE WE ARE.
YEAH... THAT'S NICE, ACTUALLY.
ALL RIGHT, SWEETIE. LET'S LEAVE DADDY TO DO HIS SULKING.

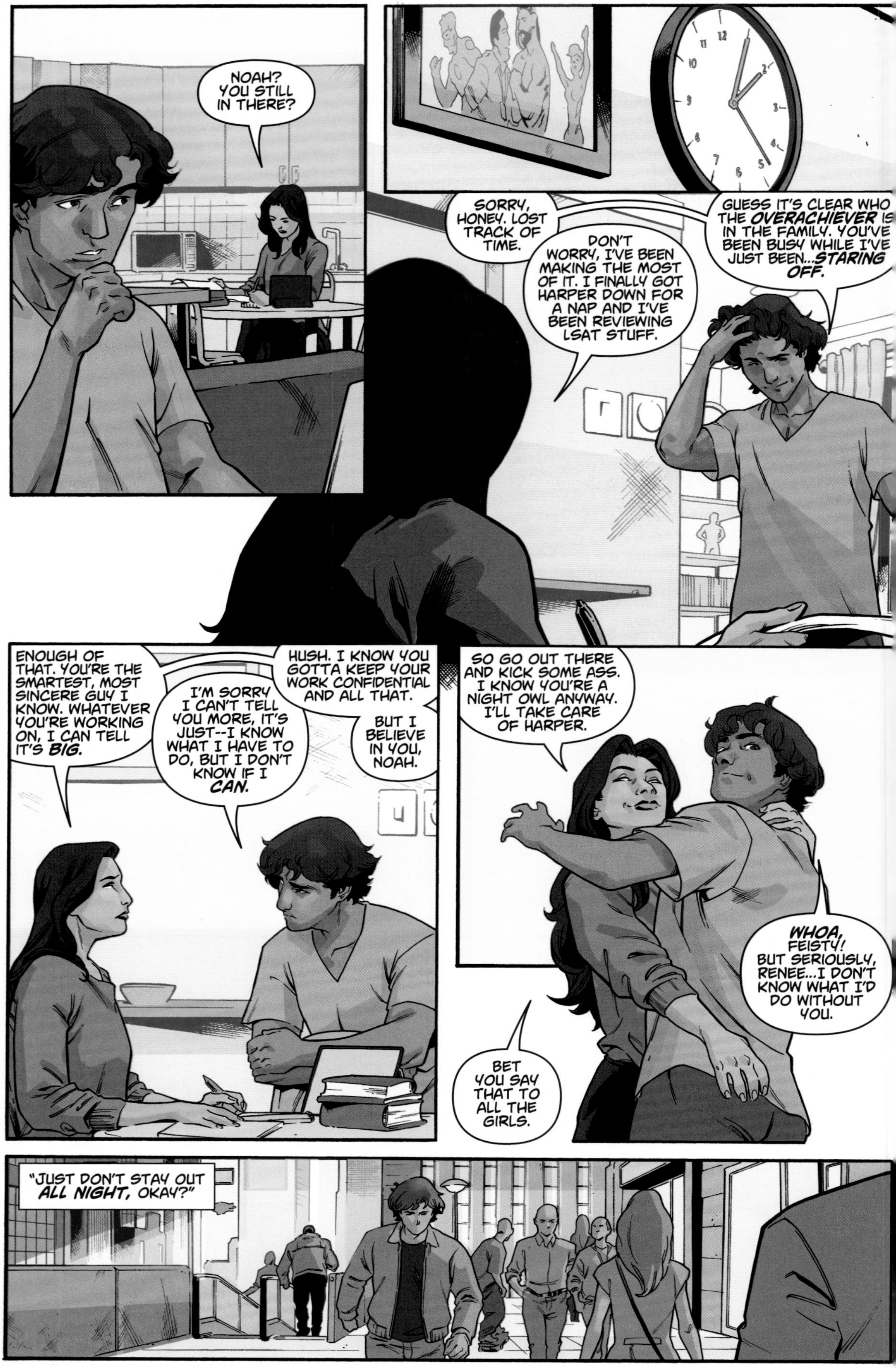
NOAH? YOU STILL IN THERE?
SORRY, HONEY. LOST TRACK OF TIME.
GUESS IT'S CLEAR WHO THE OVERACHIEVER IS IN THE FAMILY. YOU'VE BEEN BUSY WHILE I'VE JUST BEEN...STARING OFF.
DON'T WORRY, I'VE BEEN MAKING THE MOST OF IT. I FINALLY GOT HARPER DOWN FOR A NAP AND I'VE BEEN REVIEWING LSAT STUFF.
ENOUGH OF THAT. YOU'RE THE SMARTEST, MOST SINCERE GUY I KNOW. WHATEVER YOU'RE WORKING ON, I CAN TELL IT'S BIG.
I'M SORRY I CAN'T TELL YOU MORE, IT'S JUST--I KNOW WHAT I HAVE TO DO, BUT I DON'T KNOW IF I CAN.
HUSH. I KNOW YOU GOTTA KEEP YOUR WORK CONFIDENTIAL AND ALL THAT.
BUT I BELIEVE IN YOU, NOAH.
SO GO OUT THERE AND KICK SOME ASS. I KNOW YOU'RE A NIGHT OWL ANYWAY. I'LL TAKE CARE OF HARPER.
WHOA, FEISTY! BUT SERIOUSLY, RENEE...I DON'T KNOW WHAT I'D DO WITHOUT YOU.
BET YOU SAY THAT TO ALL THE GIRLS.
"JUST DON'T STAY OUT ALL NIGHT, OKAY?"

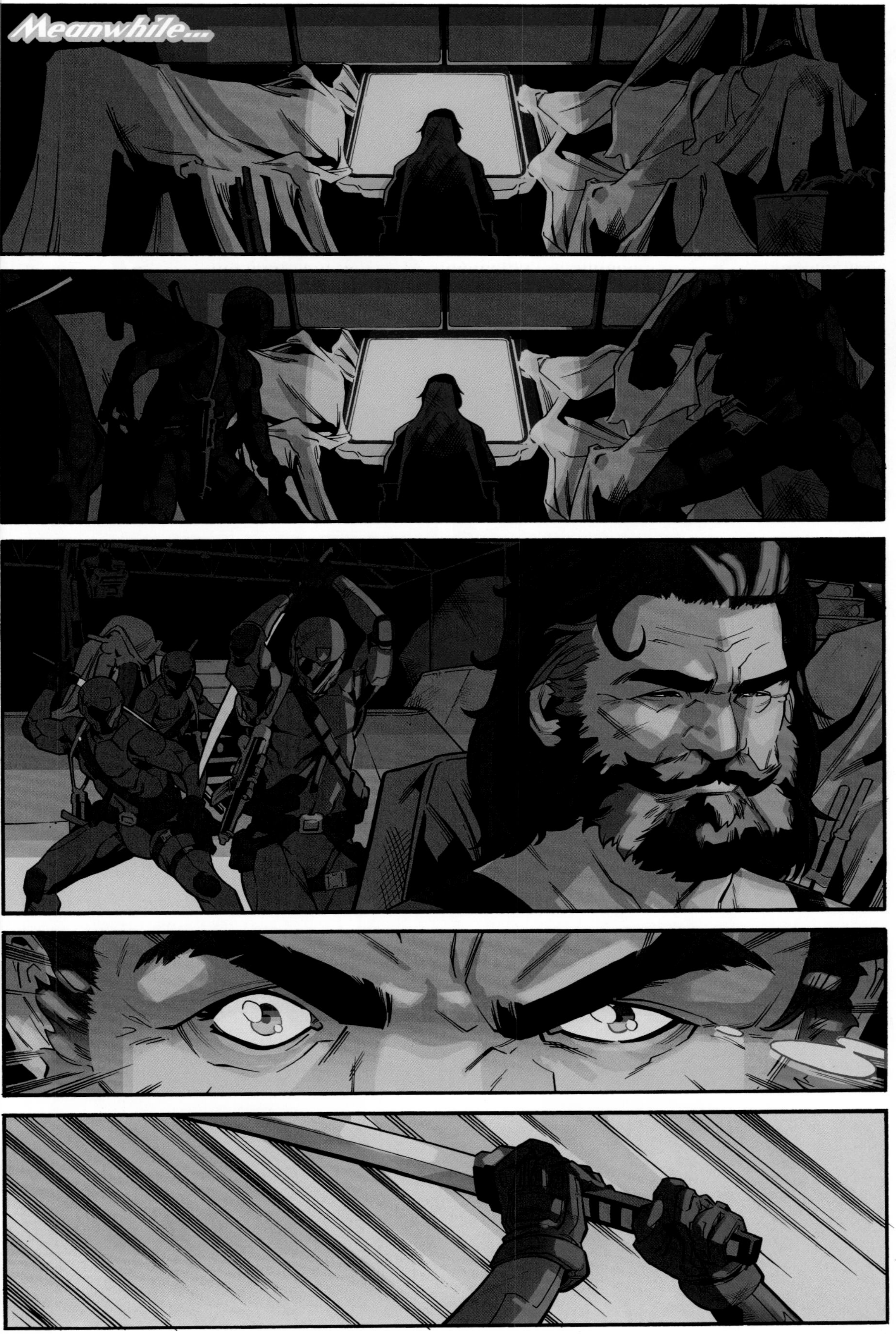
Meanwhile...

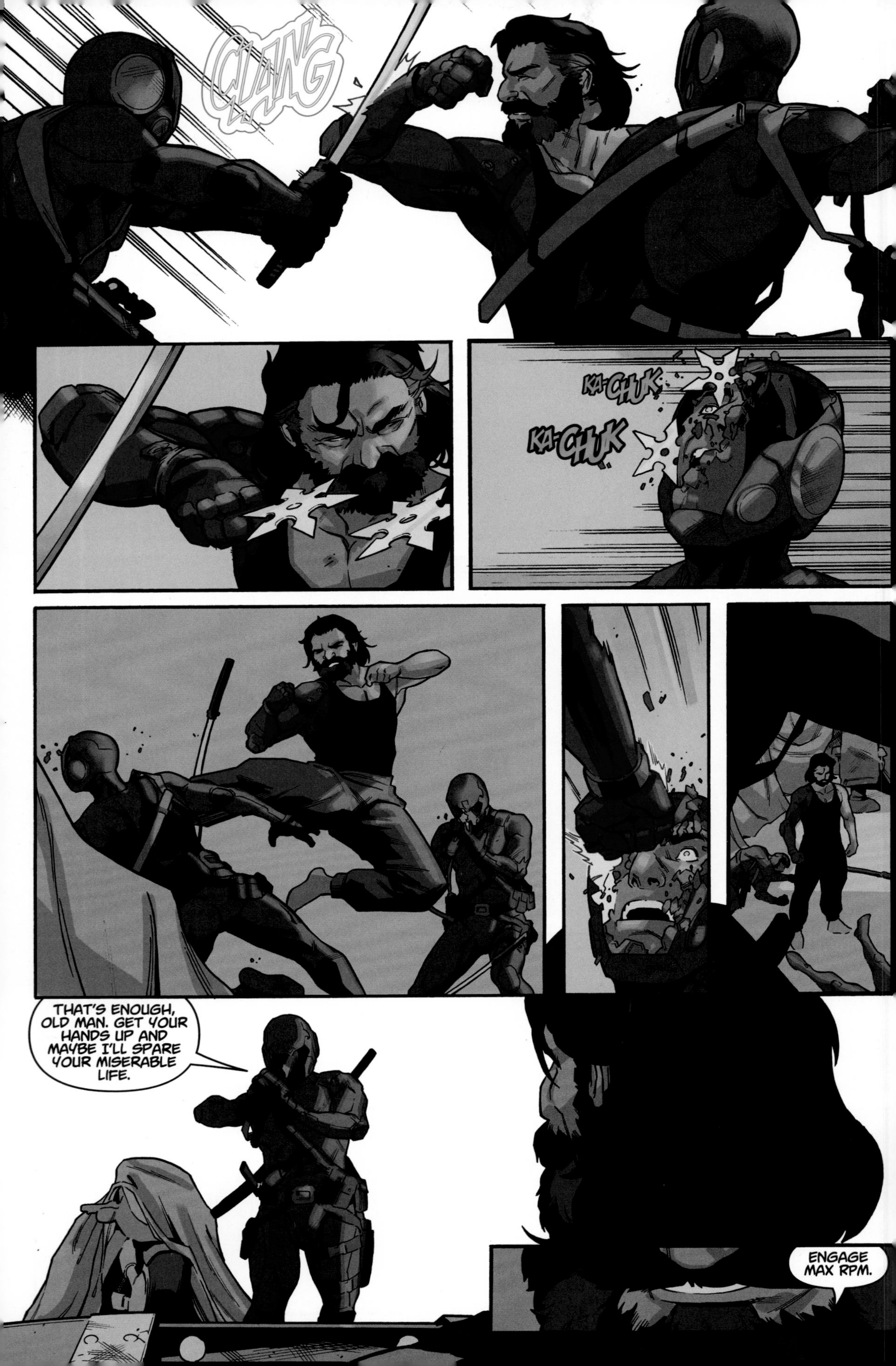
CLANG
KA-CHUK
KA-CHUK
THAT'S ENOUGH, OLD MAN. GET YOUR HANDS UP AND MAYBE I'LL SPARE YOUR MISERABLE LIFE.
ENGAGE MAX RPM.

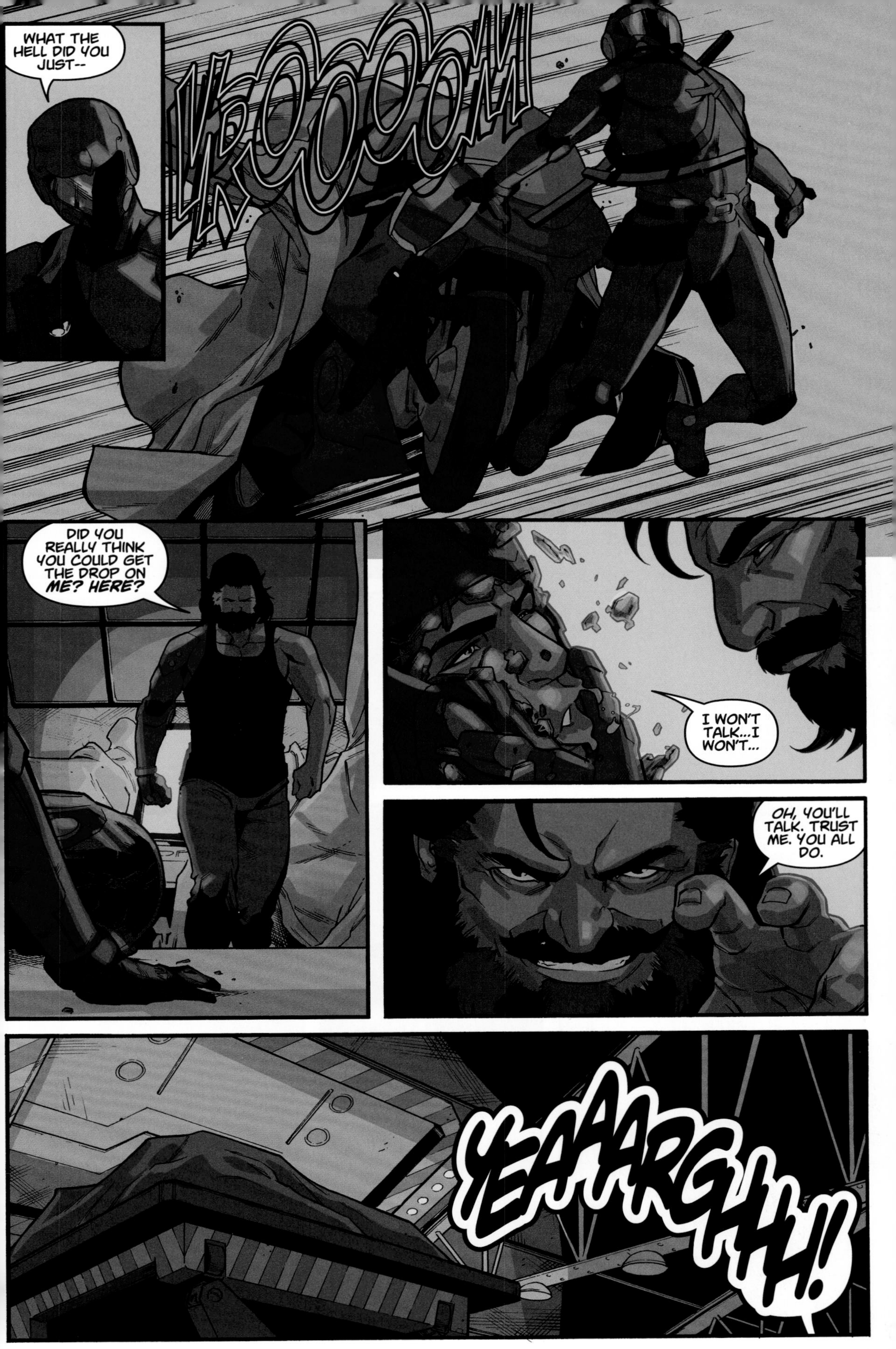
WHAT THE HELL DID YOU JUST--
VROOOOOOM
DID YOU REALLY THINK YOU COULD GET THE DROP ON ME? HERE?
I WON'T TALK...I WON'T...
OH, YOU'LL TALK. TRUST ME. YOU ALL DO.
YEAAARGHH!

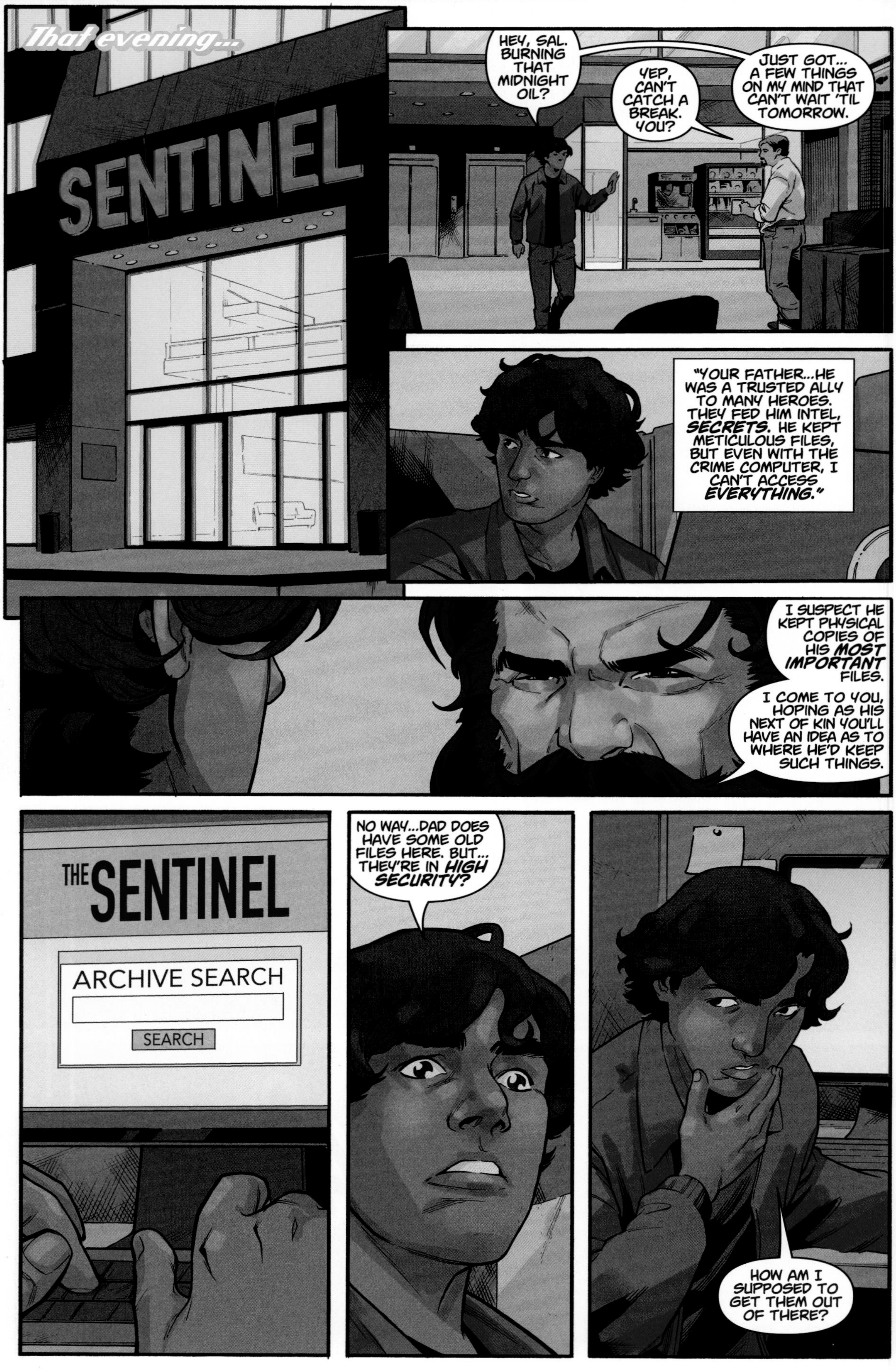
That evening...
SENTINEL
HEY, SAL. BURNING THAT MIDNIGHT OIL?
YEP, CAN'T CATCH A BREAK. YOU?
JUST GOT... A FEW THINGS ON MY MIND THAT CAN'T WAIT 'TIL TOMORROW.
"YOUR FATHER...HE WAS A TRUSTED ALLY TO MANY HEROES. THEY FED HIM INTEL, SECRETS. HE KEPT METICULOUS FILES, BUT EVEN WITH THE CRIME COMPUTER, I CAN'T ACCESS EVERYTHING."
I SUSPECT HE KEPT PHYSICAL COPIES OF HIS MOST IMPORTANT FILES.
I COME TO YOU, HOPING AS HIS NEXT OF KIN YOU'LL HAVE AN IDEA AS TO WHERE HE'D KEEP SUCH THINGS.
THE SENTINEL
ARCHIVE SEARCH
SEARCH
NO WAY...DAD DOES HAVE SOME OLD FILES HERE. BUT... THEY'RE IN HIGH SECURITY?
HOW AM I SUPPOSED TO GET THEM OUT OF THERE?

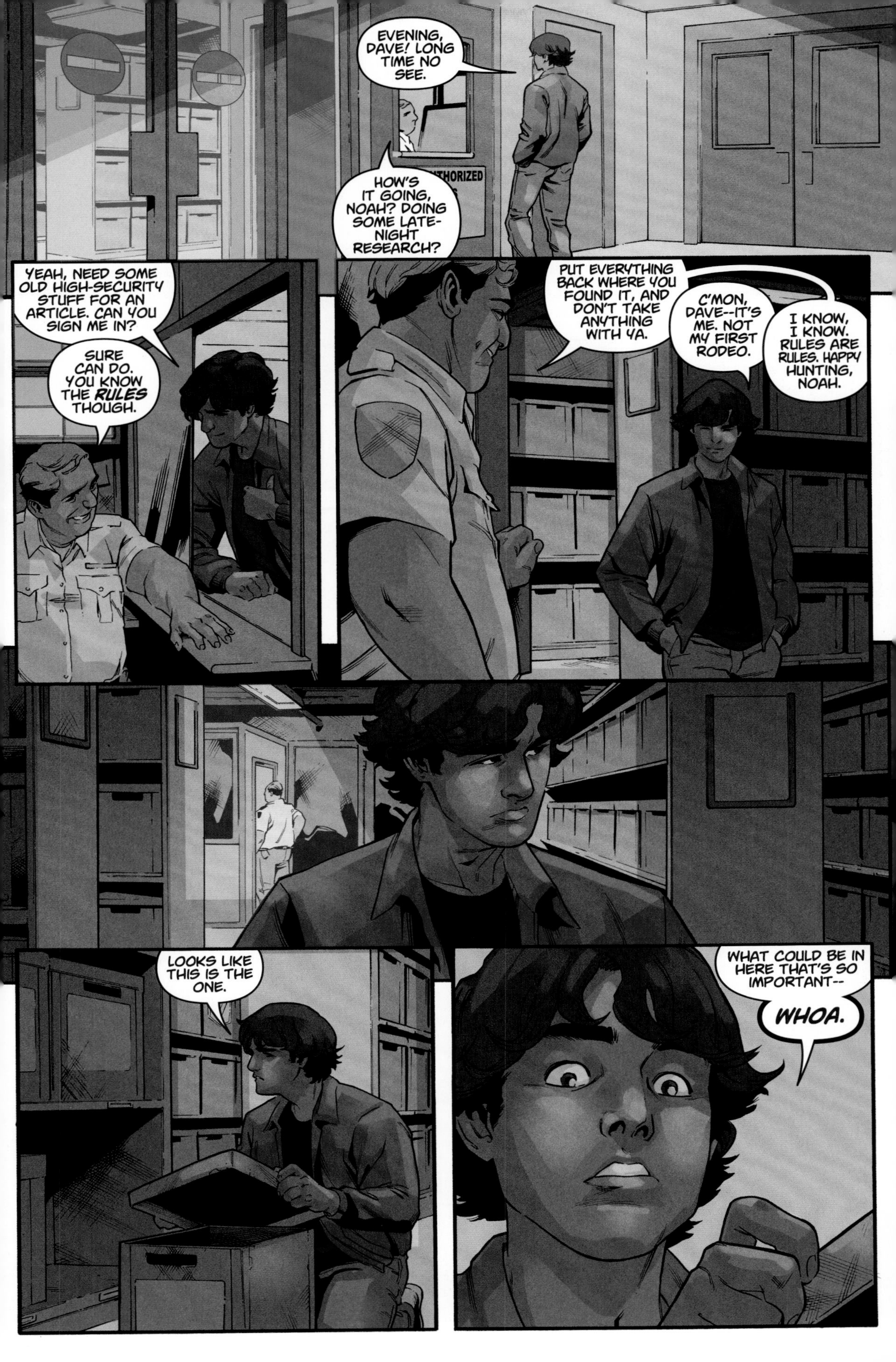

EVENING, DAVE! LONG TIME NO SEE.
HOW'S IT GOING, NOAH? DOING SOME LATE-NIGHT RESEARCH?
YEAH, NEED SOME OLD HIGH-SECURITY STUFF FOR AN ARTICLE. CAN YOU SIGN ME IN?
SURE CAN DO. YOU KNOW THE *RULES* THOUGH.
PUT EVERYTHING BACK WHERE YOU FOUND IT, AND DON'T TAKE ANYTHING WITH YA.
C'MON, DAVE--IT'S ME. NOT MY FIRST RODEO.
I KNOW, I KNOW. RULES ARE RULES. HAPPY HUNTING, NOAH.
LOOKS LIKE THIS IS THE ONE.
WHAT COULD BE IN HERE THAT'S SO IMPORTANT--
WHOA.

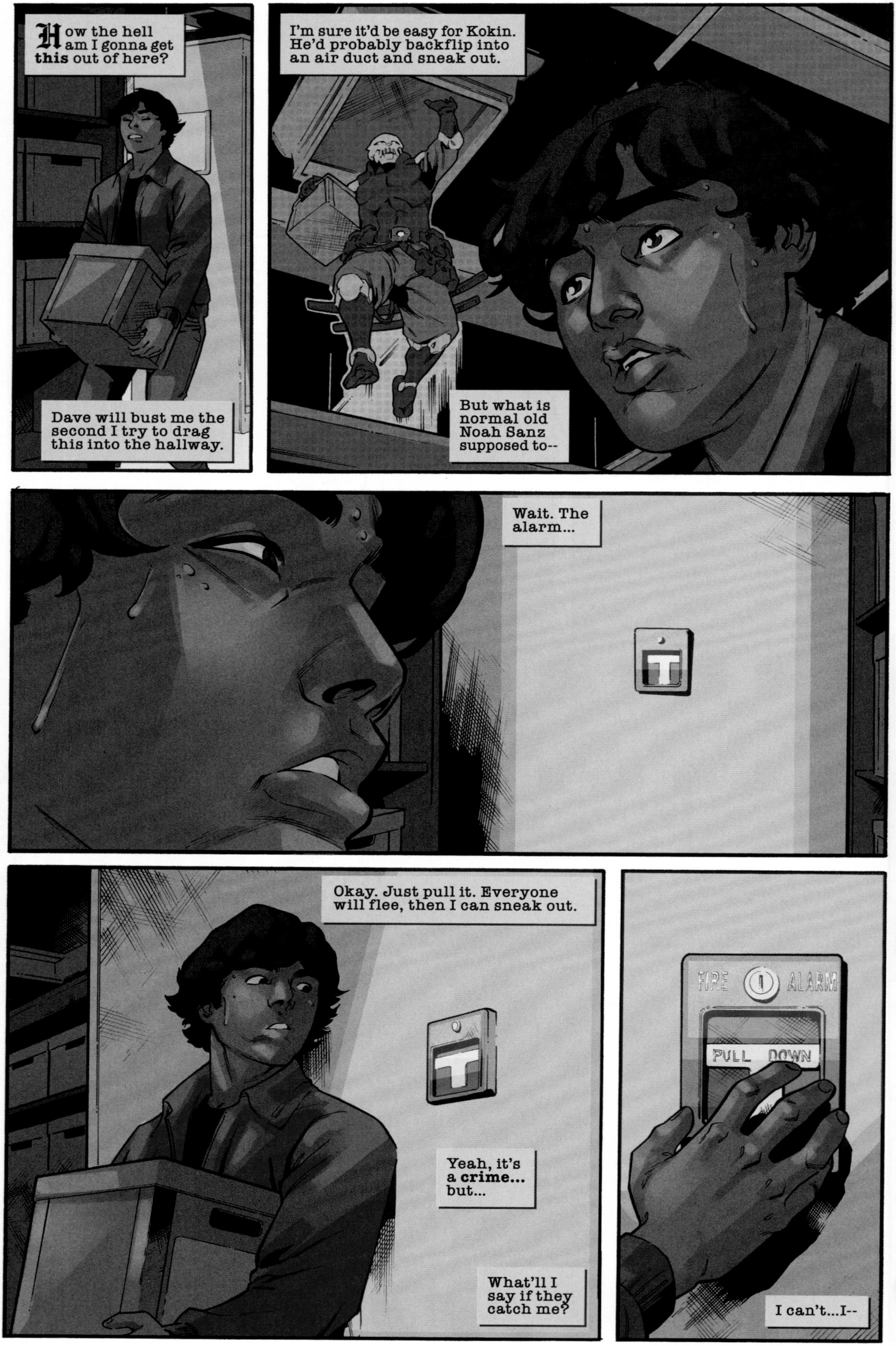
How the hell am I gonna get **this** out of here?
Dave will bust me the second I try to drag this into the hallway.
I'm sure it'd be easy for Kokin. He'd probably backflip into an air duct and sneak out.
But what is normal old Noah Sanz supposed to--
Wait. The alarm...
Okay. Just pull it. Everyone will flee, then I can sneak out.
Yeah, it's a **crime**... but...
What'll I say if they catch me?
FIRE ALARM
PULL DOWN
I can't...I--

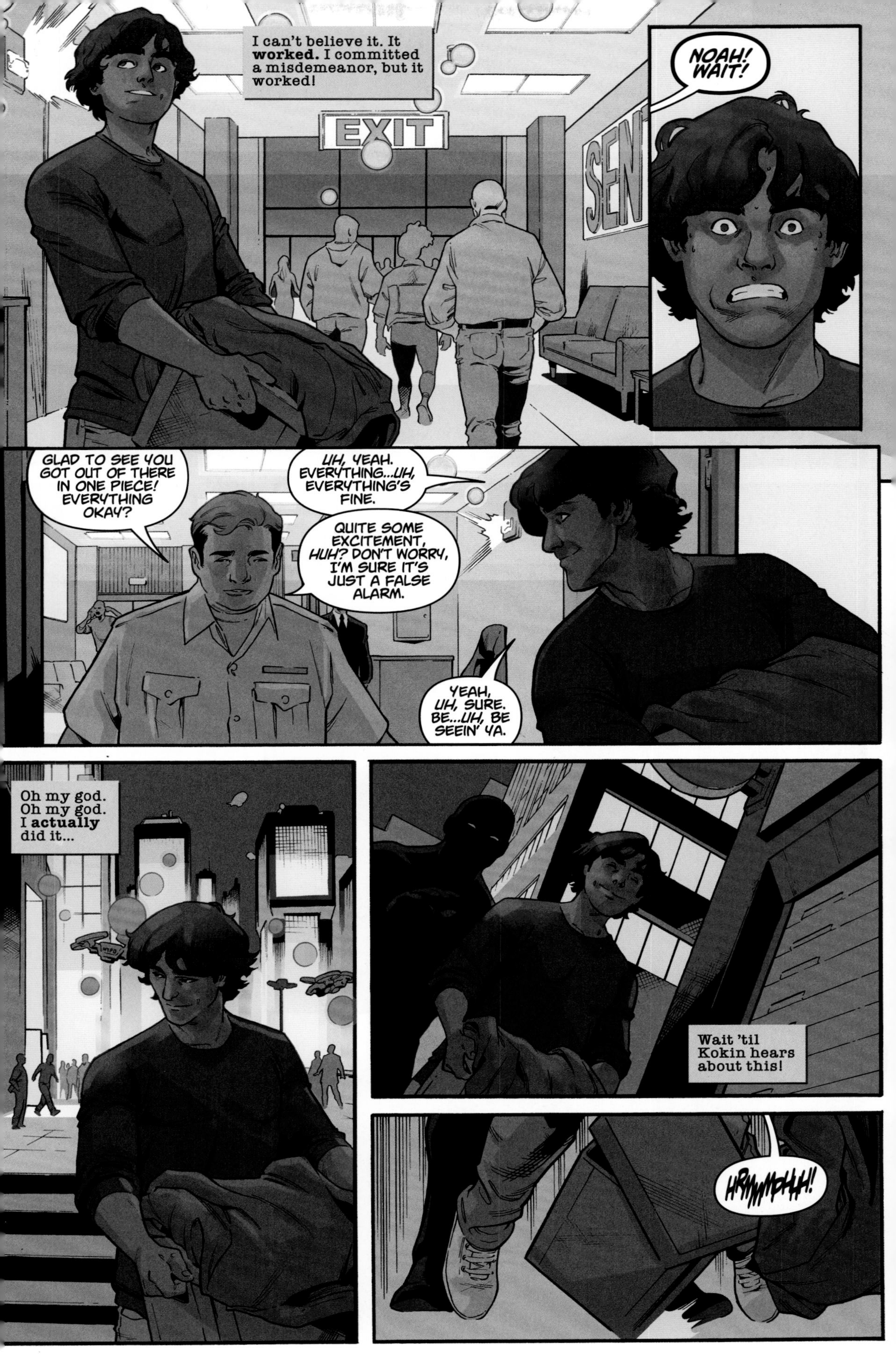
I can't believe it. It **worked.** I committed a misdemeanor, but it worked!
EXIT
NOAH! WAIT!
GLAD TO SEE YOU GOT OUT OF THERE IN ONE PIECE! EVERYTHING OKAY?
UH, YEAH. EVERYTHING...UH, EVERYTHING'S FINE.
QUITE SOME EXCITEMENT, HUH? DON'T WORRY, I'M SURE IT'S JUST A FALSE ALARM.
YEAH, UH, SURE. BE...UH, BE SEEIN' YA.
Oh my god. Oh my god. I **actually** did it...
Wait 'til Kokin hears about this!
HRMMMPHHH!

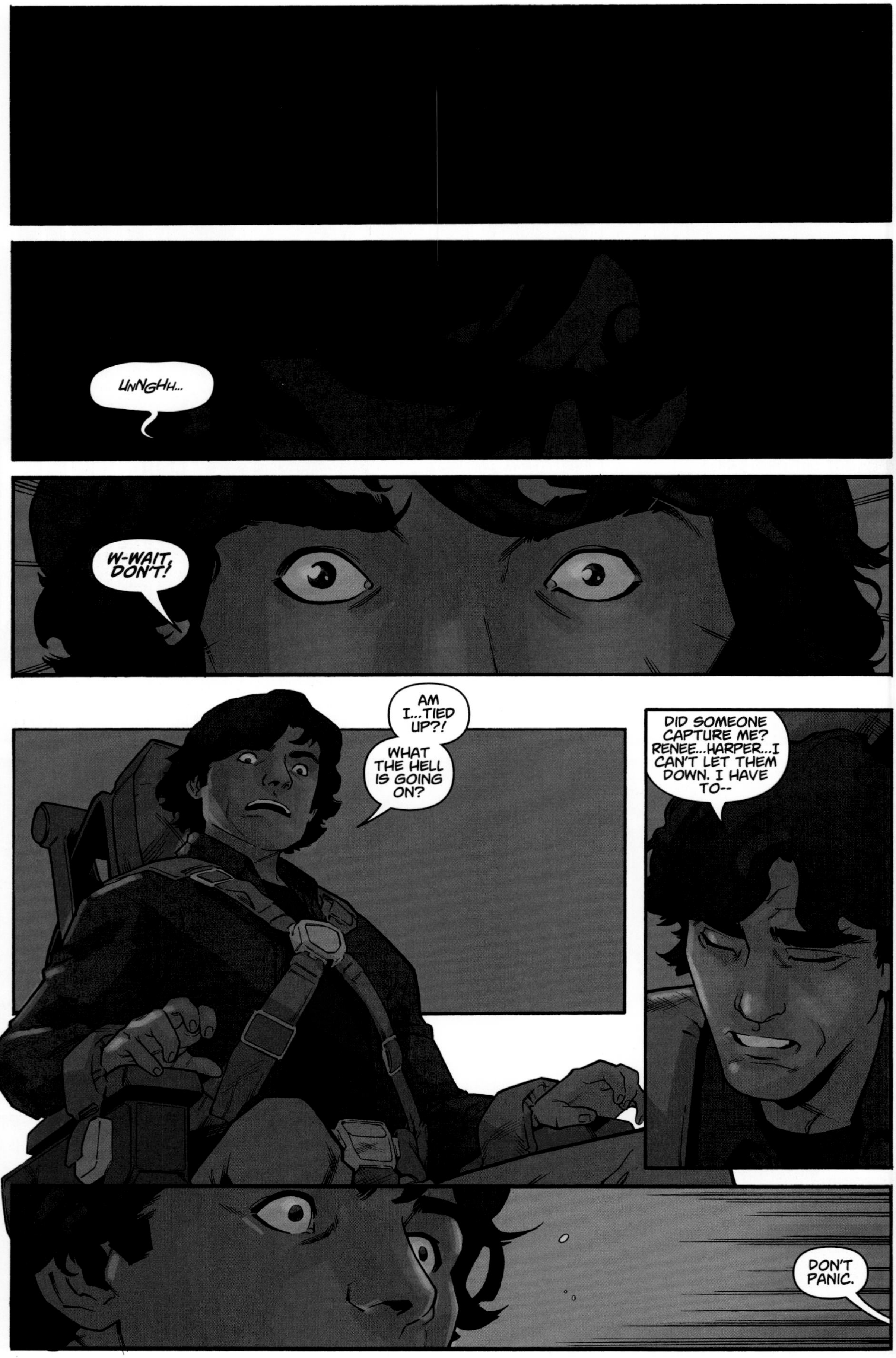

UNNGHH...
W-WAIT, DON'T!
AM I...TIED UP?!
WHAT THE HELL IS GOING ON?
DID SOMEONE CAPTURE ME? RENEE...HARPER...I CAN'T LET THEM DOWN. I HAVE TO--
DON'T PANIC.

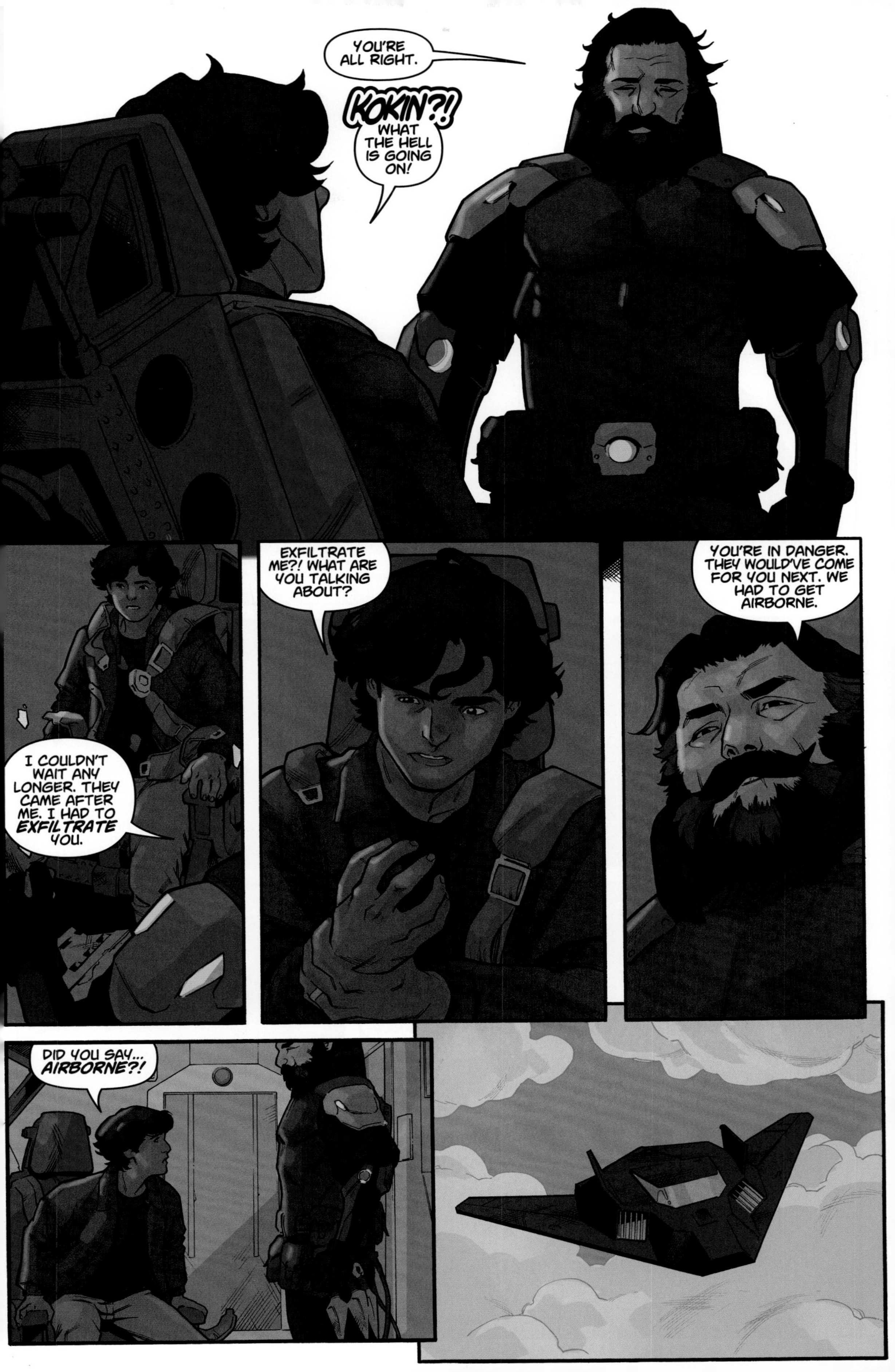
YOU'RE ALL RIGHT.
KOKIN?! WHAT THE HELL IS GOING ON!
I COULDN'T WAIT ANY LONGER. THEY CAME AFTER ME. I HAD TO EXFILTRATE YOU.
EXFILTRATE ME?! WHAT ARE YOU TALKING ABOUT?
YOU'RE IN DANGER. THEY WOULD'VE COME FOR YOU NEXT. WE HAD TO GET AIRBORNE.
DID YOU SAY... AIRBORNE?!

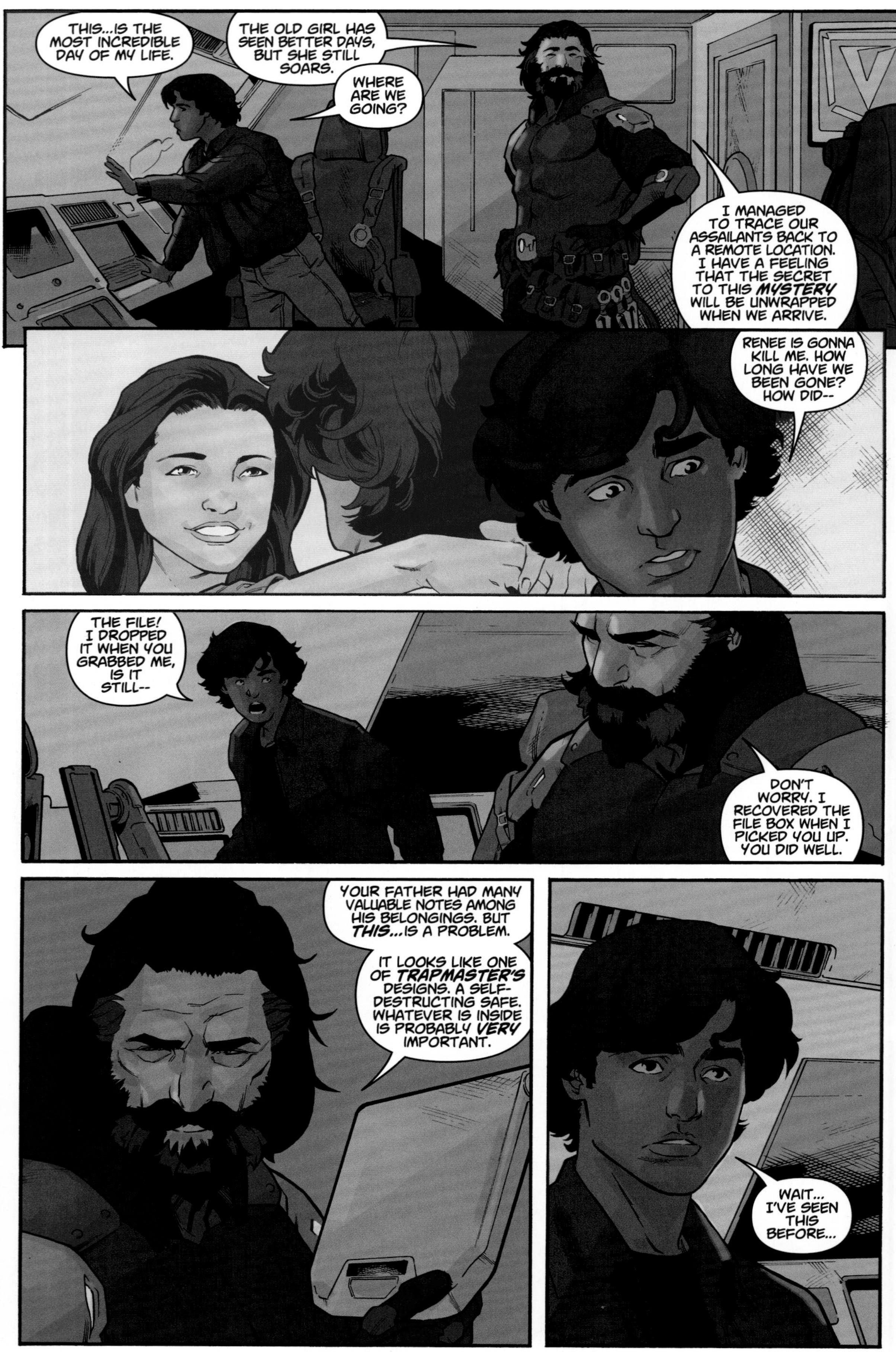
THIS...IS THE MOST INCREDIBLE DAY OF MY LIFE.
THE OLD GIRL HAS SEEN BETTER DAYS, BUT SHE STILL SOARS.
WHERE ARE WE GOING?
I MANAGED TO TRACE OUR ASSAILANTS BACK TO A REMOTE LOCATION. I HAVE A FEELING THAT THE SECRET TO THIS *MYSTERY* WILL BE UNWRAPPED WHEN WE ARRIVE.
RENEE IS GONNA KILL ME. HOW LONG HAVE WE BEEN GONE? HOW DID--
THE FILE! I DROPPED IT WHEN YOU GRABBED ME, IS IT STILL--
DON'T WORRY. I RECOVERED THE FILE BOX WHEN I PICKED YOU UP. YOU DID WELL.
YOUR FATHER HAD MANY VALUABLE NOTES AMONG HIS BELONGINGS. BUT *THIS...*IS A PROBLEM.
IT LOOKS LIKE ONE OF *TRAPMASTER'S* DESIGNS. A SELF-DESTRUCTING SAFE. WHATEVER IS INSIDE IS PROBABLY *VERY* IMPORTANT.
WAIT... I'VE SEEN THIS BEFORE...

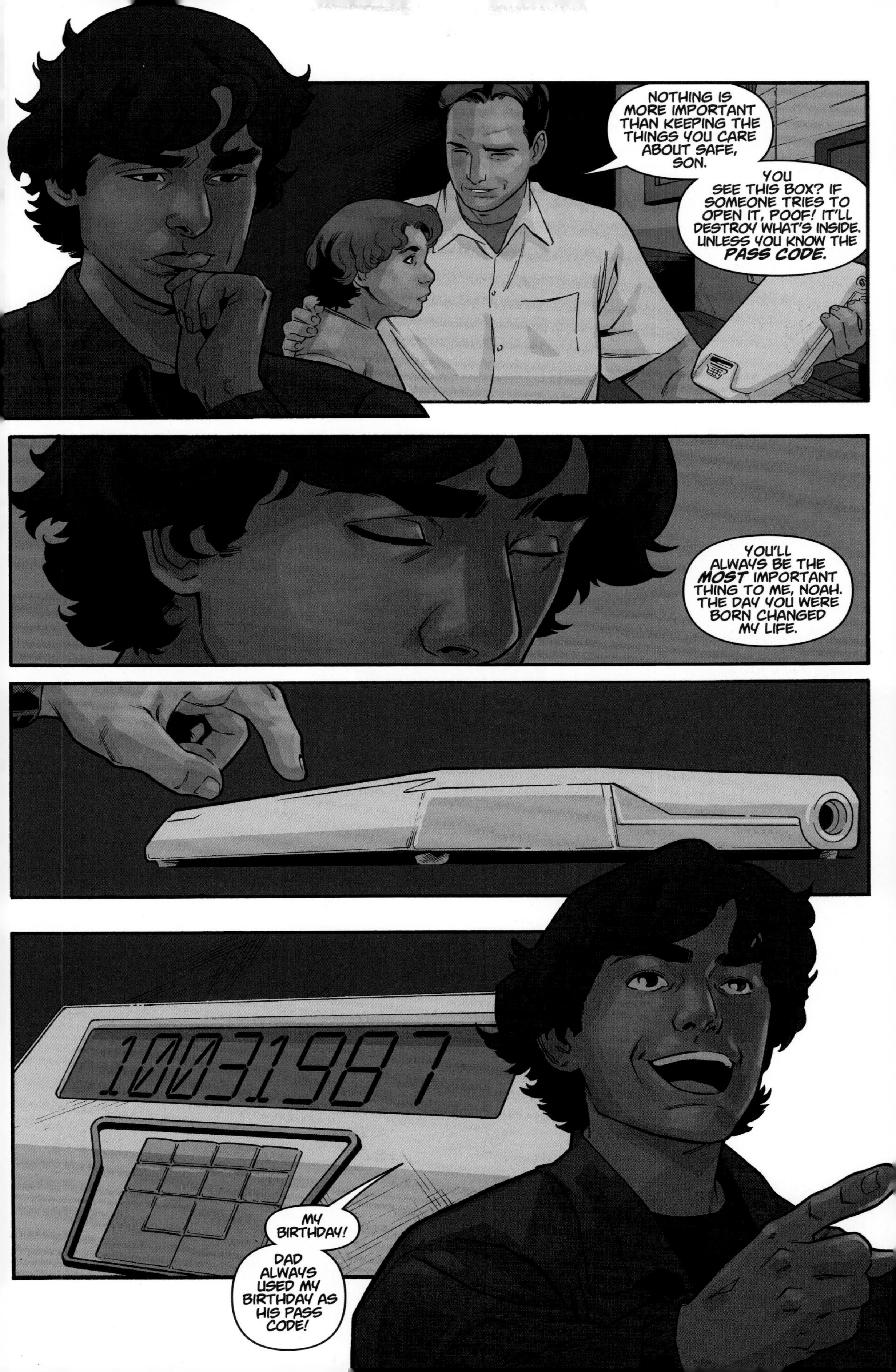
NOTHING IS MORE IMPORTANT THAN KEEPING THE THINGS YOU CARE ABOUT SAFE, SON.
YOU SEE THIS BOX? IF SOMEONE TRIES TO OPEN IT, POOF! IT'LL DESTROY WHAT'S INSIDE. UNLESS YOU KNOW THE PASS CODE.
YOU'LL ALWAYS BE THE MOST IMPORTANT THING TO ME, NOAH. THE DAY YOU WERE BORN CHANGED MY LIFE.
10031987
MY BIRTHDAY!
DAD ALWAYS USED MY BIRTHDAY AS HIS PASS CODE!

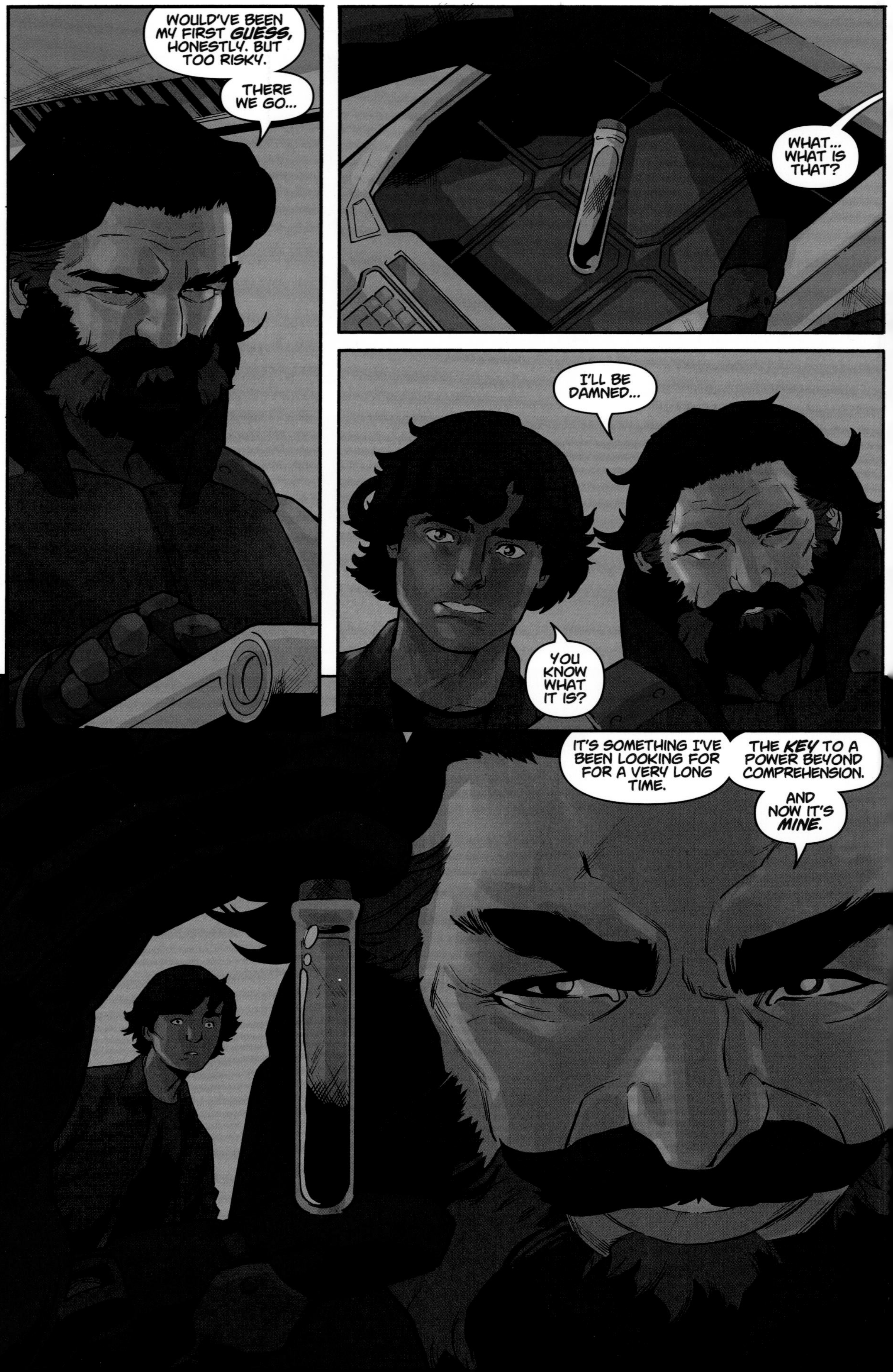
WOULD'VE BEEN MY FIRST GUESS, HONESTLY. BUT TOO RISKY.
THERE WE GO...
WHAT... WHAT IS THAT?
I'LL BE DAMNED...
YOU KNOW WHAT IT IS?
IT'S SOMETHING I'VE BEEN LOOKING FOR FOR A VERY LONG TIME.
THE KEY TO A POWER BEYOND COMPREHENSION.
AND NOW IT'S MINE.

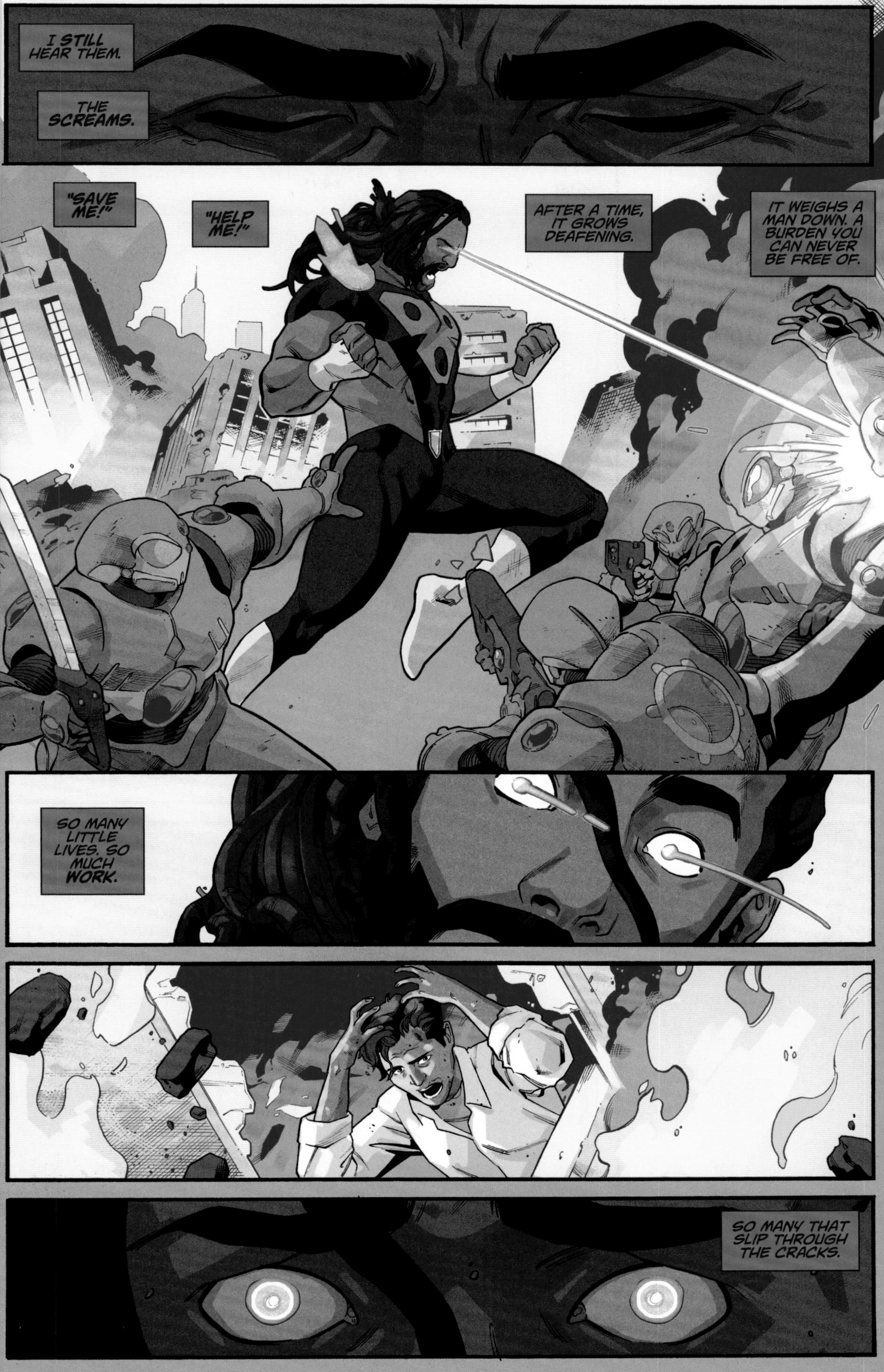
I STILL HEAR THEM.
THE SCREAMS.
"SAVE ME!"
"HELP ME!"
AFTER A TIME, IT GROWS DEAFENING.
IT WEIGHS A MAN DOWN. A BURDEN YOU CAN NEVER BE FREE OF.
SO MANY LITTLE LIVES. SO MUCH WORK.
SO MANY THAT SLIP THROUGH THE CRACKS.

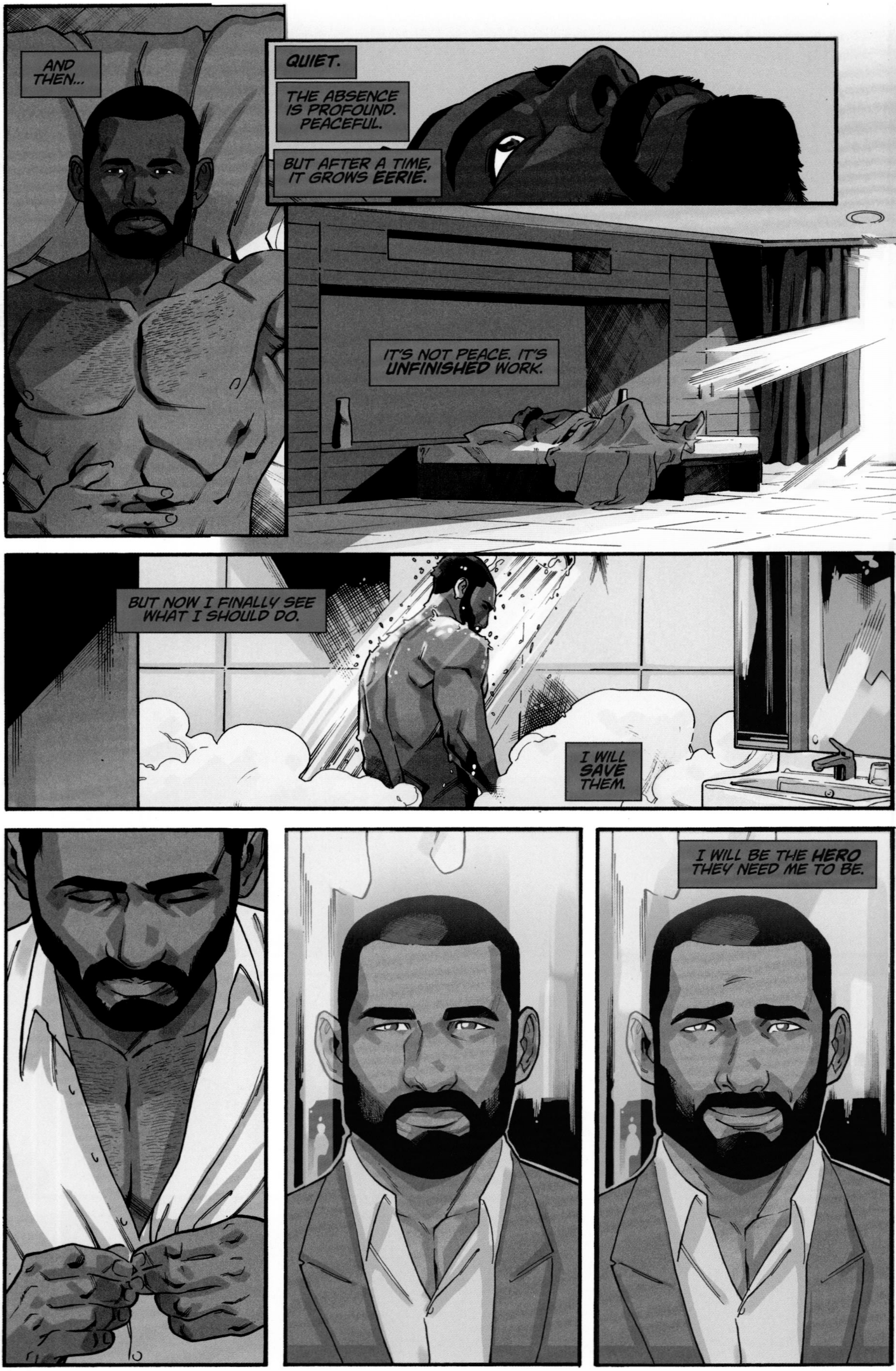
AND THEN...
QUIET.
THE ABSENCE IS PROFOUND. PEACEFUL.
BUT AFTER A TIME, IT GROWS EERIE.
IT'S NOT PEACE. IT'S UNFINISHED WORK.
BUT NOW I FINALLY SEE WHAT I SHOULD DO.
I WILL SAVE THEM.
I WILL BE THE HERO THEY NEED ME TO BE.

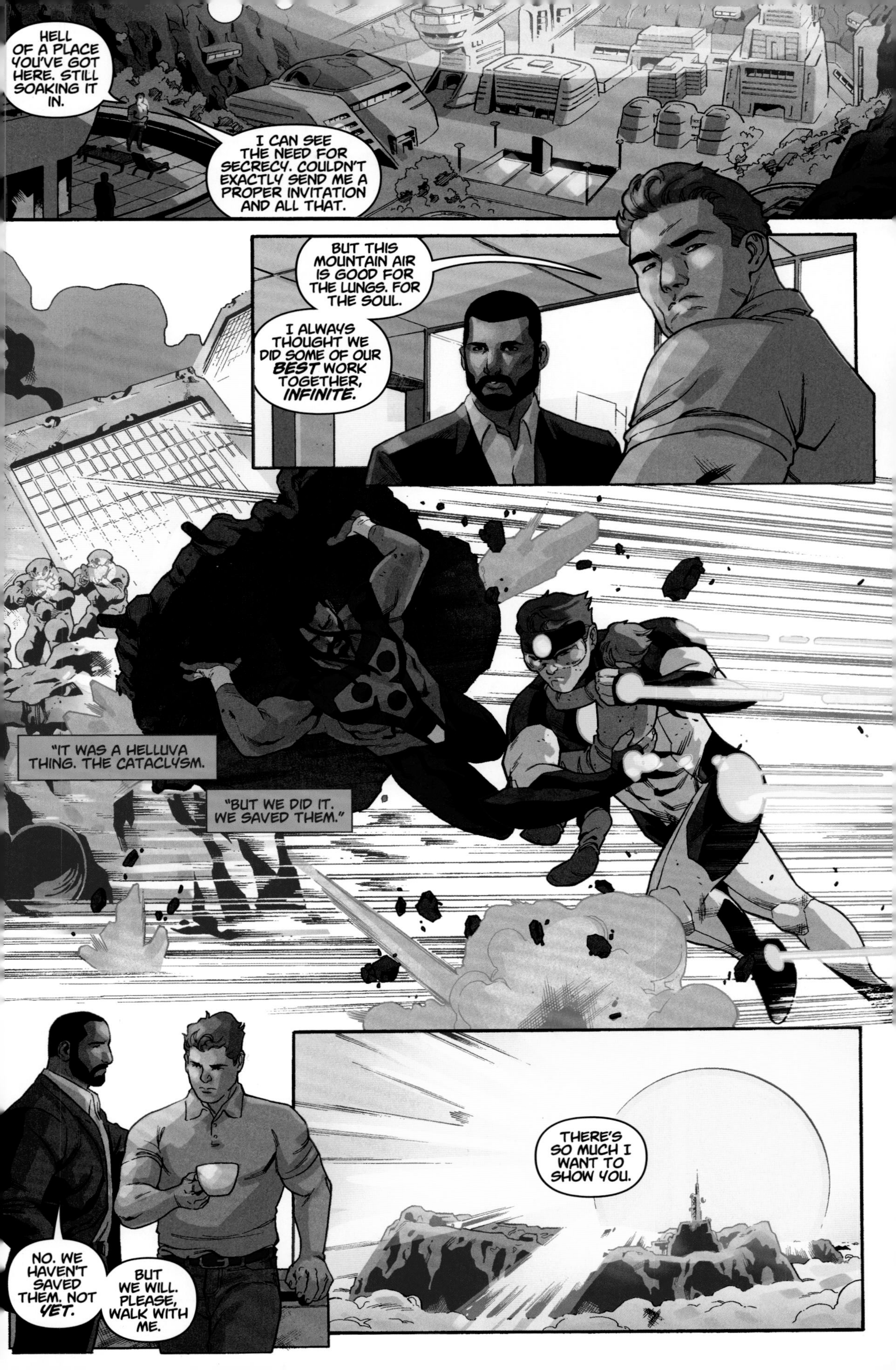
HELL OF A PLACE YOU'VE GOT HERE. STILL SOAKING IT IN.
I CAN SEE THE NEED FOR SECRECY. COULDN'T EXACTLY SEND ME A PROPER INVITATION AND ALL THAT.
BUT THIS MOUNTAIN AIR IS GOOD FOR THE LUNGS. FOR THE SOUL.
I ALWAYS THOUGHT WE DID SOME OF OUR BEST WORK TOGETHER, INFINITE.
"IT WAS A HELLUVA THING. THE CATACLYSM.
"BUT WE DID IT. WE SAVED THEM."
NO. WE HAVEN'T SAVED THEM. NOT YET.
BUT WE WILL. PLEASE, WALK WITH ME.
THERE'S SO MUCH I WANT TO SHOW YOU.

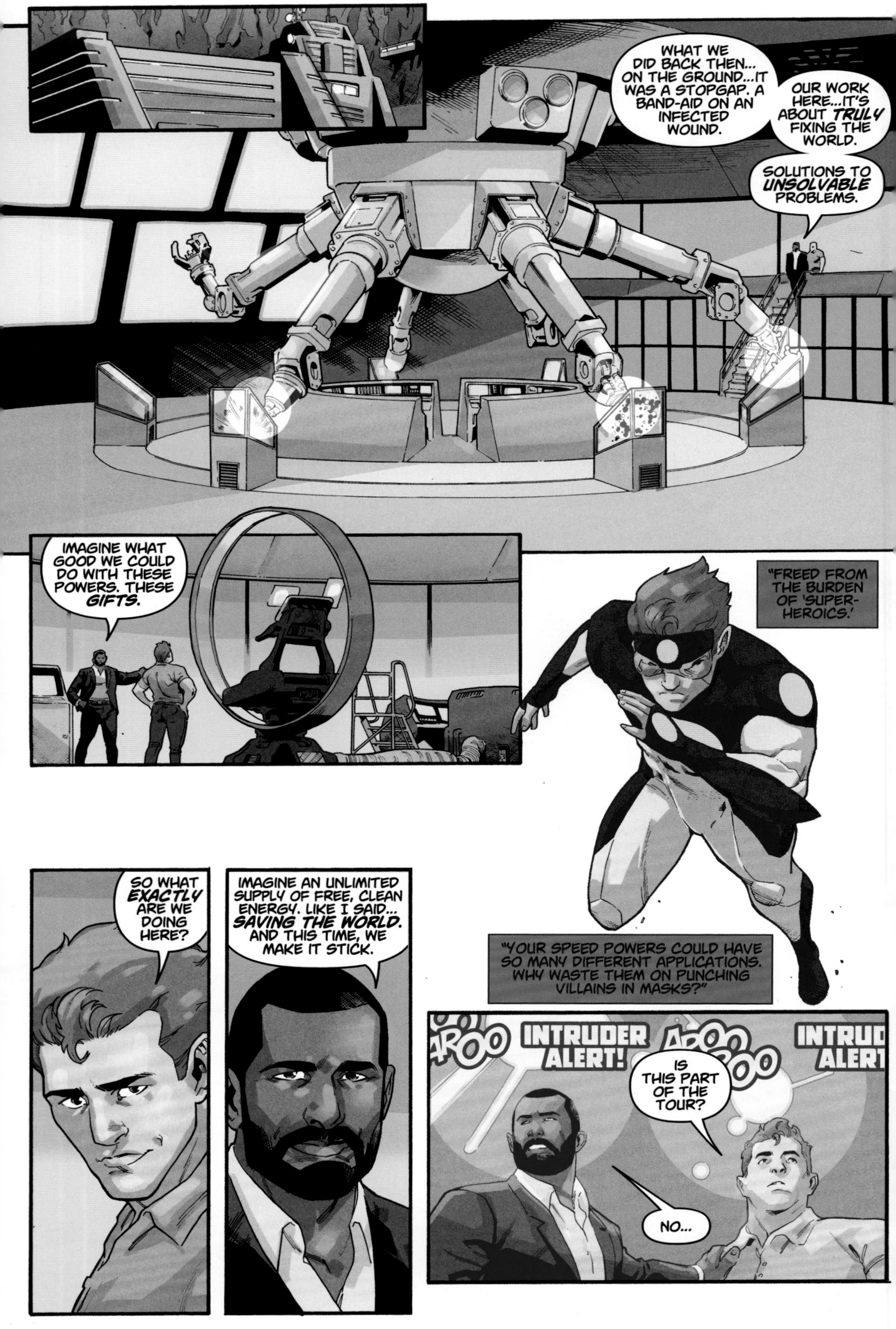
WHAT WE DID BACK THEN... ON THE GROUND...IT WAS A STOPGAP. A BAND-AID ON AN INFECTED WOUND.
OUR WORK HERE...IT'S ABOUT TRULY FIXING THE WORLD.
SOLUTIONS TO UNSOLVABLE PROBLEMS.
IMAGINE WHAT GOOD WE COULD DO WITH THESE POWERS. THESE GIFTS.
"FREED FROM THE BURDEN OF 'SUPER-HEROICS.'
"YOUR SPEED POWERS COULD HAVE SO MANY DIFFERENT APPLICATIONS. WHY WASTE THEM ON PUNCHING VILLAINS IN MASKS?"
SO WHAT EXACTLY ARE WE DOING HERE?
IMAGINE AN UNLIMITED SUPPLY OF FREE, CLEAN ENERGY. LIKE I SAID... SAVING THE WORLD. AND THIS TIME, WE MAKE IT STICK.
INTRUDER ALERT!
IS THIS PART OF THE TOUR?
NO...

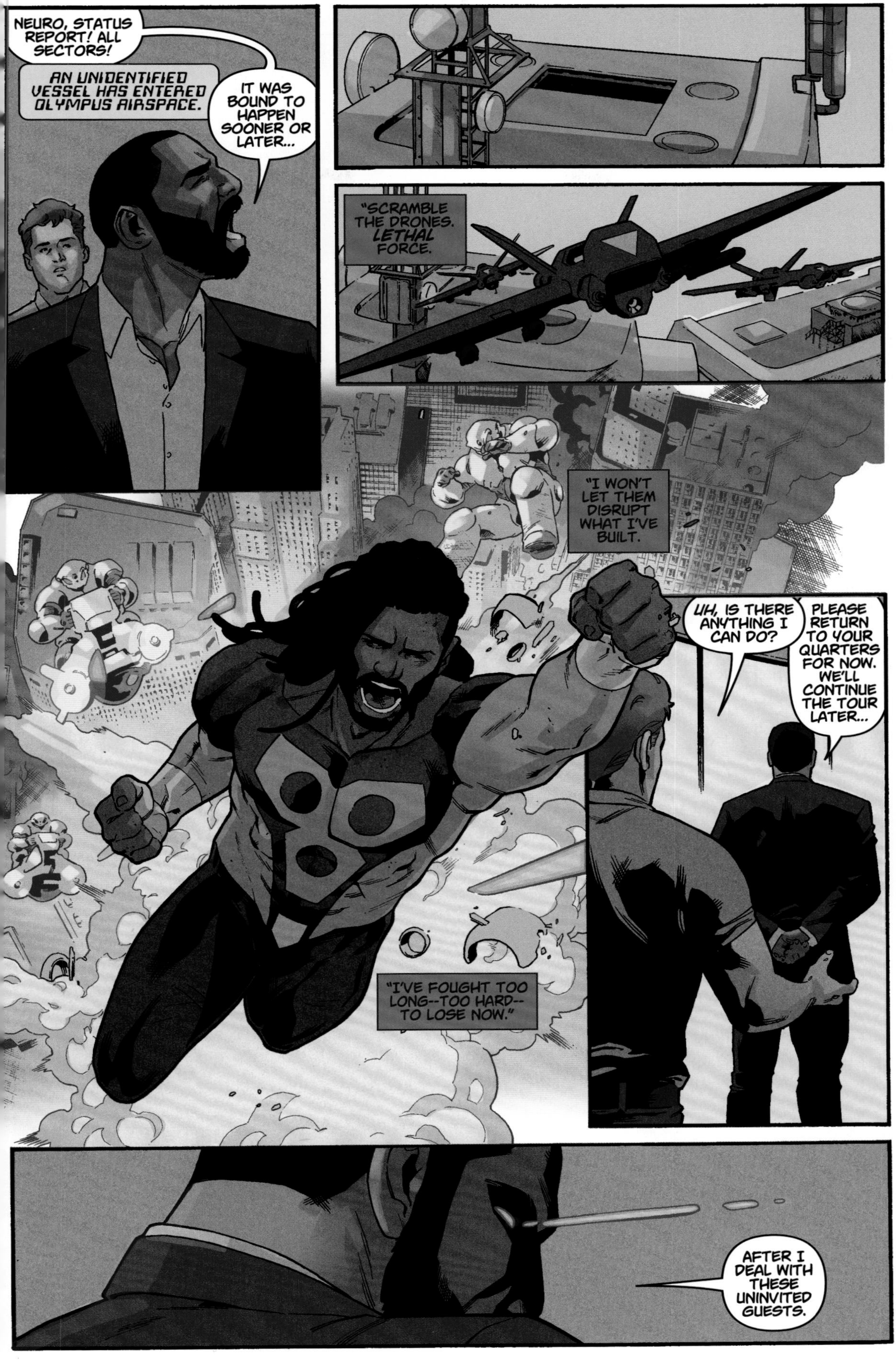
NEURO, STATUS REPORT! ALL SECTORS!
AN UNIDENTIFIED VESSEL HAS ENTERED OLYMPUS AIRSPACE.
IT WAS BOUND TO HAPPEN SOONER OR LATER...
"SCRAMBLE THE DRONES. LETHAL FORCE.
"I WON'T LET THEM DISRUPT WHAT I'VE BUILT.
"I'VE FOUGHT TOO LONG--TOO HARD--TO LOSE NOW."
UH, IS THERE ANYTHING I CAN DO?
PLEASE RETURN TO YOUR QUARTERS FOR NOW. WE'LL CONTINUE THE TOUR LATER...
AFTER I DEAL WITH THESE UNINVITED GUESTS.

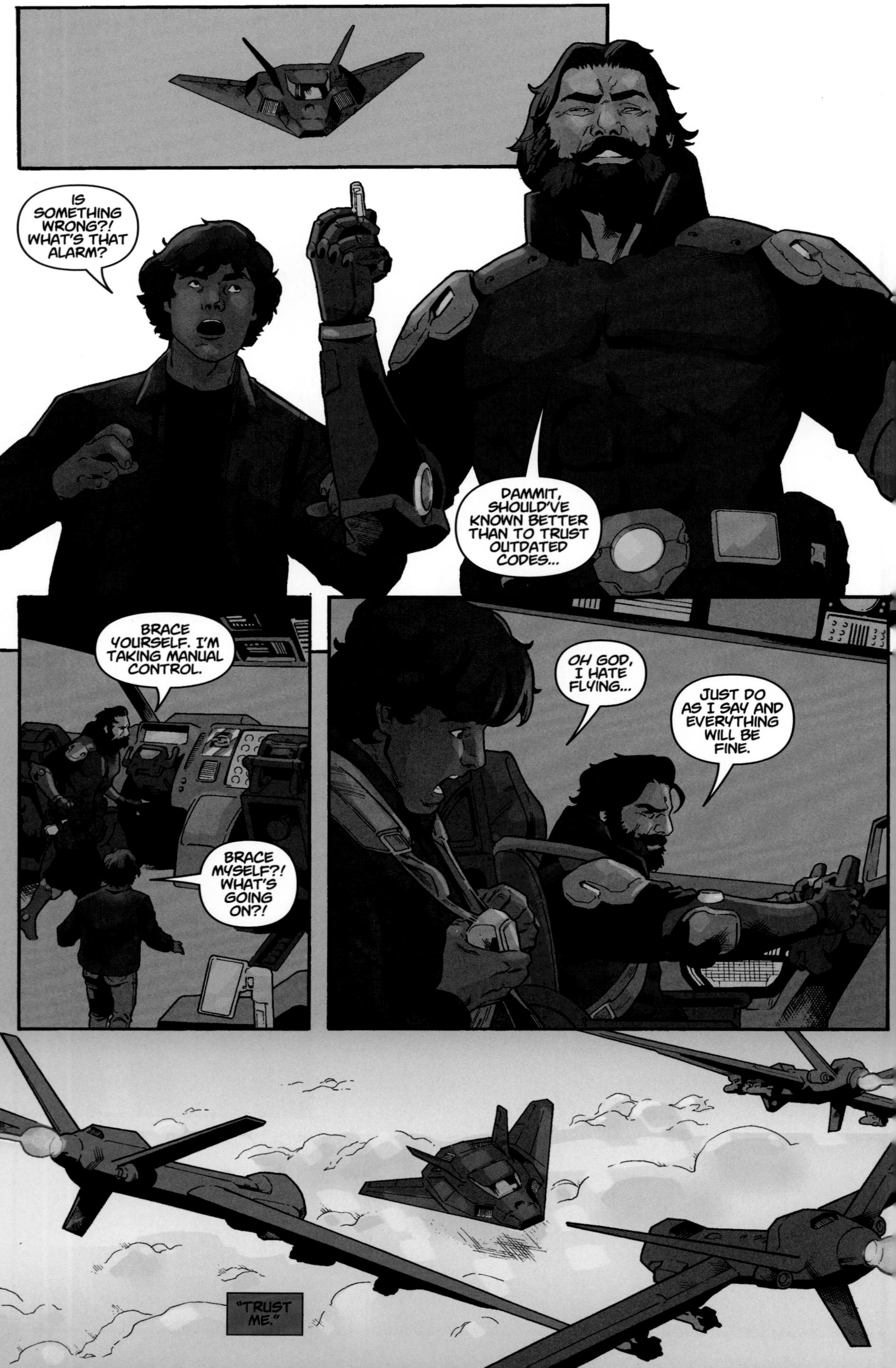
IS SOMETHING WRONG?! WHAT'S THAT ALARM?
DAMMIT, SHOULD'VE KNOWN BETTER THAN TO TRUST OUTDATED CODES...
BRACE YOURSELF. I'M TAKING MANUAL CONTROL.
BRACE MYSELF?! WHAT'S GOING ON?!
OH GOD, I HATE FLYING...
JUST DO AS I SAY AND EVERYTHING WILL BE FINE.
"TRUST ME."

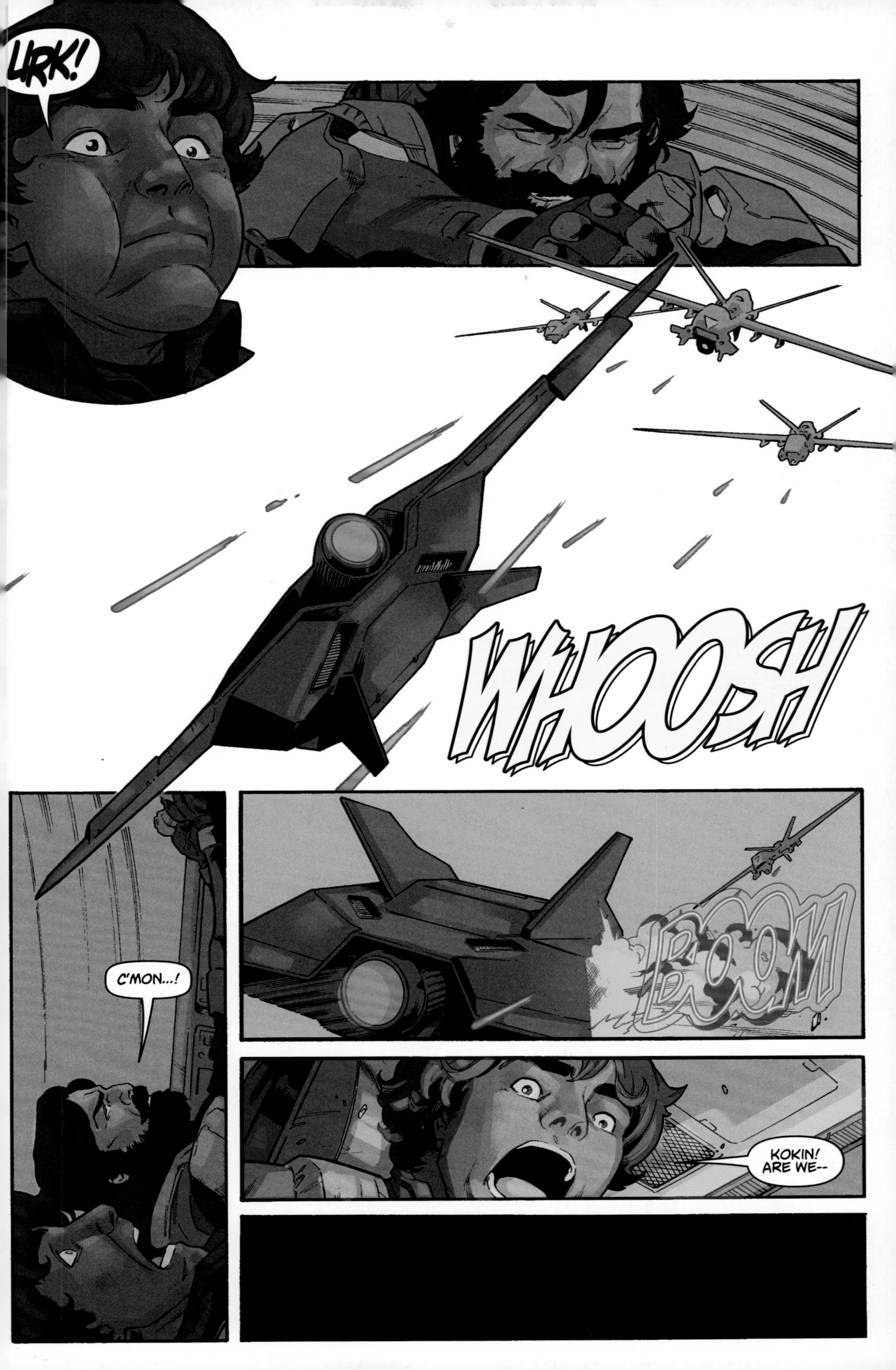
URK!
WHOOSH
C'MON...!
BOOM
KOKIN! ARE WE--

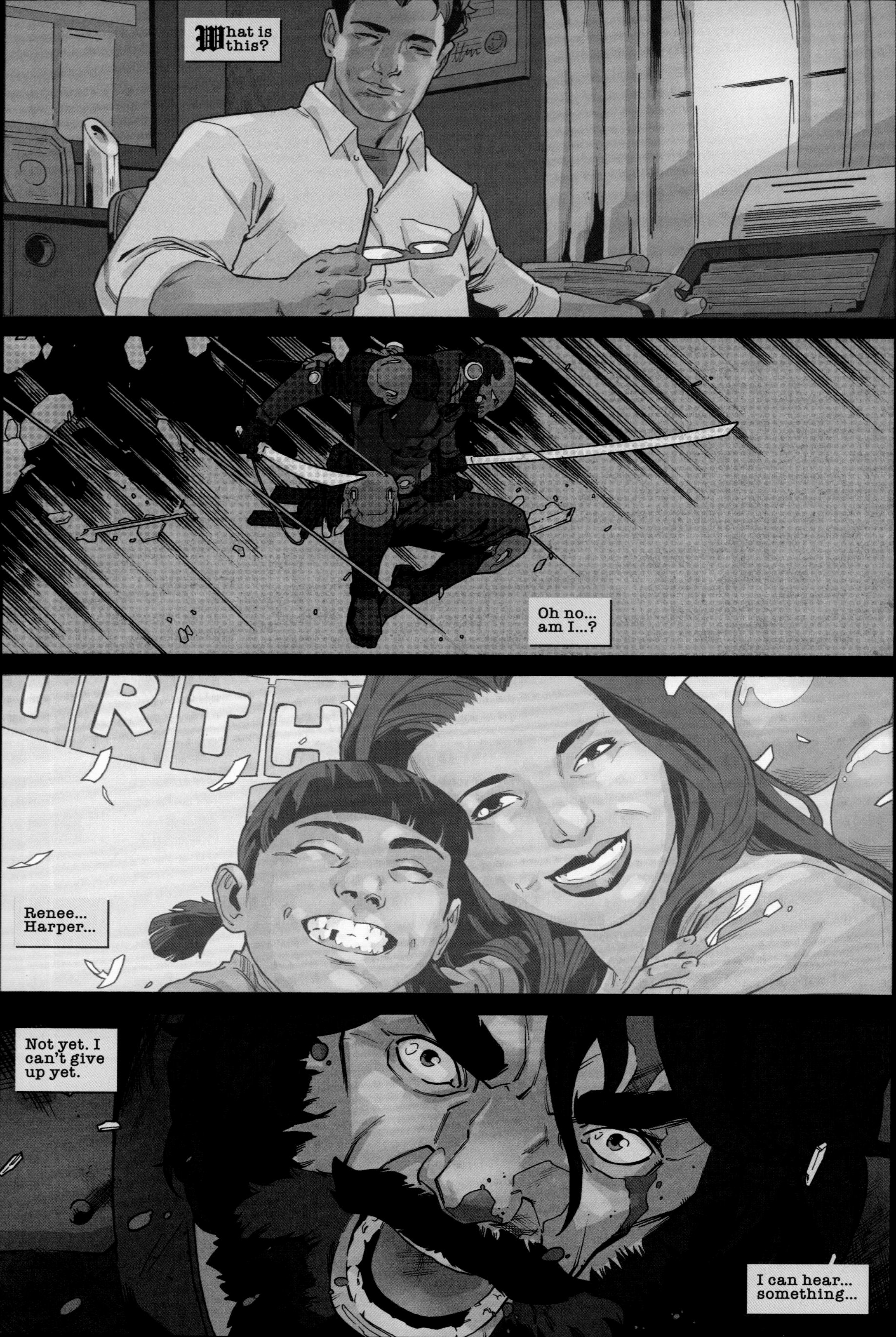
What is this?
Oh no... am I...?
Renee... Harper...
Not yet. I can't give up yet.
I can hear... something...

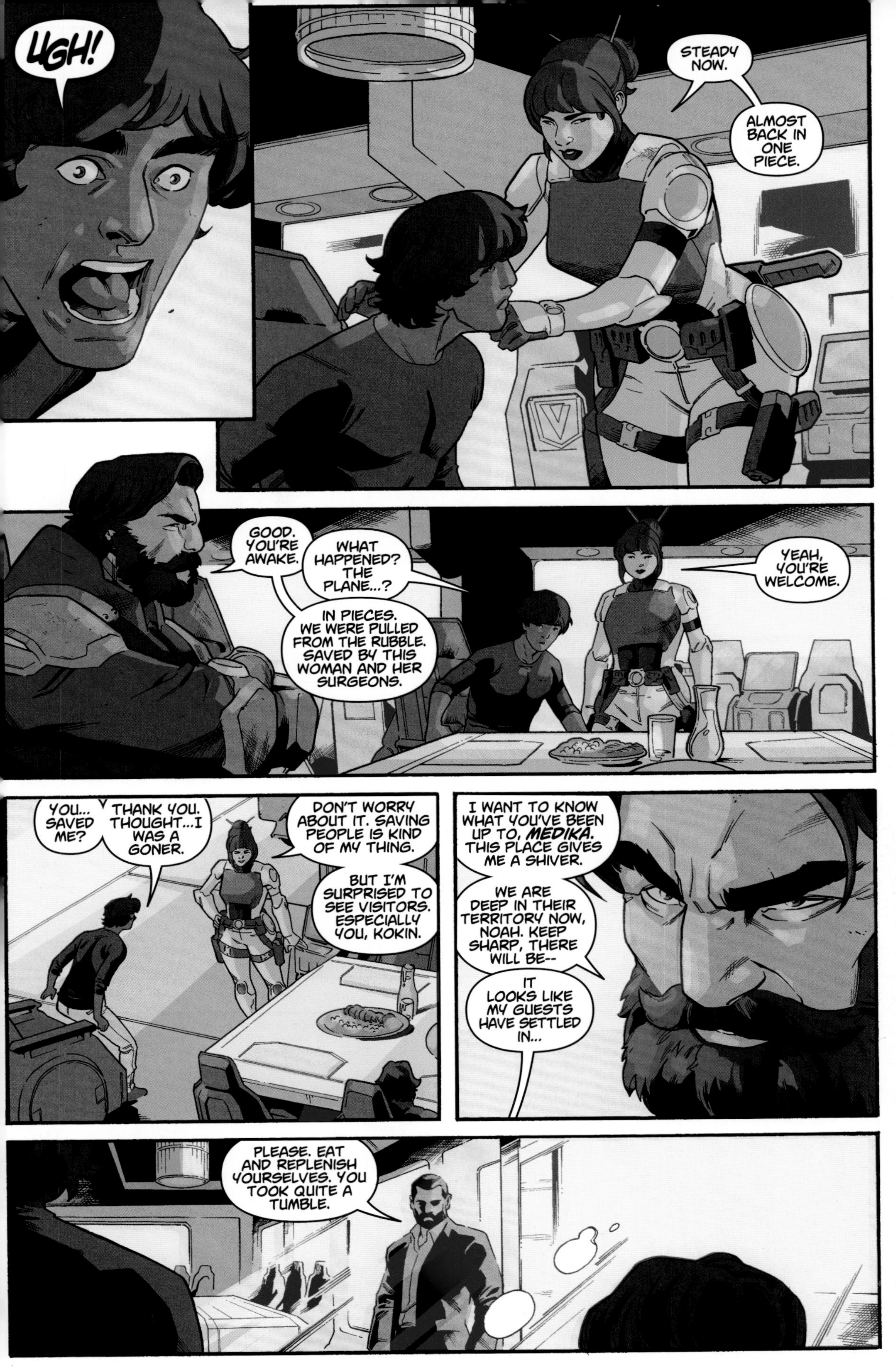
UGH!
STEADY NOW.
ALMOST BACK IN ONE PIECE.
GOOD. YOU'RE AWAKE.
WHAT HAPPENED? THE PLANE...?
IN PIECES. WE WERE PULLED FROM THE RUBBLE. SAVED BY THIS WOMAN AND HER SURGEONS.
YEAH, YOU'RE WELCOME.
YOU... SAVED ME?
THANK YOU. THOUGHT...I WAS A GONER.
DON'T WORRY ABOUT IT. SAVING PEOPLE IS KIND OF MY THING.
BUT I'M SURPRISED TO SEE VISITORS. ESPECIALLY YOU, KOKIN.
I WANT TO KNOW WHAT YOU'VE BEEN UP TO, MEDIKA. THIS PLACE GIVES ME A SHIVER.
WE ARE DEEP IN THEIR TERRITORY NOW, NOAH. KEEP SHARP, THERE WILL BE--
IT LOOKS LIKE MY GUESTS HAVE SETTLED IN...
PLEASE. EAT AND REPLENISH YOURSELVES. YOU TOOK QUITE A TUMBLE.

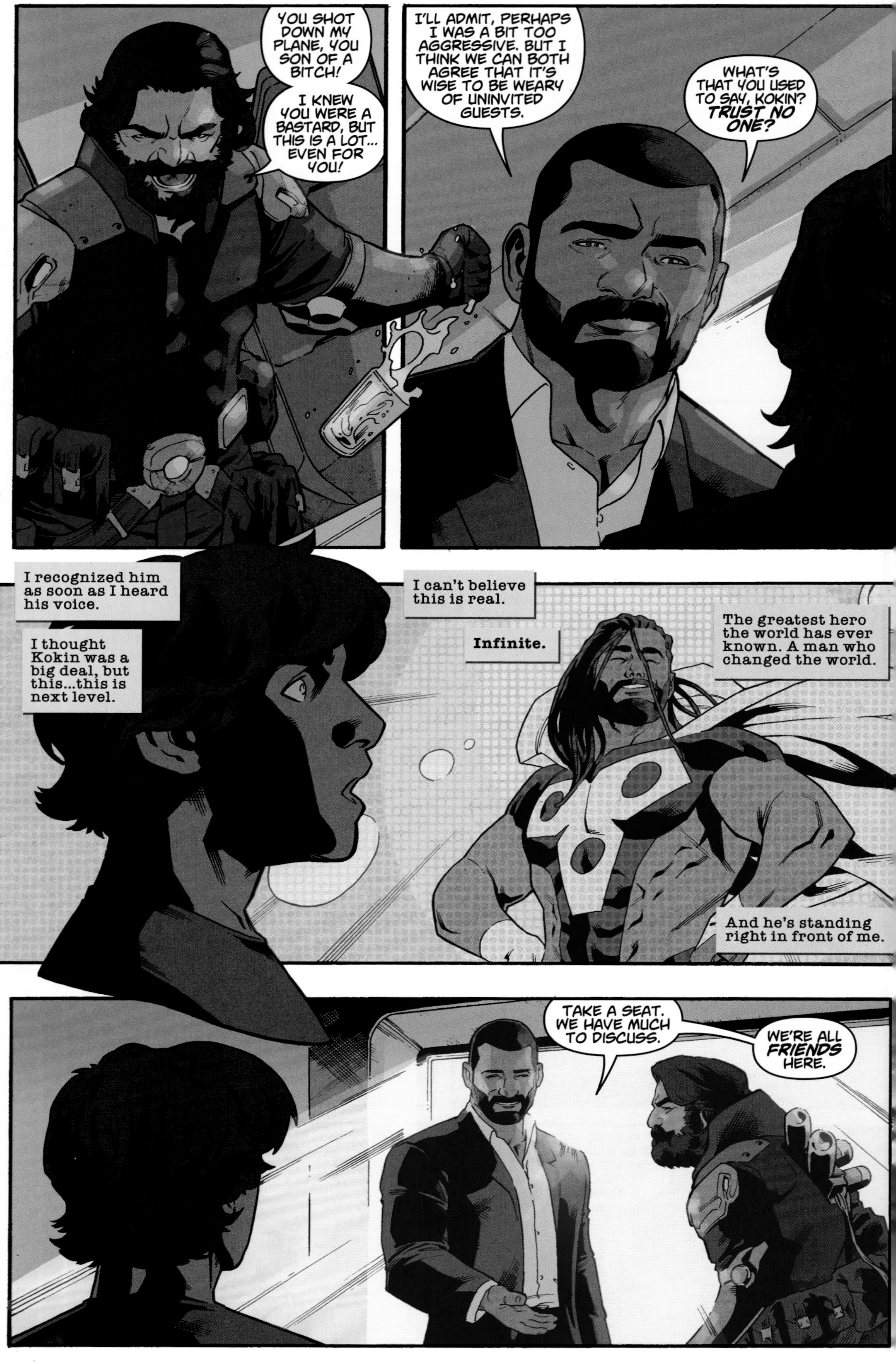
YOU SHOT DOWN MY PLANE, YOU SON OF A BITCH!
I KNEW YOU WERE A BASTARD, BUT THIS IS A LOT... EVEN FOR YOU!
I'LL ADMIT, PERHAPS I WAS A BIT TOO AGGRESSIVE. BUT I THINK WE CAN BOTH AGREE THAT IT'S WISE TO BE WEARY OF UNINVITED GUESTS.
WHAT'S THAT YOU USED TO SAY, KOKIN? *TRUST NO ONE?*
I recognized him as soon as I heard his voice.
I thought Kokin was a big deal, but this...this is next level.
I can't believe this is real.
Infinite.
The greatest hero the world has ever known. A man who changed the world.
And he's standing right in front of me.
TAKE A SEAT. WE HAVE MUCH TO DISCUSS.
WE'RE ALL *FRIENDS* HERE.

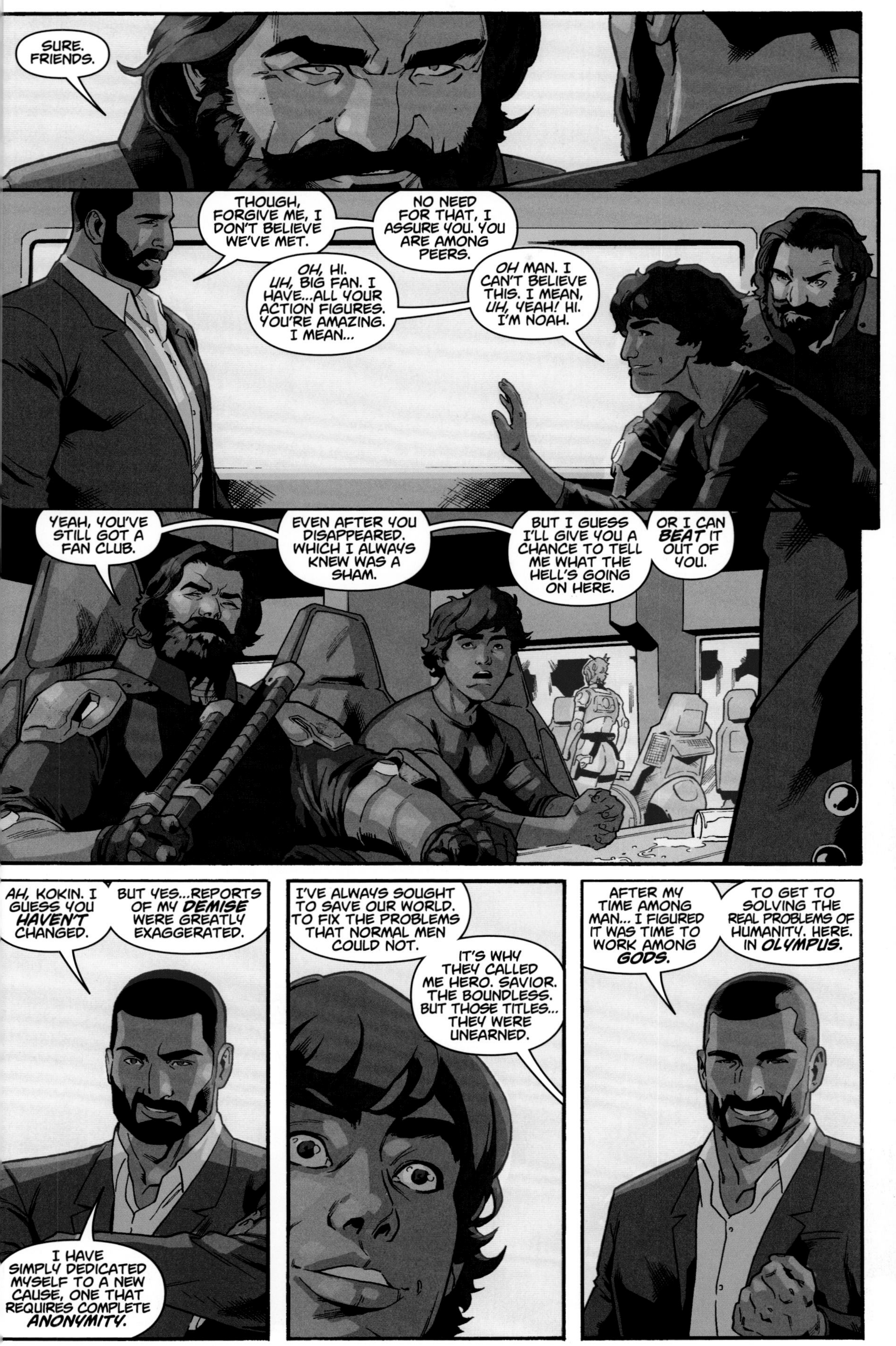
SURE. FRIENDS.
THOUGH, FORGIVE ME, I DON'T BELIEVE WE'VE MET.
NO NEED FOR THAT, I ASSURE YOU. YOU ARE AMONG PEERS.
OH, HI. UH, BIG FAN. I HAVE...ALL YOUR ACTION FIGURES. YOU'RE AMAZING. I MEAN...
OH MAN. I CAN'T BELIEVE THIS. I MEAN, UH, YEAH! HI. I'M NOAH.
YEAH, YOU'VE STILL GOT A FAN CLUB.
EVEN AFTER YOU DISAPPEARED. WHICH I ALWAYS KNEW WAS A SHAM.
BUT I GUESS I'LL GIVE YOU A CHANCE TO TELL ME WHAT THE HELL'S GOING ON HERE.
OR I CAN BEAT IT OUT OF YOU.
AH, KOKIN. I GUESS YOU HAVEN'T CHANGED.
BUT YES...REPORTS OF MY DEMISE WERE GREATLY EXAGGERATED.
I HAVE SIMPLY DEDICATED MYSELF TO A NEW CAUSE, ONE THAT REQUIRES COMPLETE ANONYMITY.
I'VE ALWAYS SOUGHT TO SAVE OUR WORLD. TO FIX THE PROBLEMS THAT NORMAL MEN COULD NOT.
IT'S WHY THEY CALLED ME HERO. SAVIOR. THE BOUNDLESS. BUT THOSE TITLES... THEY WERE UNEARNED.
AFTER MY TIME AMONG MAN... I FIGURED IT WAS TIME TO WORK AMONG GODS.
TO GET TO SOLVING THE REAL PROBLEMS OF HUMANITY. HERE. IN OLYMPUS.

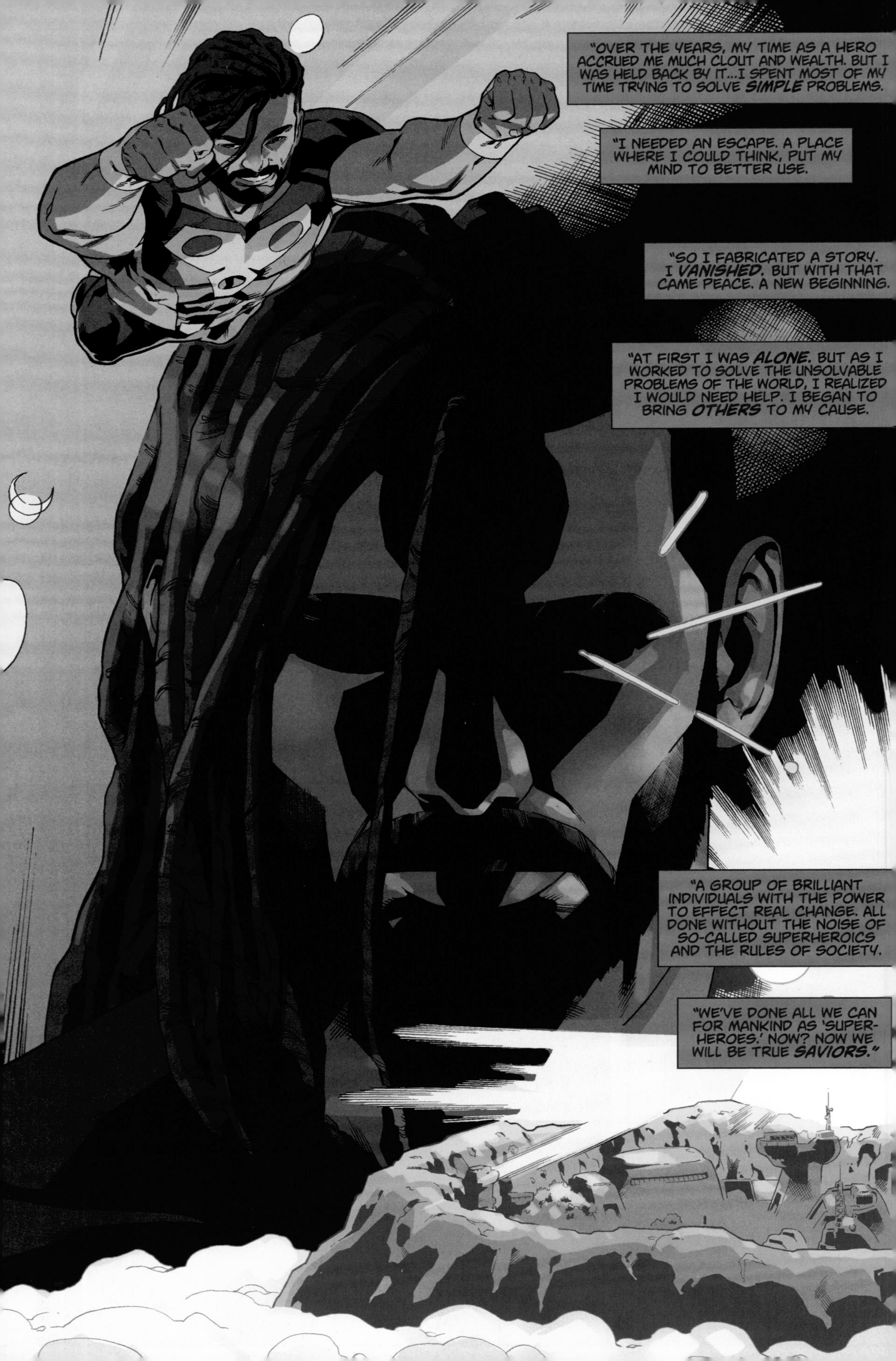
"OVER THE YEARS, MY TIME AS A HERO ACCRUED ME MUCH CLOUT AND WEALTH. BUT I WAS HELD BACK BY IT...I SPENT MOST OF MY TIME TRYING TO SOLVE *SIMPLE* PROBLEMS.
"I NEEDED AN ESCAPE. A PLACE WHERE I COULD THINK, PUT MY MIND TO BETTER USE.
"SO I FABRICATED A STORY. I *VANISHED.* BUT WITH THAT CAME PEACE. A NEW BEGINNING.
"AT FIRST I WAS *ALONE.* BUT AS I WORKED TO SOLVE THE UNSOLVABLE PROBLEMS OF THE WORLD, I REALIZED I WOULD NEED HELP. I BEGAN TO BRING *OTHERS* TO MY CAUSE.
"A GROUP OF BRILLIANT INDIVIDUALS WITH THE POWER TO EFFECT REAL CHANGE. ALL DONE WITHOUT THE NOISE OF SO-CALLED SUPERHEROICS AND THE RULES OF SOCIETY.
"WE'VE DONE ALL WE CAN FOR MANKIND AS 'SUPER-HEROES.' NOW? NOW WE WILL BE TRUE *SAVIORS.*"

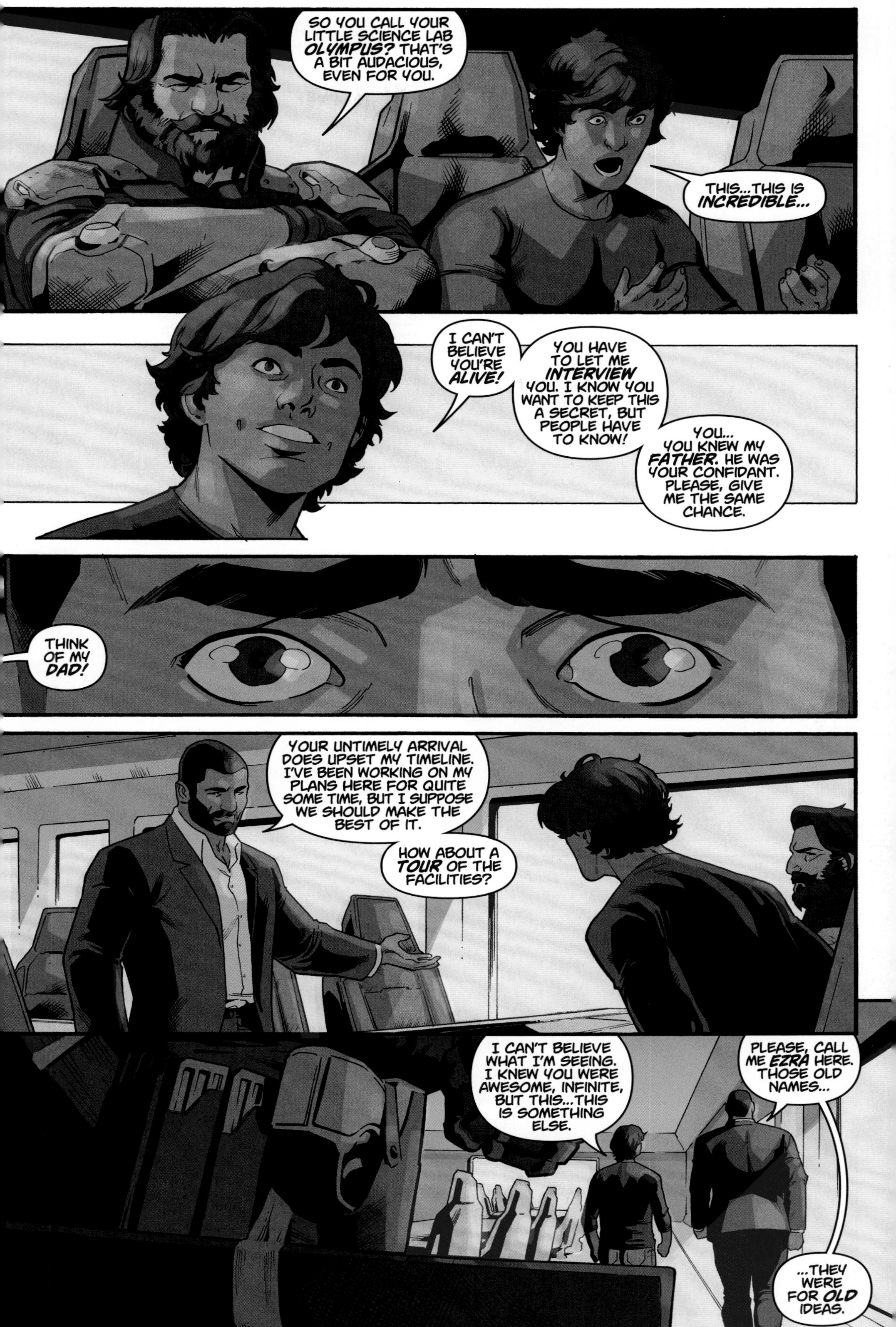
SO YOU CALL YOUR LITTLE SCIENCE LAB OLYMPUS? THAT'S A BIT AUDACIOUS, EVEN FOR YOU.
THIS...THIS IS INCREDIBLE...
I CAN'T BELIEVE YOU'RE ALIVE!
YOU HAVE TO LET ME INTERVIEW YOU. I KNOW YOU WANT TO KEEP THIS A SECRET, BUT PEOPLE HAVE TO KNOW!
YOU... YOU KNEW MY FATHER. HE WAS YOUR CONFIDANT. PLEASE, GIVE ME THE SAME CHANCE.
THINK OF MY DAD!
YOUR UNTIMELY ARRIVAL DOES UPSET MY TIMELINE. I'VE BEEN WORKING ON MY PLANS HERE FOR QUITE SOME TIME, BUT I SUPPOSE WE SHOULD MAKE THE BEST OF IT.
HOW ABOUT A TOUR OF THE FACILITIES?
I CAN'T BELIEVE WHAT I'M SEEING. I KNEW YOU WERE AWESOME, INFINITE, BUT THIS...THIS IS SOMETHING ELSE.
PLEASE, CALL ME EZRA HERE. THOSE OLD NAMES...
...THEY WERE FOR OLD IDEAS.

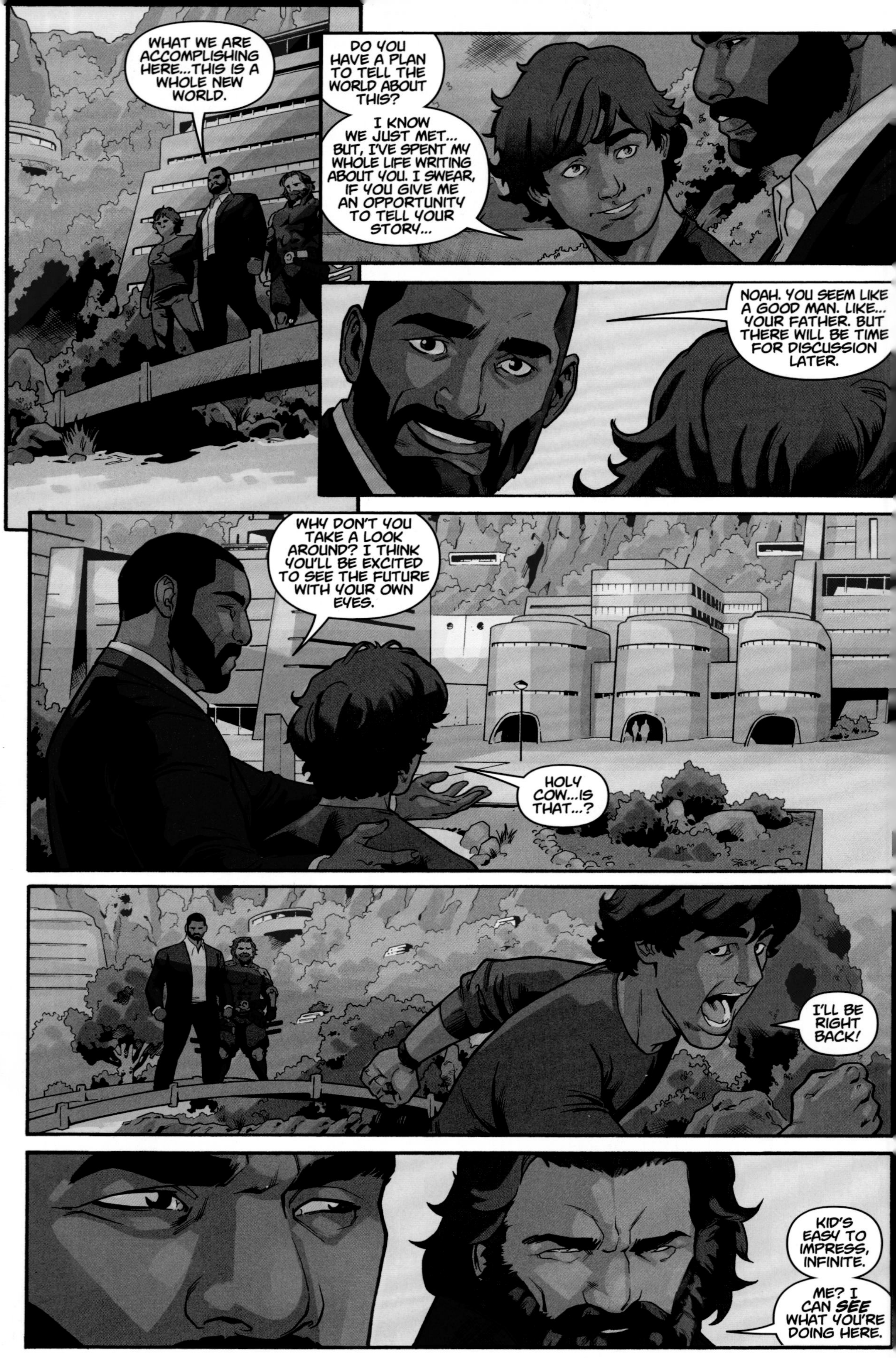
WHAT WE ARE ACCOMPLISHING HERE...THIS IS A WHOLE NEW WORLD.
DO YOU HAVE A PLAN TO TELL THE WORLD ABOUT THIS?
I KNOW WE JUST MET... BUT, I'VE SPENT MY WHOLE LIFE WRITING ABOUT YOU. I SWEAR, IF YOU GIVE ME AN OPPORTUNITY TO TELL YOUR STORY...
NOAH. YOU SEEM LIKE A GOOD MAN. LIKE... YOUR FATHER. BUT THERE WILL BE TIME FOR DISCUSSION LATER.
WHY DON'T YOU TAKE A LOOK AROUND? I THINK YOU'LL BE EXCITED TO SEE THE FUTURE WITH YOUR OWN EYES.
HOLY COW...IS THAT...?
I'LL BE RIGHT BACK!
KID'S EASY TO IMPRESS, INFINITE.
ME? I CAN *SEE* WHAT YOU'RE DOING HERE.

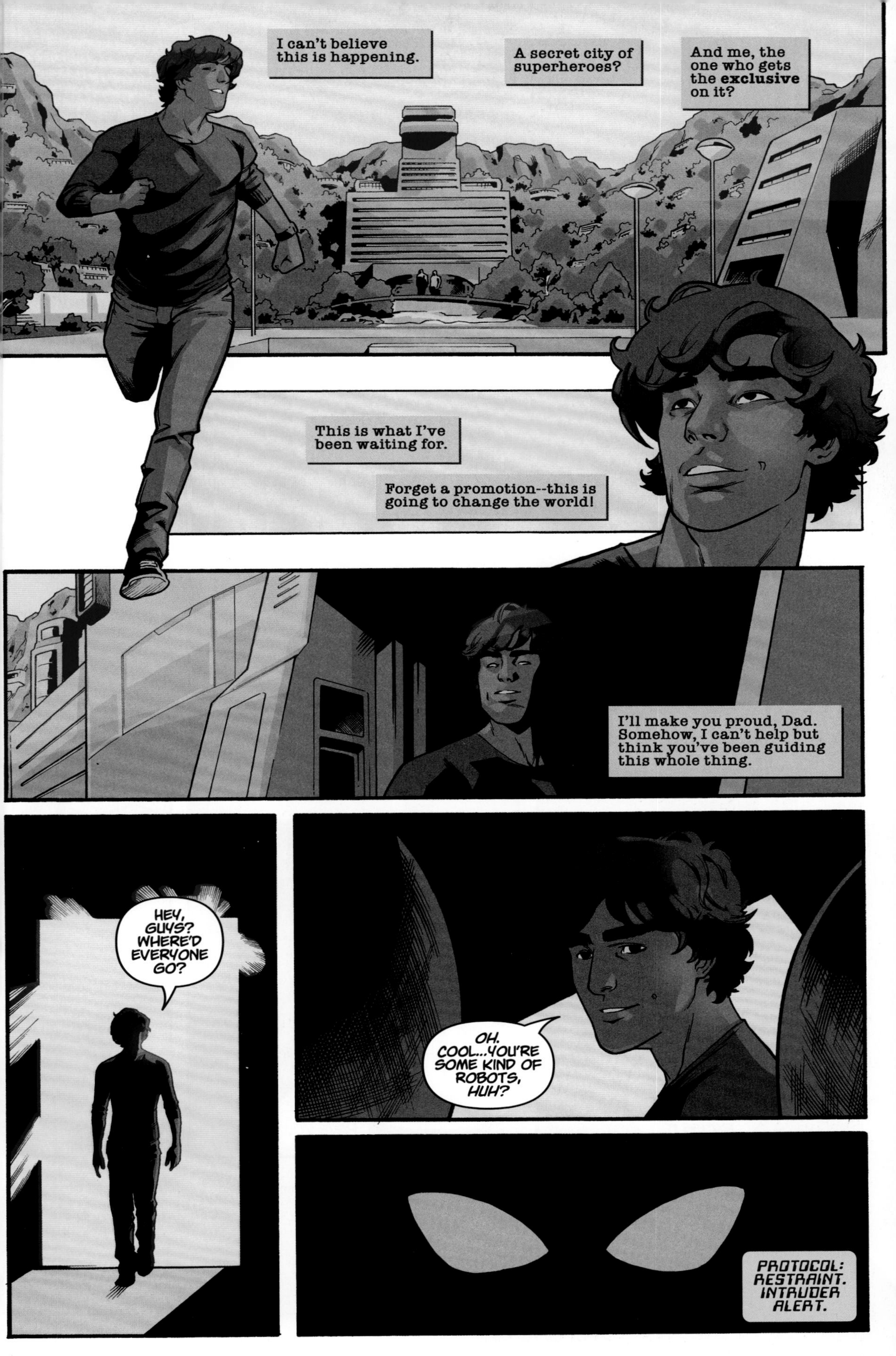
I can't believe this is happening.
A secret city of superheroes?
And me, the one who gets the **exclusive** on it?
This is what I've been waiting for.
Forget a promotion--this is going to change the world!
I'll make you proud, Dad. Somehow, I can't help but think you've been guiding this whole thing.
HEY, GUYS? WHERE'D EVERYONE GO?
OH. COOL...YOU'RE SOME KIND OF ROBOTS, HUH?
PROTOCOL: RESTRAINT. INTRUDER ALERT.

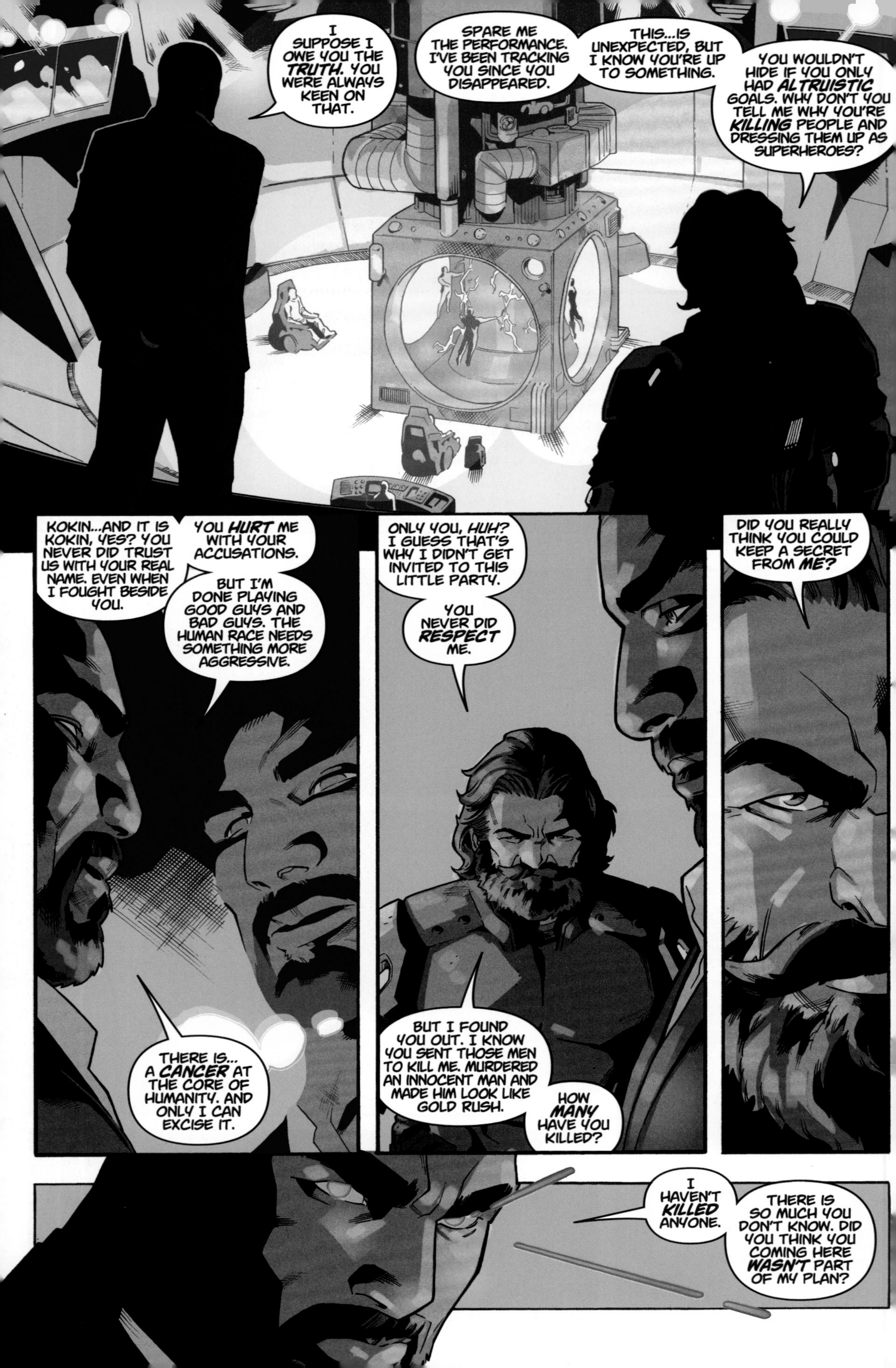
I SUPPOSE I OWE YOU THE TRUTH. YOU WERE ALWAYS KEEN ON THAT.
SPARE ME THE PERFORMANCE. I'VE BEEN TRACKING YOU SINCE YOU DISAPPEARED.
THIS...IS UNEXPECTED, BUT I KNOW YOU'RE UP TO SOMETHING.
YOU WOULDN'T HIDE IF YOU ONLY HAD ALTRUISTIC GOALS. WHY DON'T YOU TELL ME WHY YOU'RE KILLING PEOPLE AND DRESSING THEM UP AS SUPERHEROES?
KOKIN...AND IT IS KOKIN, YES? YOU NEVER DID TRUST US WITH YOUR REAL NAME. EVEN WHEN I FOUGHT BESIDE YOU.
YOU HURT ME WITH YOUR ACCUSATIONS.
BUT I'M DONE PLAYING GOOD GUYS AND BAD GUYS. THE HUMAN RACE NEEDS SOMETHING MORE AGGRESSIVE.
THERE IS... A CANCER AT THE CORE OF HUMANITY. AND ONLY I CAN EXCISE IT.
ONLY YOU, HUH? I GUESS THAT'S WHY I DIDN'T GET INVITED TO THIS LITTLE PARTY.
YOU NEVER DID RESPECT ME.
BUT I FOUND YOU OUT. I KNOW YOU SENT THOSE MEN TO KILL ME. MURDERED AN INNOCENT MAN AND MADE HIM LOOK LIKE GOLD RUSH.
HOW MANY HAVE YOU KILLED?
DID YOU REALLY THINK YOU COULD KEEP A SECRET FROM ME?
I HAVEN'T KILLED ANYONE.
THERE IS SO MUCH YOU DON'T KNOW. DID YOU THINK YOU COMING HERE WASN'T PART OF MY PLAN?

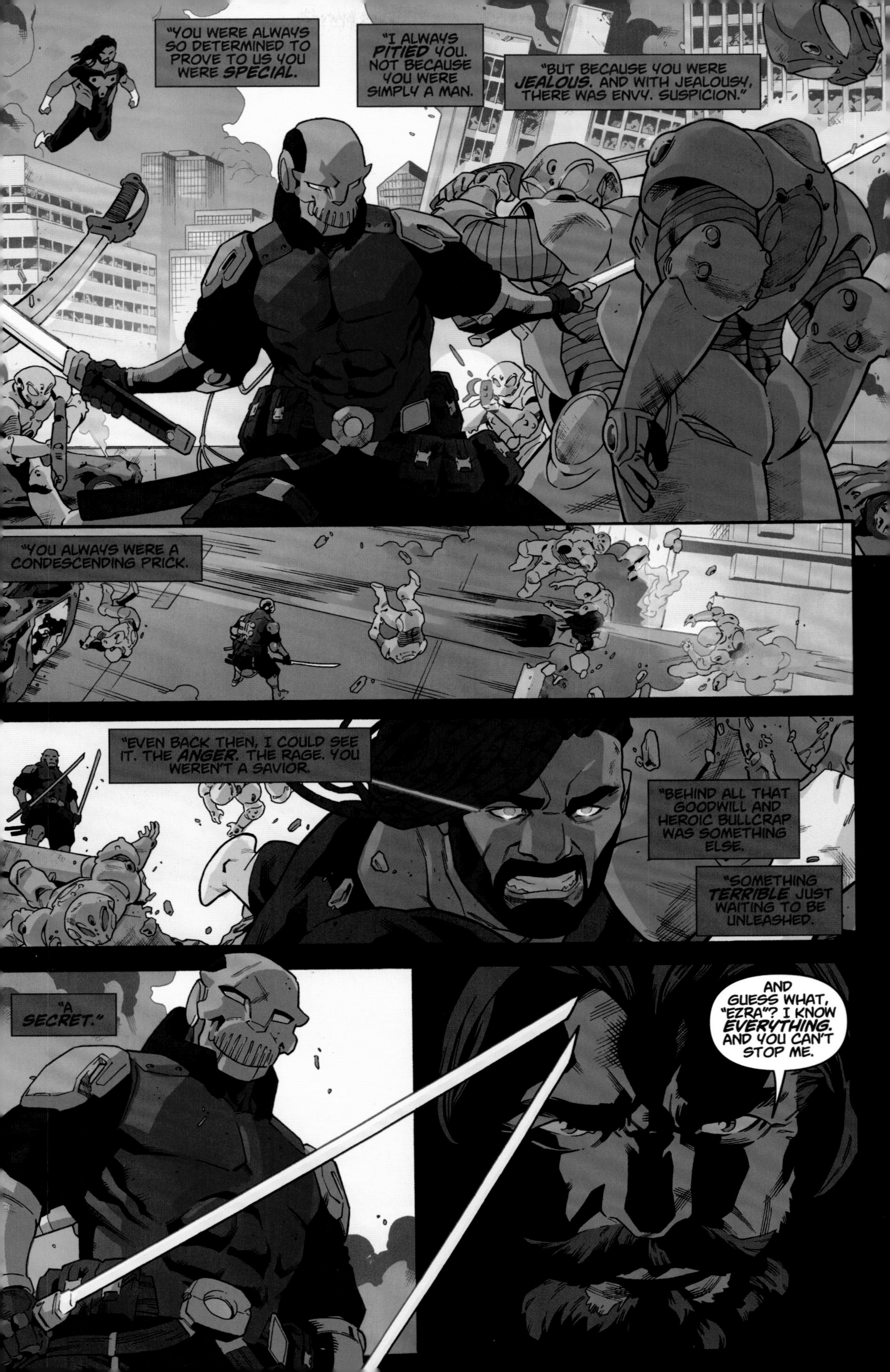
"YOU WERE ALWAYS SO DETERMINED TO PROVE TO US YOU WERE SPECIAL.
"I ALWAYS PITIED YOU. NOT BECAUSE YOU WERE SIMPLY A MAN.
"BUT BECAUSE YOU WERE JEALOUS. AND WITH JEALOUSY, THERE WAS ENVY. SUSPICION."
"YOU ALWAYS WERE A CONDESCENDING PRICK.
"EVEN BACK THEN, I COULD SEE IT. THE ANGER. THE RAGE. YOU WEREN'T A SAVIOR.
"BEHIND ALL THAT GOODWILL AND HEROIC BULLCRAP WAS SOMETHING ELSE.
"SOMETHING TERRIBLE JUST WAITING TO BE UNLEASHED.
"A SECRET."
AND GUESS WHAT, "EZRA"? I KNOW EVERYTHING. AND YOU CAN'T STOP ME.

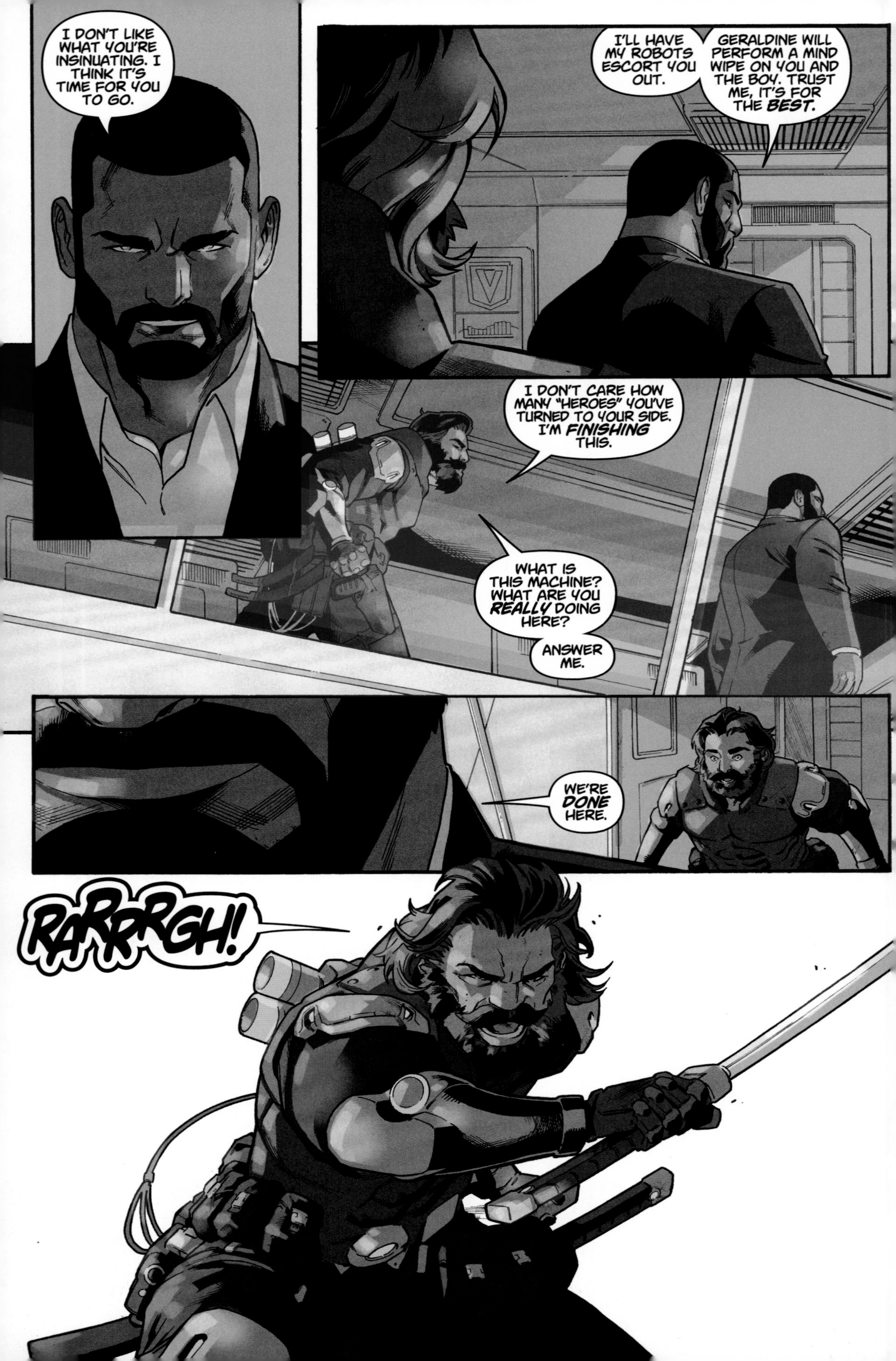

I DON'T LIKE WHAT YOU'RE INSINUATING. I THINK IT'S TIME FOR YOU TO GO.
I'LL HAVE MY ROBOTS ESCORT YOU OUT.
GERALDINE WILL PERFORM A MIND WIPE ON YOU AND THE BOY. TRUST ME, IT'S FOR THE BEST.
I DON'T CARE HOW MANY "HEROES" YOU'VE TURNED TO YOUR SIDE. I'M FINISHING THIS.
WHAT IS THIS MACHINE? WHAT ARE YOU REALLY DOING HERE?
ANSWER ME.
WE'RE DONE HERE.
RARRRGH!

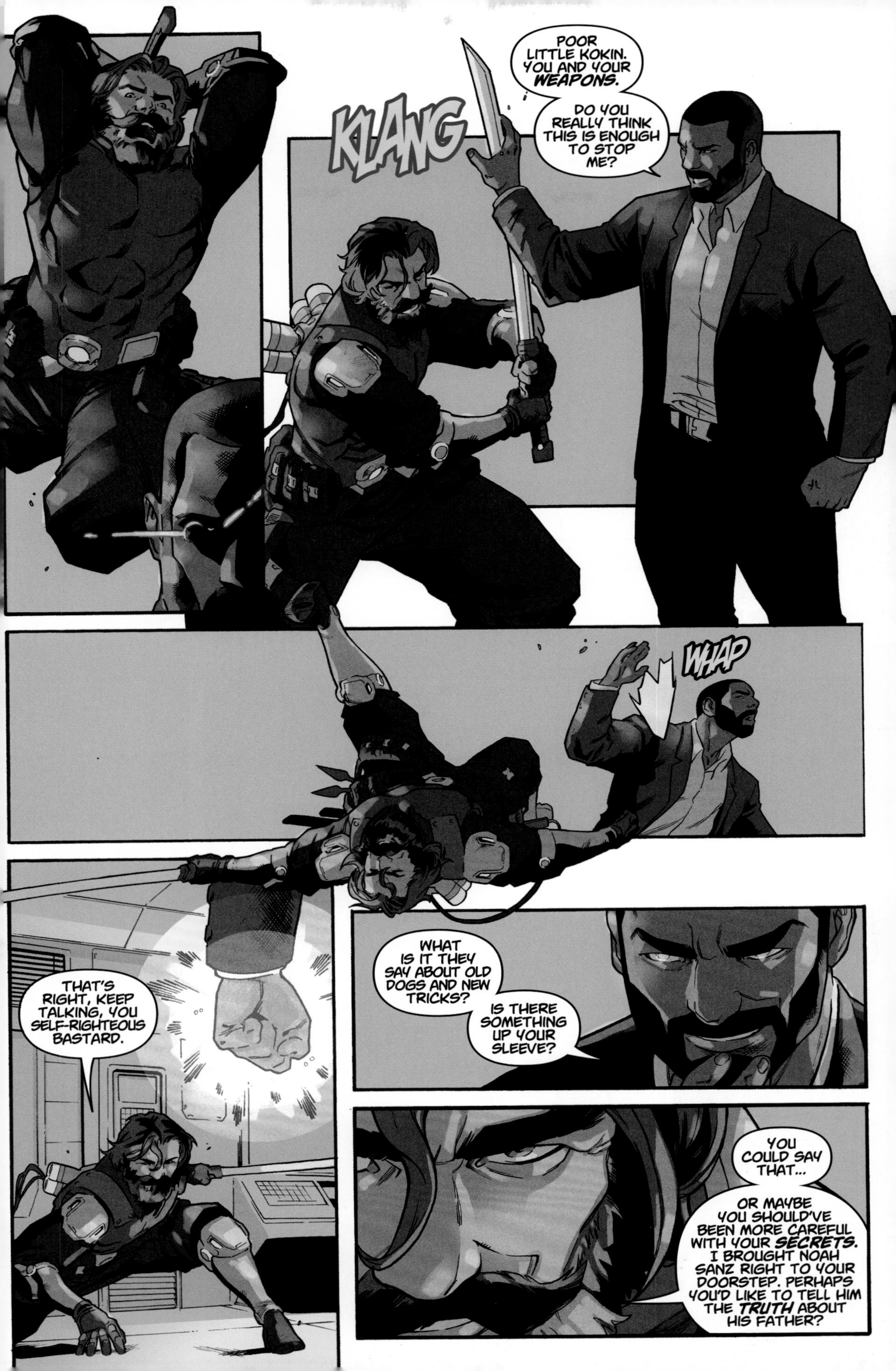
KLANG
POOR LITTLE KOKIN. YOU AND YOUR WEAPONS.
DO YOU REALLY THINK THIS IS ENOUGH TO STOP ME?
WHAP
WHAT IS IT THEY SAY ABOUT OLD DOGS AND NEW TRICKS?
IS THERE SOMETHING UP YOUR SLEEVE?
THAT'S RIGHT, KEEP TALKING, YOU SELF-RIGHTEOUS BASTARD.
YOU COULD SAY THAT...
OR MAYBE YOU SHOULD'VE BEEN MORE CAREFUL WITH YOUR SECRETS. I BROUGHT NOAH SANZ RIGHT TO YOUR DOORSTEP. PERHAPS YOU'D LIKE TO TELL HIM THE TRUTH ABOUT HIS FATHER?

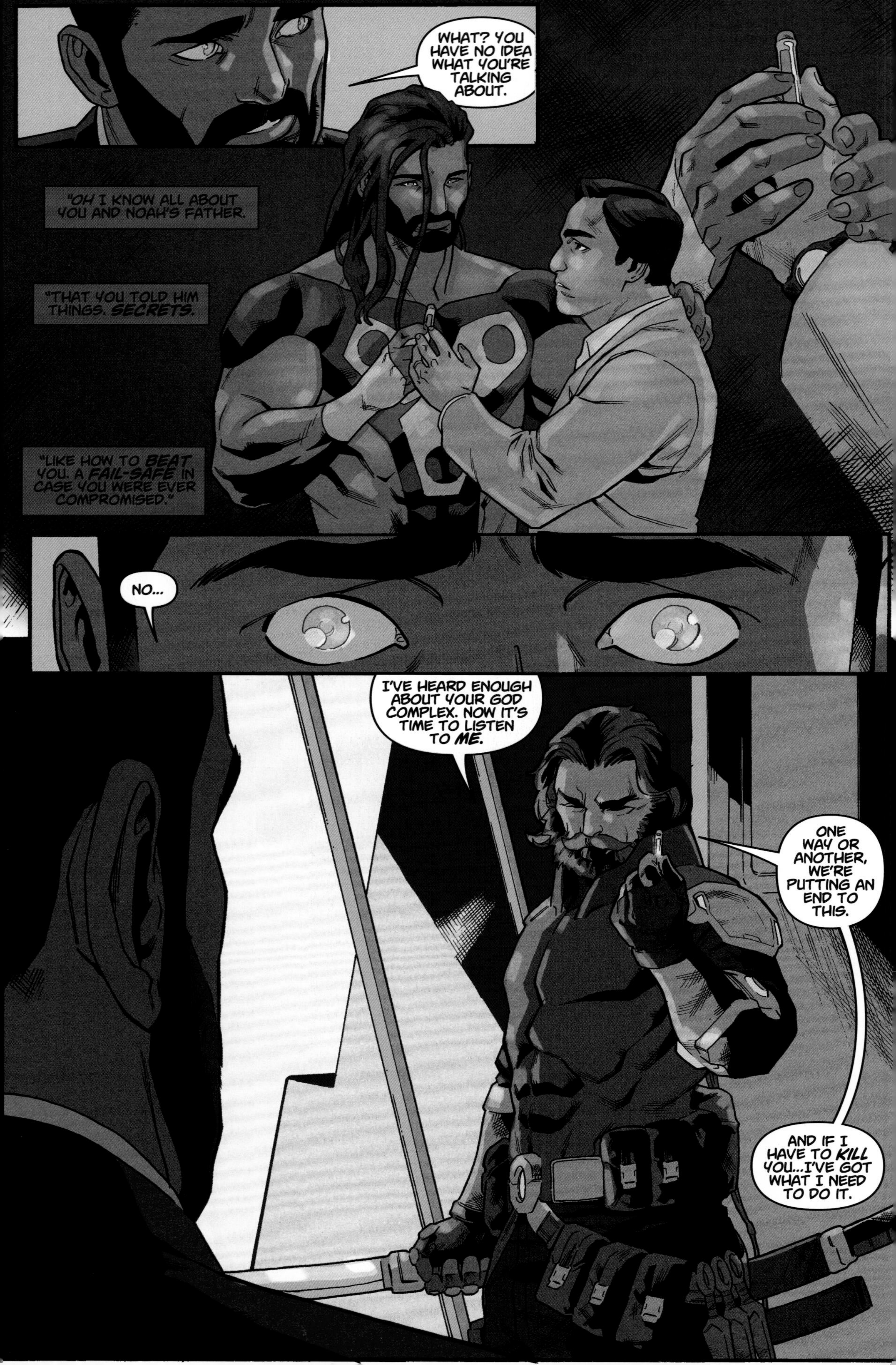
WHAT? YOU HAVE NO IDEA WHAT YOU'RE TALKING ABOUT.
"OH I KNOW ALL ABOUT YOU AND NOAH'S FATHER.
"THAT YOU TOLD HIM THINGS. SECRETS.
"LIKE HOW TO BEAT YOU. A FAIL-SAFE IN CASE YOU WERE EVER COMPROMISED."
NO...
I'VE HEARD ENOUGH ABOUT YOUR GOD COMPLEX. NOW IT'S TIME TO LISTEN TO ME.
ONE WAY OR ANOTHER, WE'RE PUTTING AN END TO THIS.
AND IF I HAVE TO KILL YOU...I'VE GOT WHAT I NEED TO DO IT.

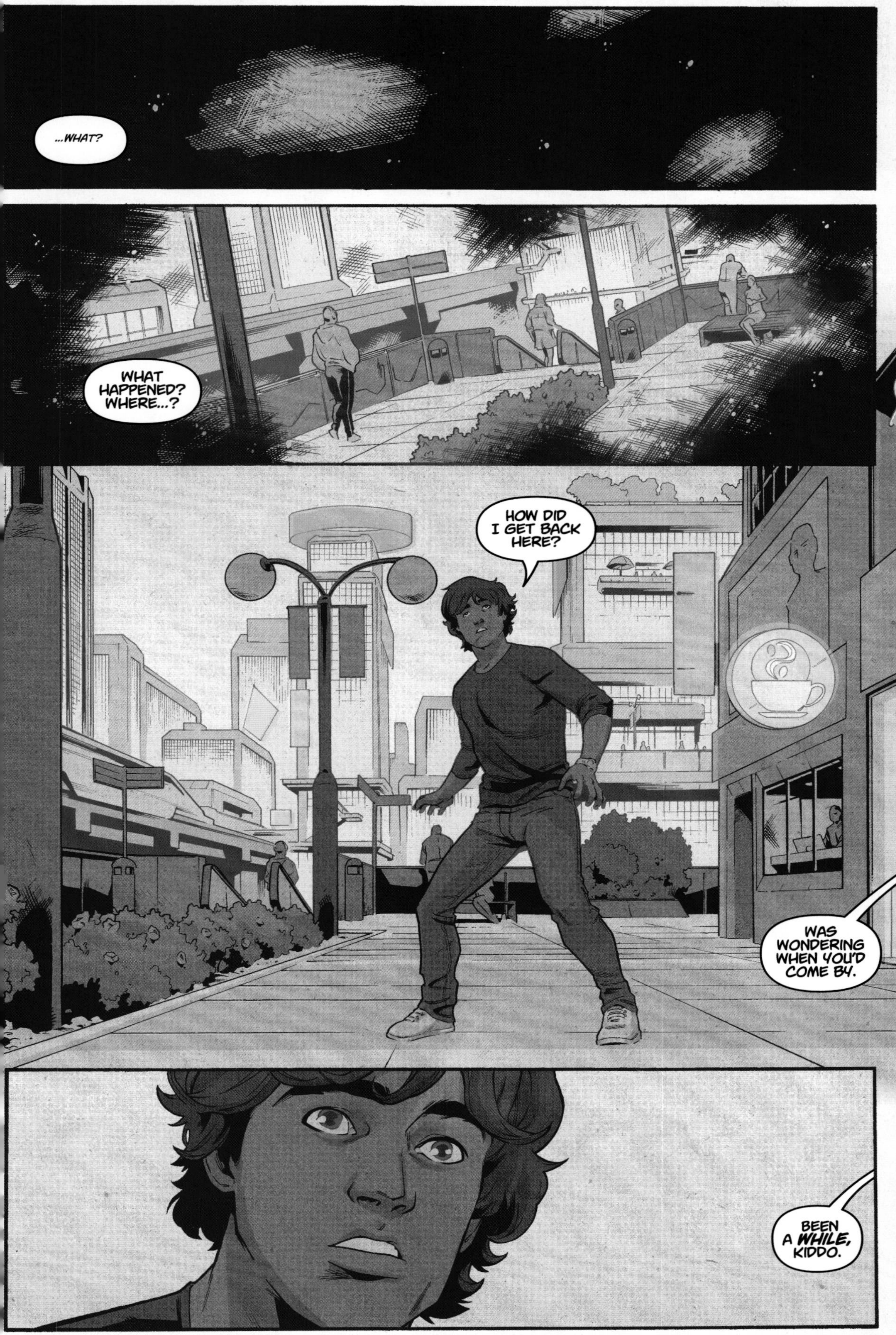
...WHAT?
WHAT HAPPENED? WHERE...?
HOW DID I GET BACK HERE?
WAS WONDERING WHEN YOU'D COME BY.
BEEN A WHILE, KIDDO.

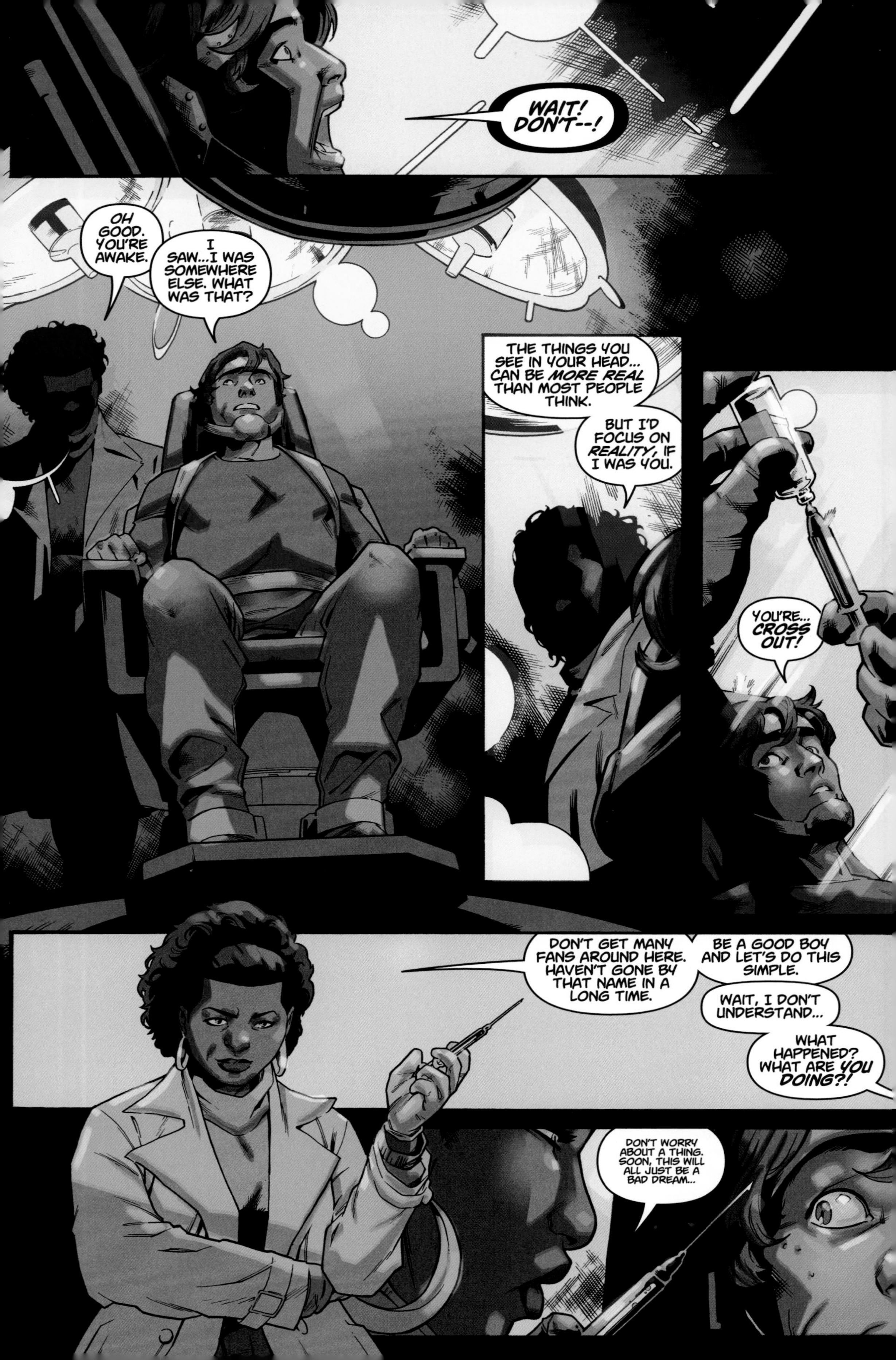
WAIT! DON'T--!
OH GOOD. YOU'RE AWAKE.
I SAW...I WAS SOMEWHERE ELSE. WHAT WAS THAT?
THE THINGS YOU SEE IN YOUR HEAD... CAN BE MORE REAL THAN MOST PEOPLE THINK.
BUT I'D FOCUS ON REALITY, IF I WAS YOU.
YOU'RE... CROSS OUT!
DON'T GET MANY FANS AROUND HERE. HAVEN'T GONE BY THAT NAME IN A LONG TIME.
BE A GOOD BOY AND LET'S DO THIS SIMPLE.
WAIT, I DON'T UNDERSTAND...
WHAT HAPPENED? WHAT ARE YOU DOING?!
DON'T WORRY ABOUT A THING. SOON, THIS WILL ALL JUST BE A BAD DREAM...

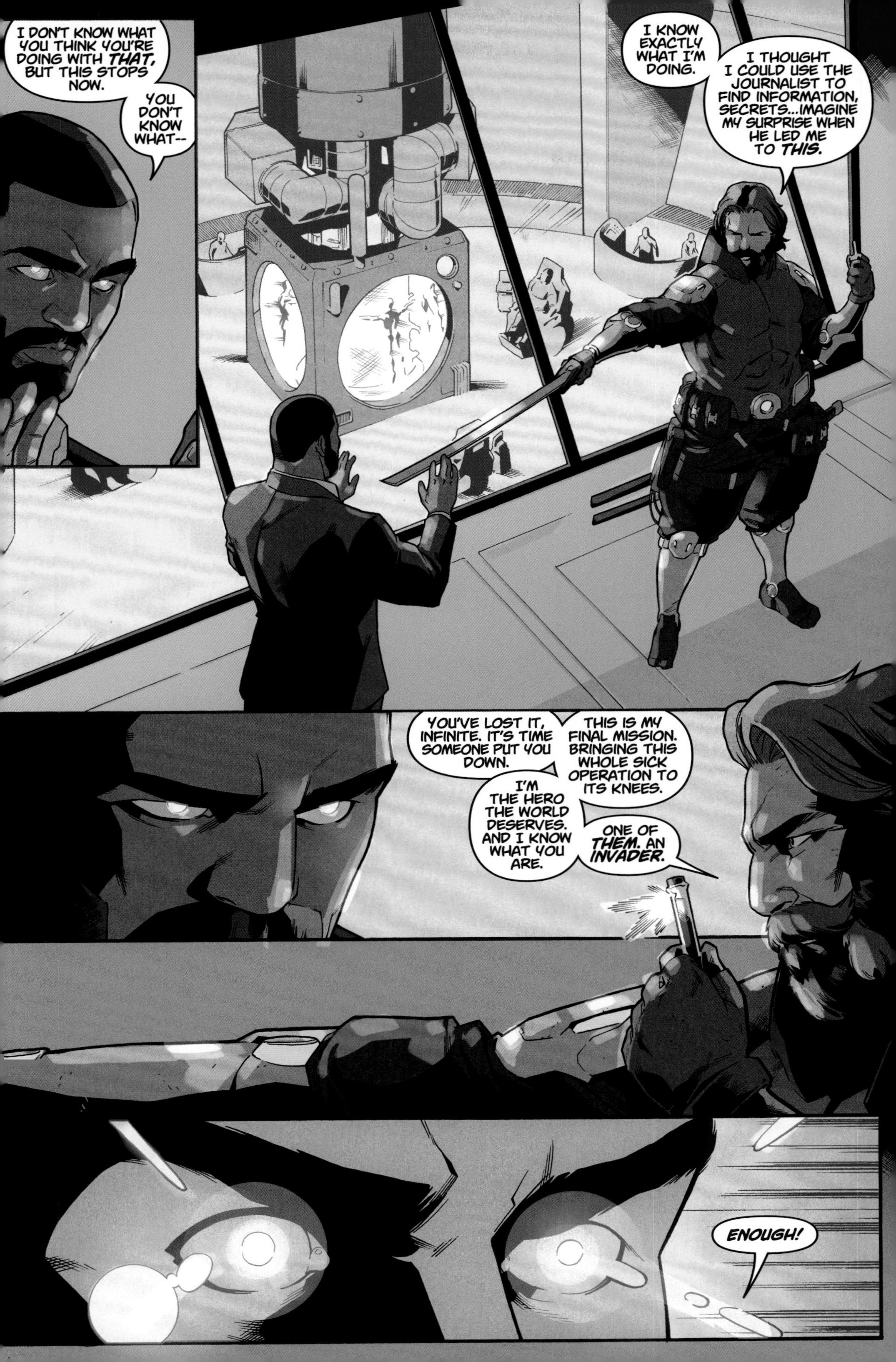

I DON'T KNOW WHAT YOU THINK YOU'RE DOING WITH *THAT*, BUT THIS STOPS NOW.
YOU DON'T KNOW WHAT--
I KNOW EXACTLY WHAT I'M DOING.
I THOUGHT I COULD USE THE JOURNALIST TO FIND INFORMATION, SECRETS...IMAGINE MY SURPRISE WHEN HE LED ME TO *THIS*.
YOU'VE LOST IT, INFINITE. IT'S TIME SOMEONE PUT YOU DOWN.
THIS IS MY FINAL MISSION. BRINGING THIS WHOLE SICK OPERATION TO ITS KNEES.
I'M THE HERO THE WORLD DESERVES. AND I KNOW WHAT YOU ARE.
ONE OF *THEM*. AN *INVADER*.
ENOUGH!

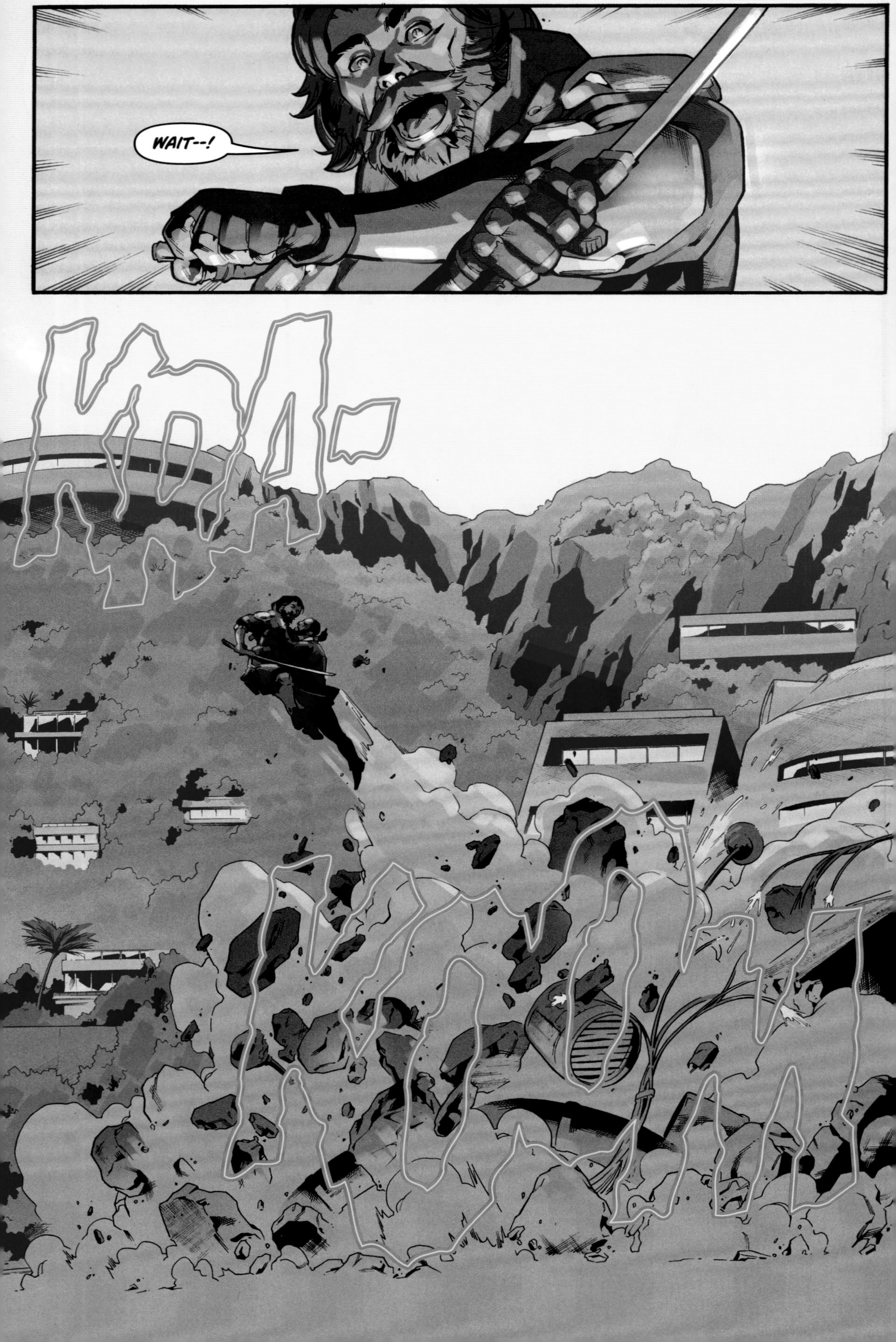
WAIT--!
KRA-
KOOM

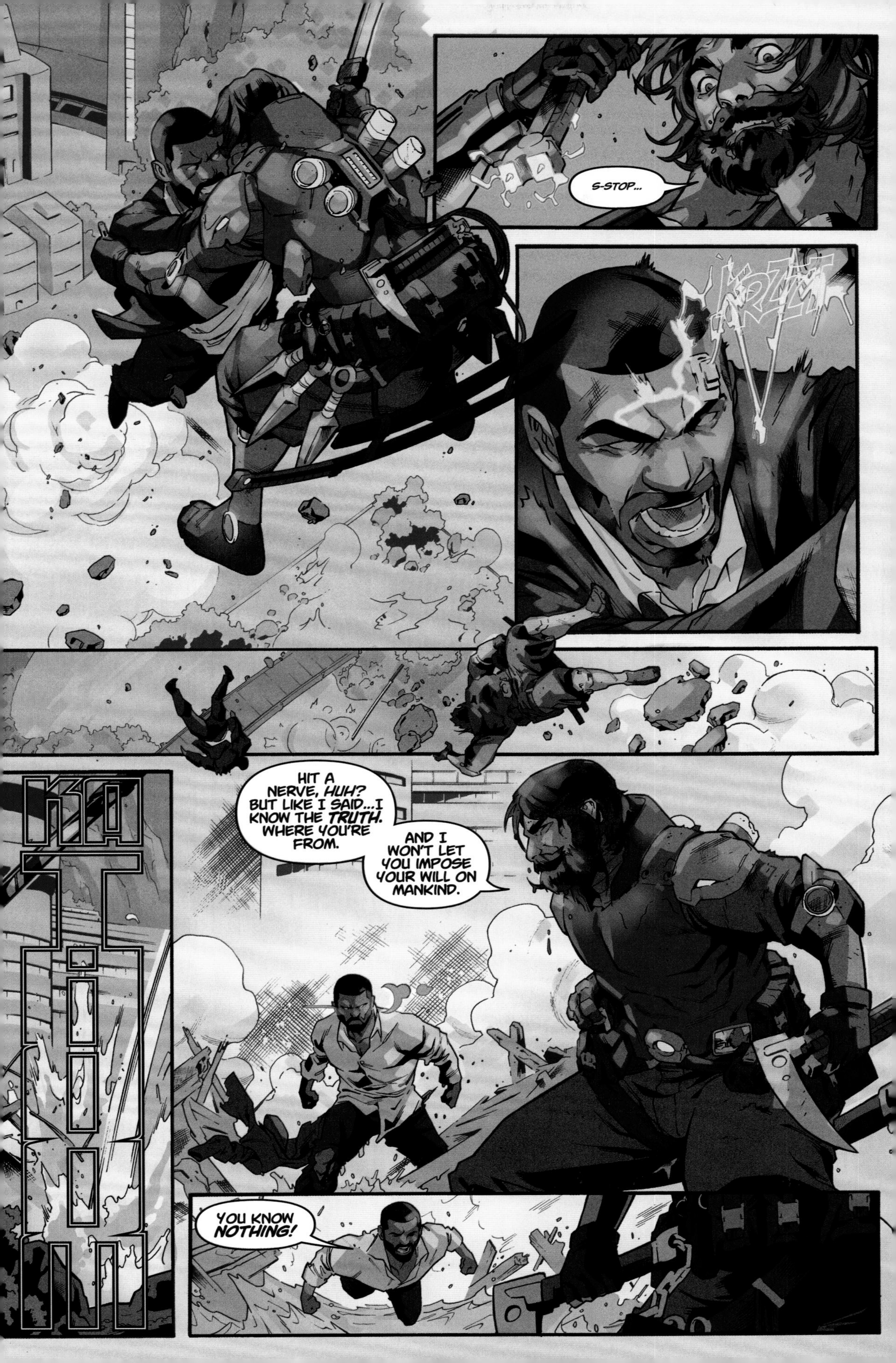
S-STOP...
KRZZT
HIT A NERVE, HUH? BUT LIKE I SAID...I KNOW THE TRUTH. WHERE YOU'RE FROM.
AND I WON'T LET YOU IMPOSE YOUR WILL ON MANKIND.
KA-THOOM
YOU KNOW NOTHING!

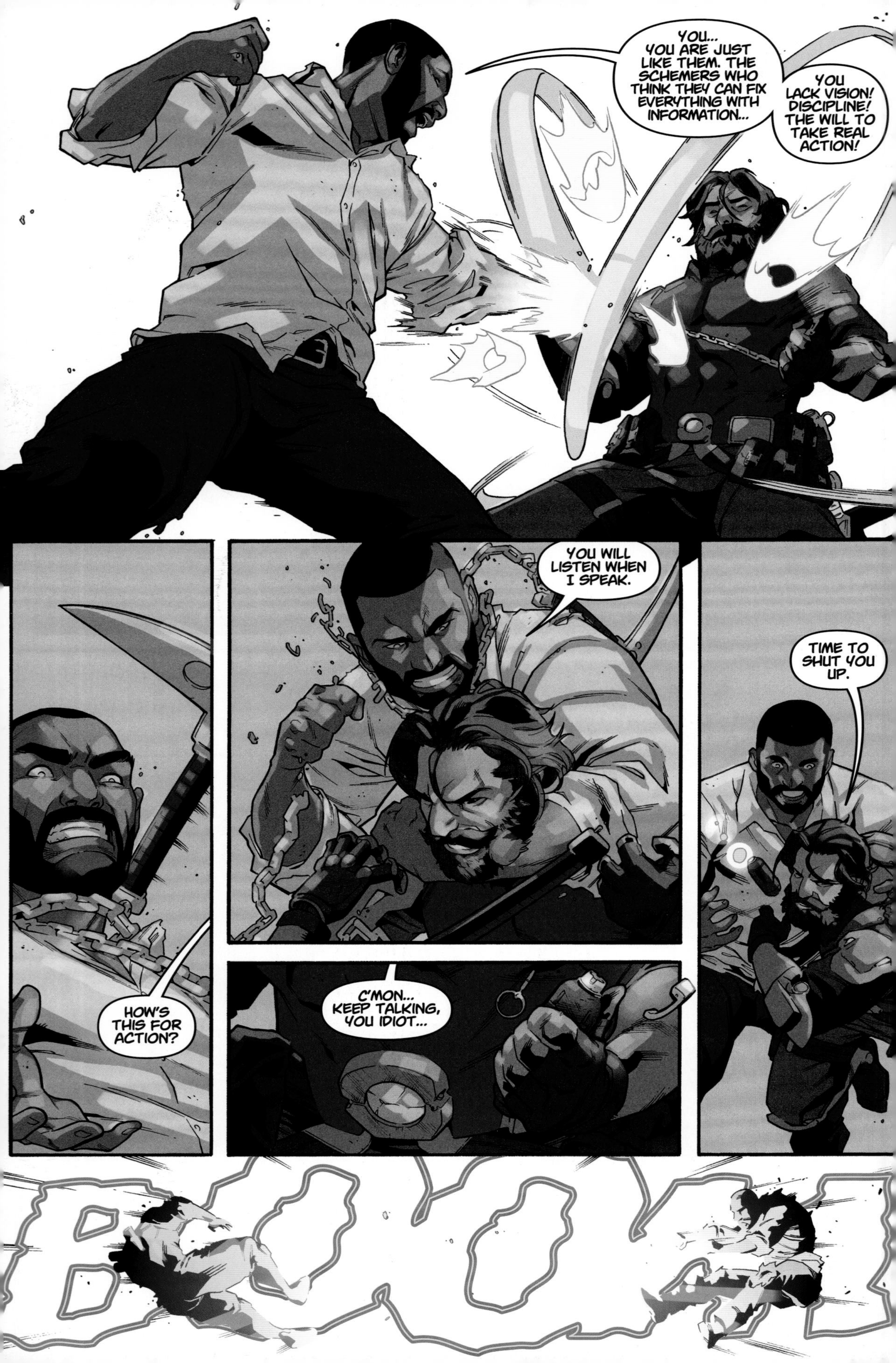
YOU... YOU ARE JUST LIKE THEM. THE SCHEMERS WHO THINK THEY CAN FIX EVERYTHING WITH INFORMATION...
YOU LACK VISION! DISCIPLINE! THE WILL TO TAKE REAL ACTION!
YOU WILL LISTEN WHEN I SPEAK.
TIME TO SHUT YOU UP.
HOW'S THIS FOR ACTION?
C'MON... KEEP TALKING, YOU IDIOT...
BOOM

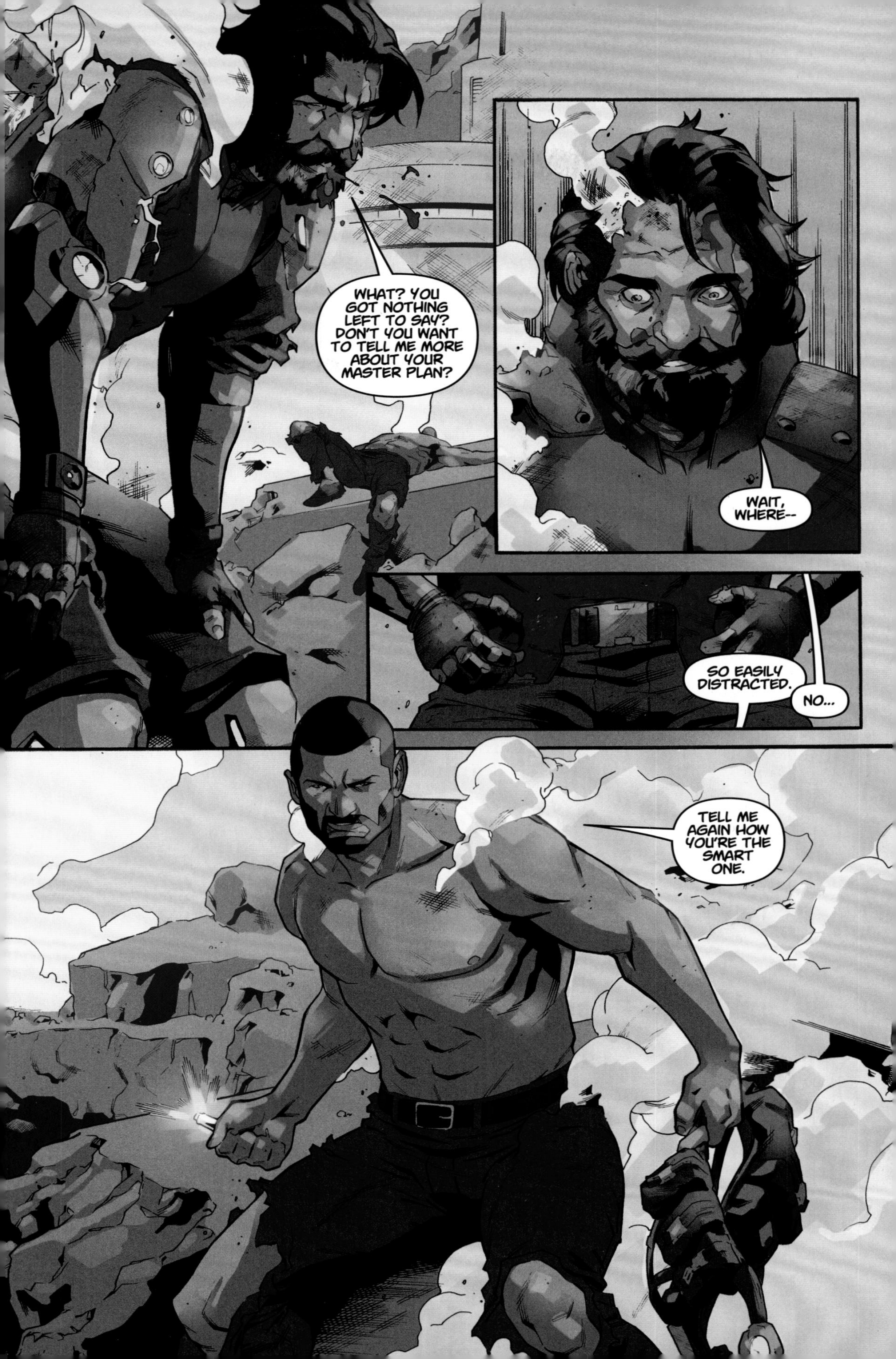
WHAT? YOU GOT NOTHING LEFT TO SAY? DON'T YOU WANT TO TELL ME MORE ABOUT YOUR MASTER PLAN?
WAIT, WHERE--
SO EASILY DISTRACTED.
NO...
TELL ME AGAIN HOW YOU'RE THE SMART ONE.

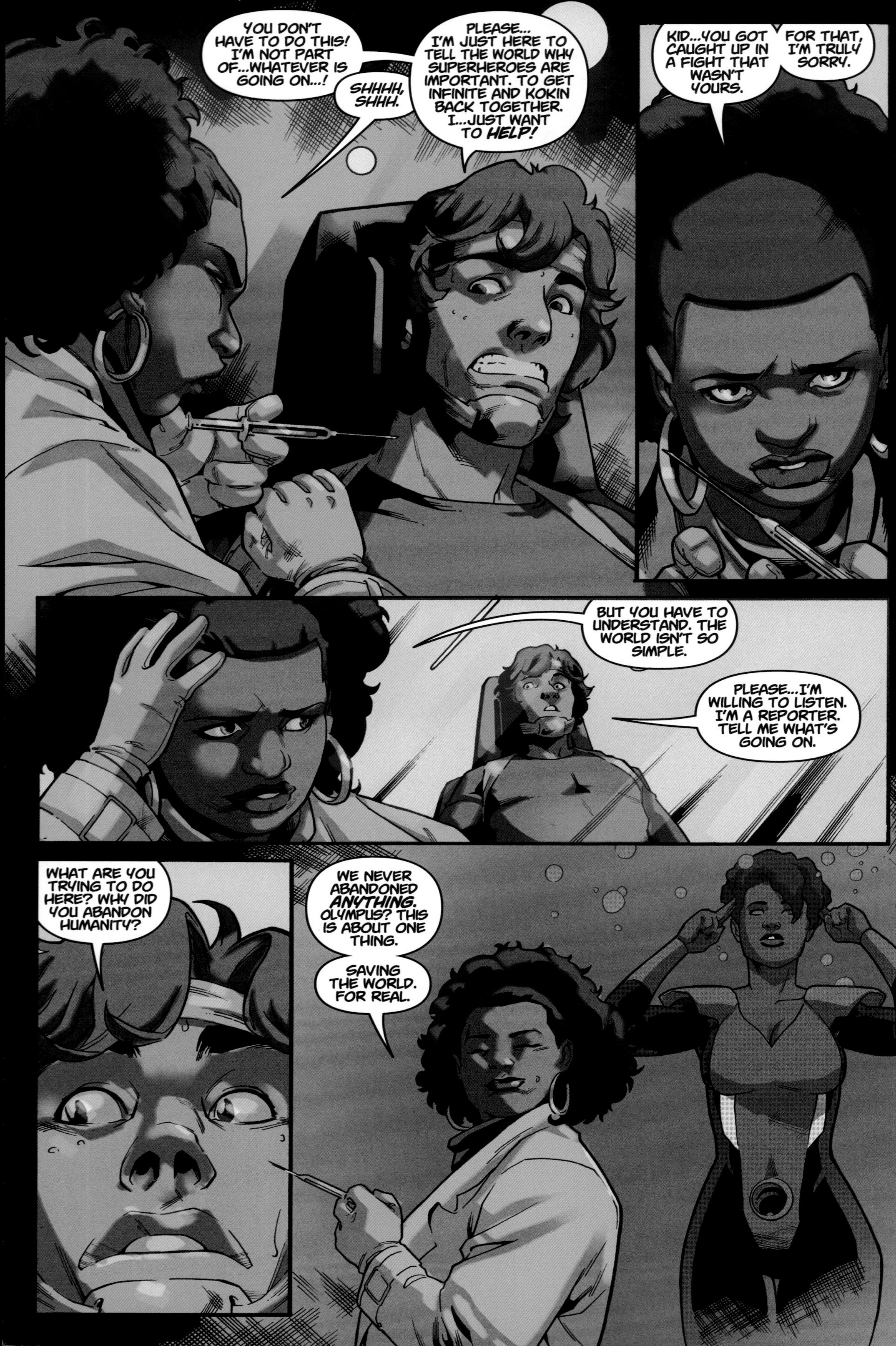
YOU DON'T HAVE TO DO THIS! I'M NOT PART OF...WHATEVER IS GOING ON...!
SHHHH, SHHH.
PLEASE... I'M JUST HERE TO TELL THE WORLD WHY SUPERHEROES ARE IMPORTANT. TO GET INFINITE AND KOKIN BACK TOGETHER. I...JUST WANT TO HELP!
KID...YOU GOT CAUGHT UP IN A FIGHT THAT WASN'T YOURS.
FOR THAT, I'M TRULY SORRY.
BUT YOU HAVE TO UNDERSTAND. THE WORLD ISN'T SO SIMPLE.
PLEASE...I'M WILLING TO LISTEN. I'M A REPORTER. TELL ME WHAT'S GOING ON.
WHAT ARE YOU TRYING TO DO HERE? WHY DID YOU ABANDON HUMANITY?
WE NEVER ABANDONED ANYTHING. OLYMPUS? THIS IS ABOUT ONE THING.
SAVING THE WORLD. FOR REAL.

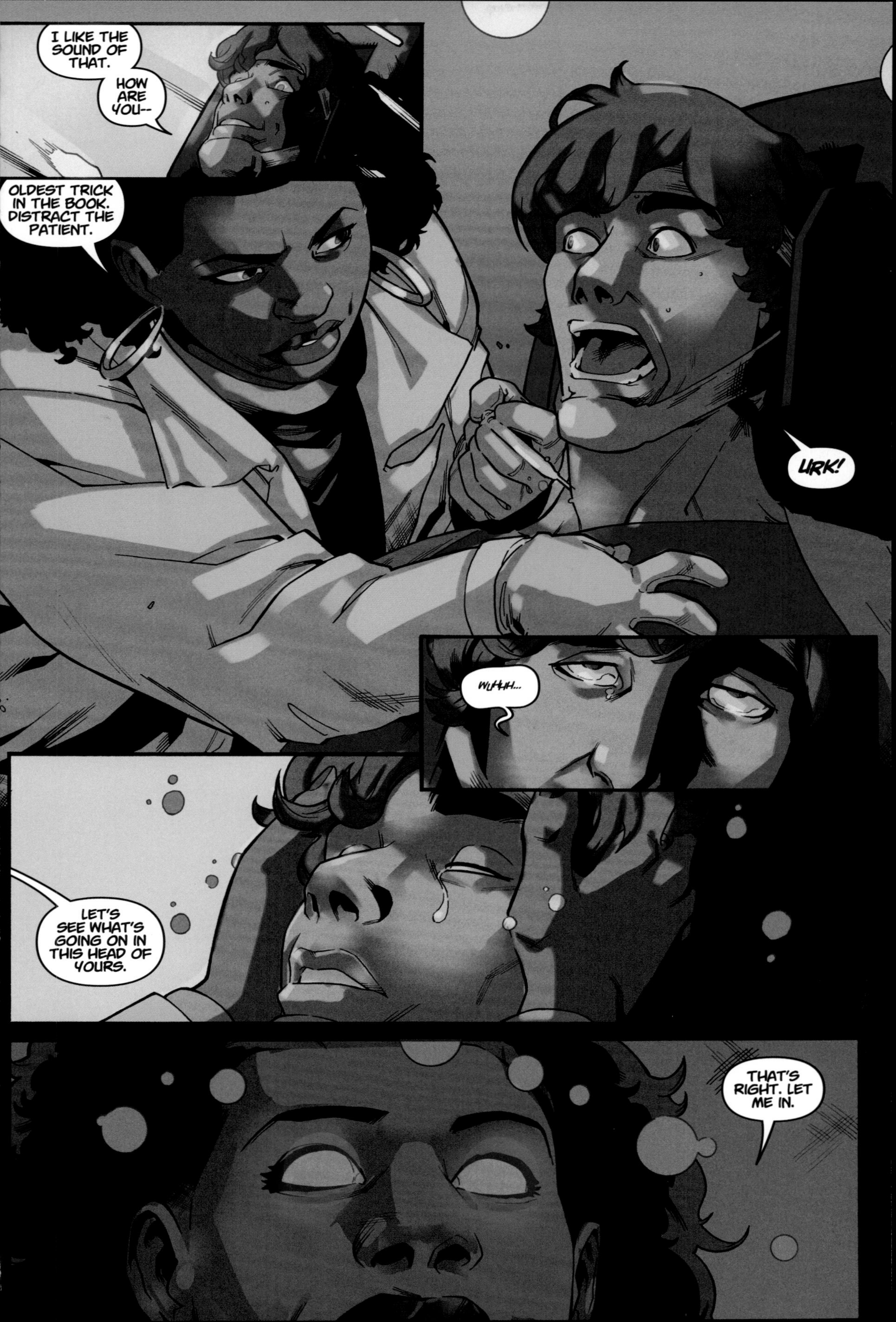
I LIKE THE SOUND OF THAT.
HOW ARE YOU--
OLDEST TRICK IN THE BOOK. DISTRACT THE PATIENT.
URK!
WUHHH...
LET'S SEE WHAT'S GOING ON IN THIS HEAD OF YOURS.
THAT'S RIGHT. LET ME IN.

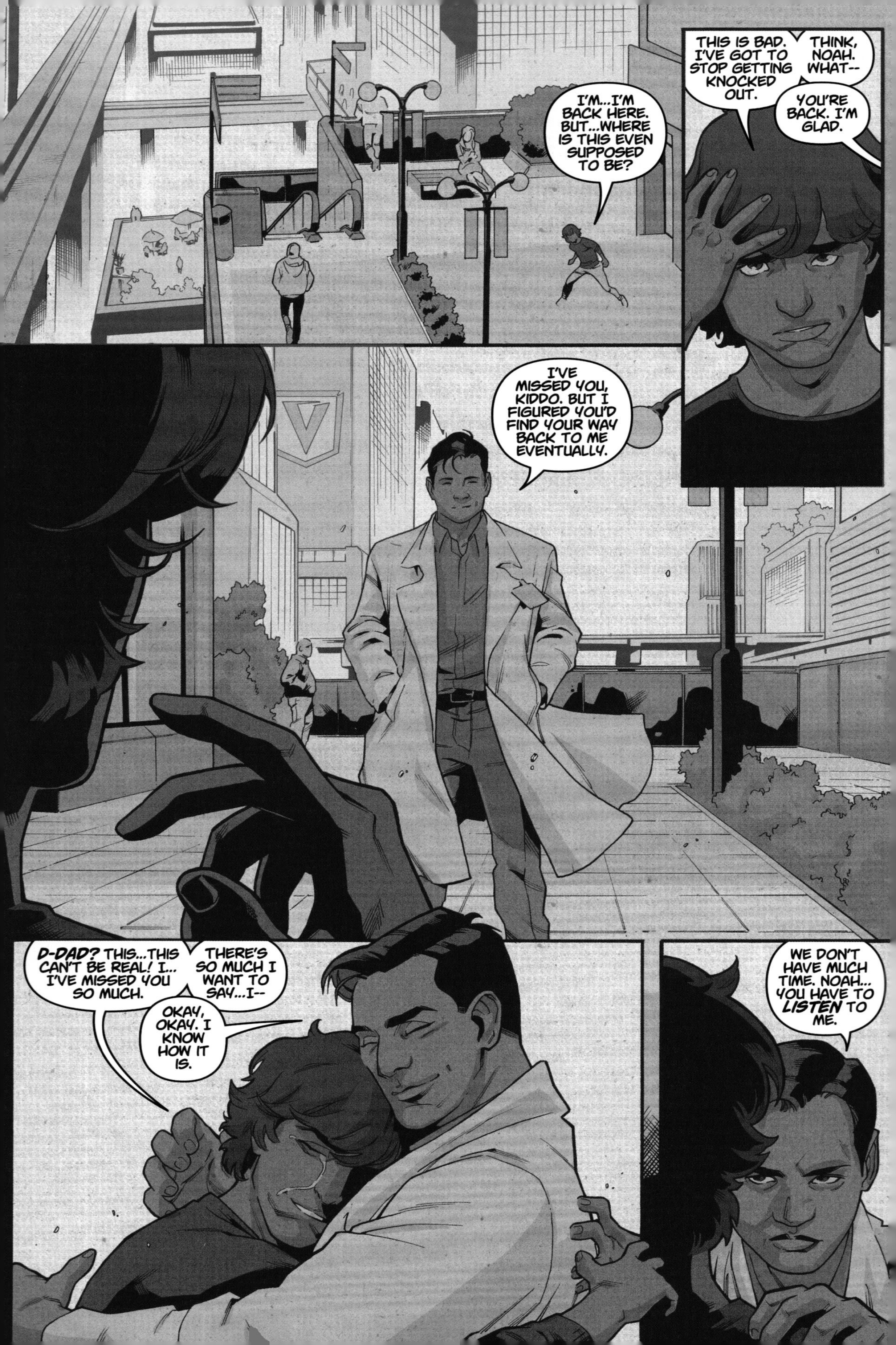
I'M...I'M BACK HERE. BUT...WHERE IS THIS EVEN SUPPOSED TO BE?
THIS IS BAD. I'VE GOT TO STOP GETTING KNOCKED OUT.
THINK, NOAH. WHAT--
YOU'RE BACK. I'M GLAD.
I'VE MISSED YOU, KIDDO. BUT I FIGURED YOU'D FIND YOUR WAY BACK TO ME EVENTUALLY.
D-DAD? THIS...THIS CAN'T BE REAL! I... I'VE MISSED YOU SO MUCH.
THERE'S SO MUCH I WANT TO SAY...I--
OKAY, OKAY. I KNOW HOW IT IS.
WE DON'T HAVE MUCH TIME. NOAH... YOU HAVE TO LISTEN TO ME.

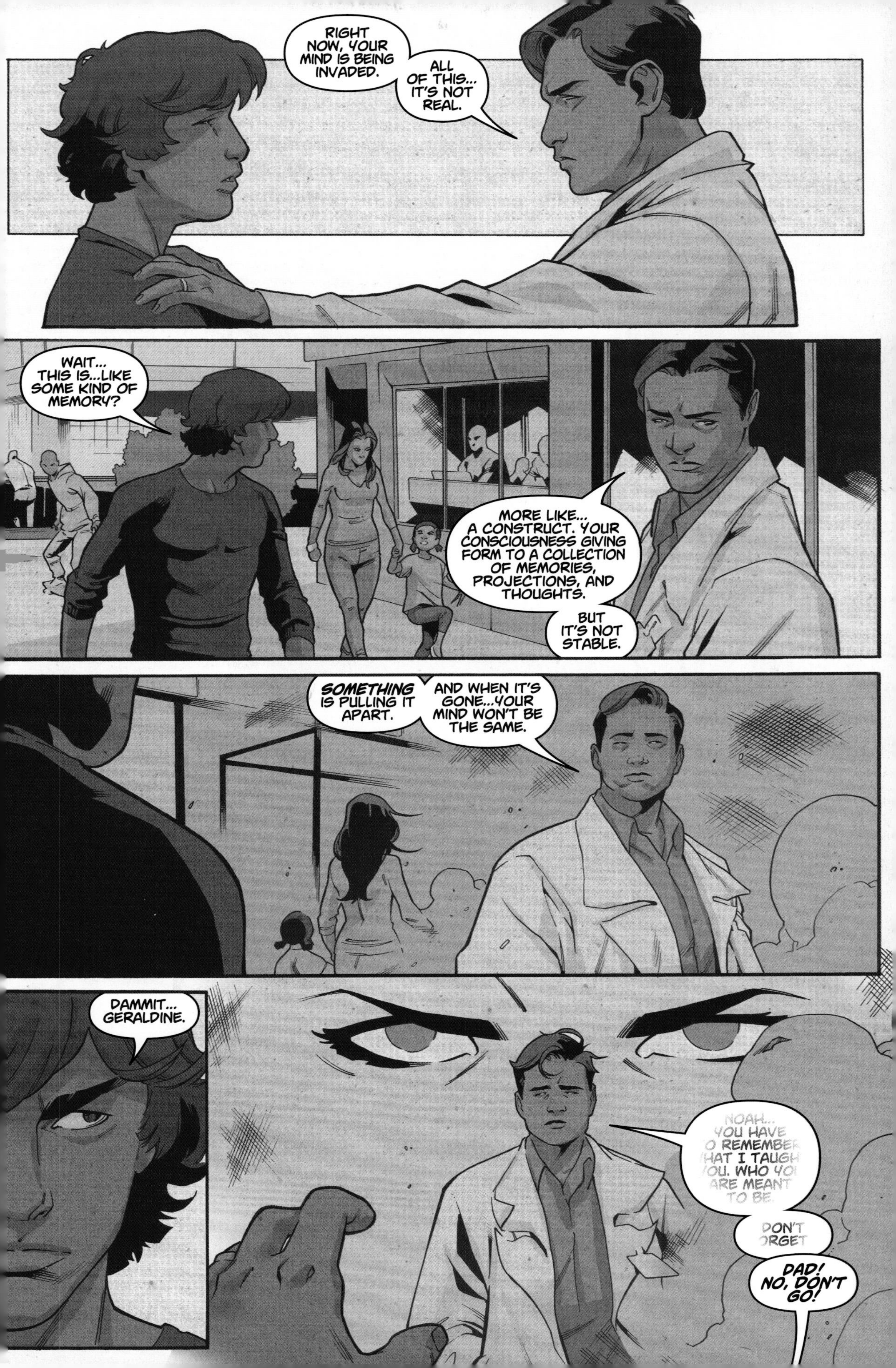
RIGHT NOW, YOUR MIND IS BEING INVADED.
ALL OF THIS... IT'S NOT REAL.
WAIT... THIS IS...LIKE SOME KIND OF MEMORY?
MORE LIKE... A CONSTRUCT. YOUR CONSCIOUSNESS GIVING FORM TO A COLLECTION OF MEMORIES, PROJECTIONS, AND THOUGHTS.
BUT IT'S NOT STABLE.
SOMETHING IS PULLING IT APART.
AND WHEN IT'S GONE...YOUR MIND WON'T BE THE SAME.
DAMMIT... GERALDINE.
NOAH... YOU HAVE O REMEMBER HAT I TAUGH OU. WHO YO ARE MEANT TO BE.
DON'T ORGET
DAD! NO, DON'T GO!

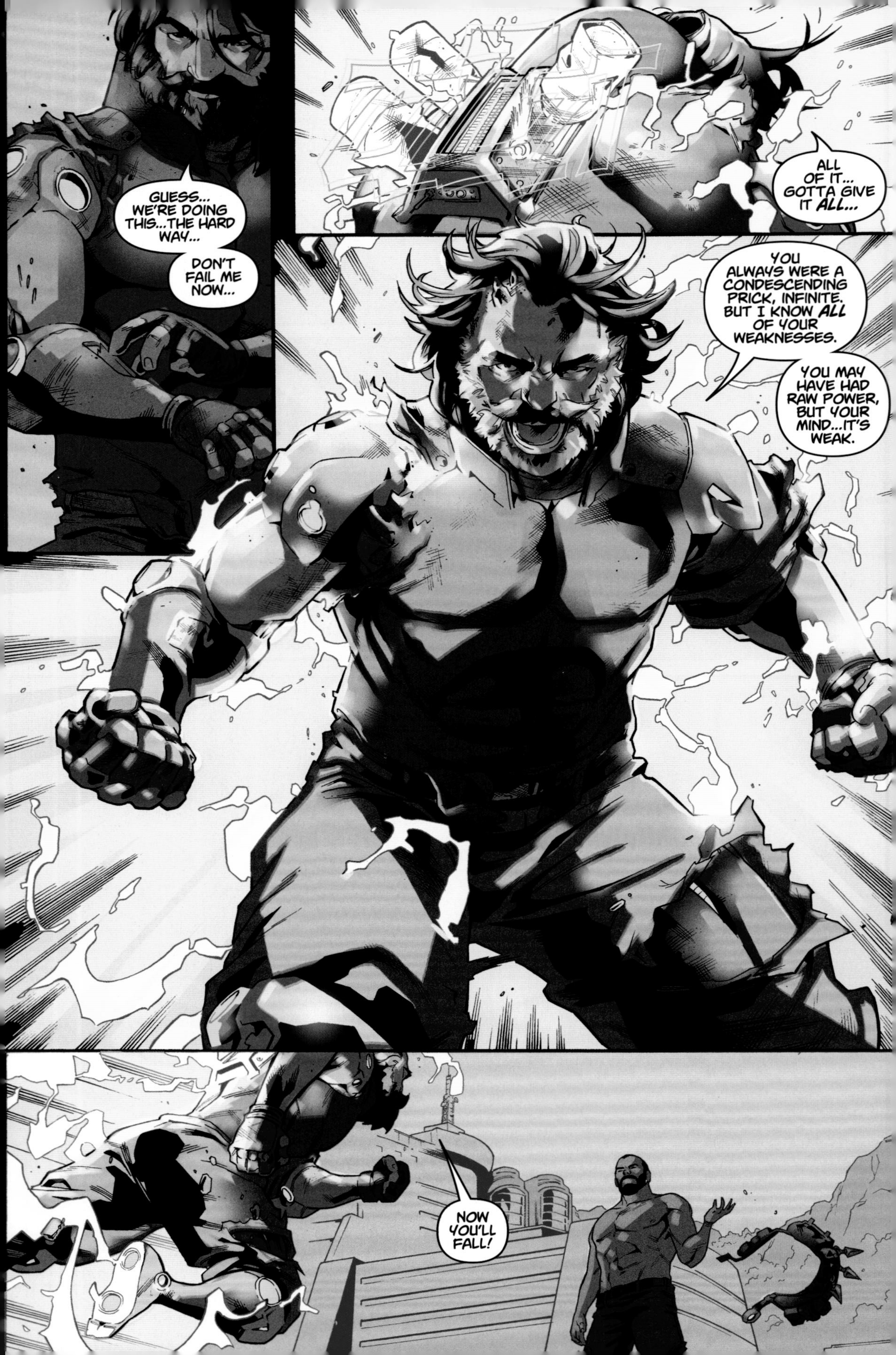
GUESS... WE'RE DOING THIS...THE HARD WAY...
DON'T FAIL ME NOW...
ALL OF IT... GOTTA GIVE IT ALL...
YOU ALWAYS WERE A CONDESCENDING PRICK, INFINITE. BUT I KNOW ALL OF YOUR WEAKNESSES.
YOU MAY HAVE HAD RAW POWER, BUT YOUR MIND...IT'S WEAK.
NOW YOU'LL FALL!

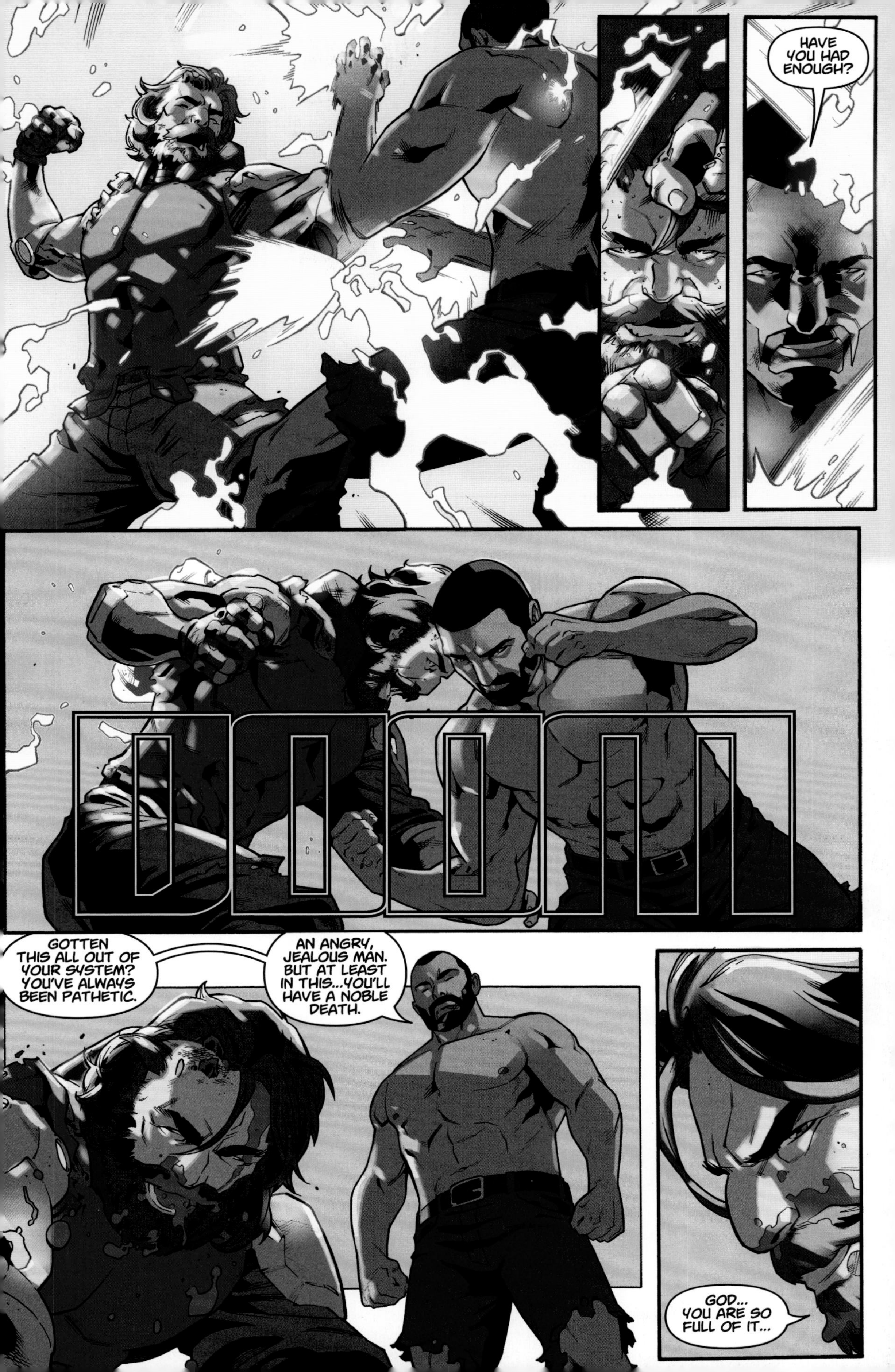
HAVE YOU HAD ENOUGH?
GOTTEN THIS ALL OUT OF YOUR SYSTEM? YOU'VE ALWAYS BEEN PATHETIC.
AN ANGRY, JEALOUS MAN. BUT AT LEAST IN THIS...YOU'LL HAVE A NOBLE DEATH.
GOD... YOU ARE SO FULL OF IT...

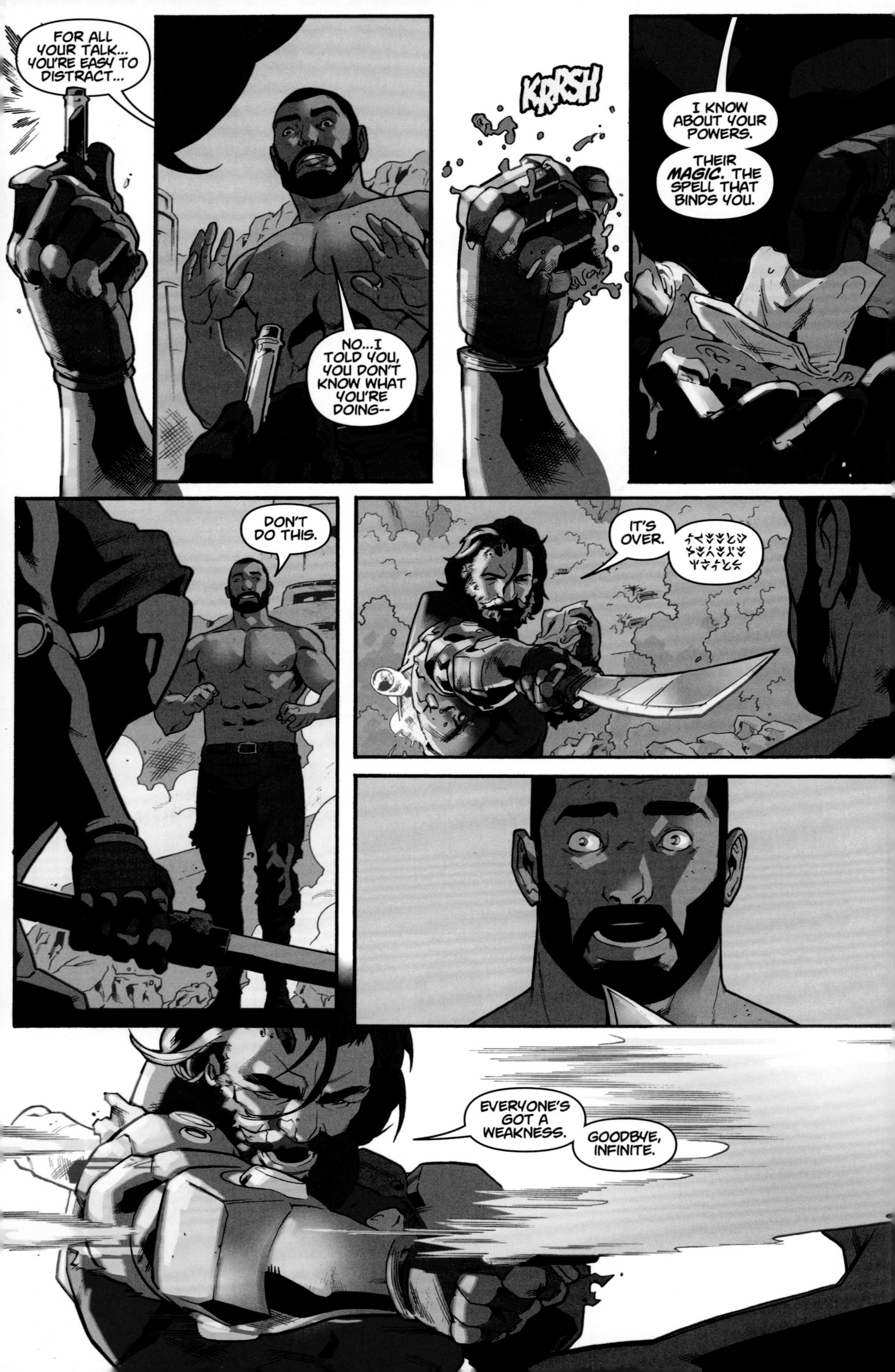
FOR ALL YOUR TALK... YOU'RE EASY TO DISTRACT...
NO...I TOLD YOU, YOU DON'T KNOW WHAT YOU'RE DOING--
KRRSH
I KNOW ABOUT YOUR POWERS.
THEIR MAGIC. THE SPELL THAT BINDS YOU.
DON'T DO THIS.
IT'S OVER.
EVERYONE'S GOT A WEAKNESS.
GOODBYE, INFINITE.

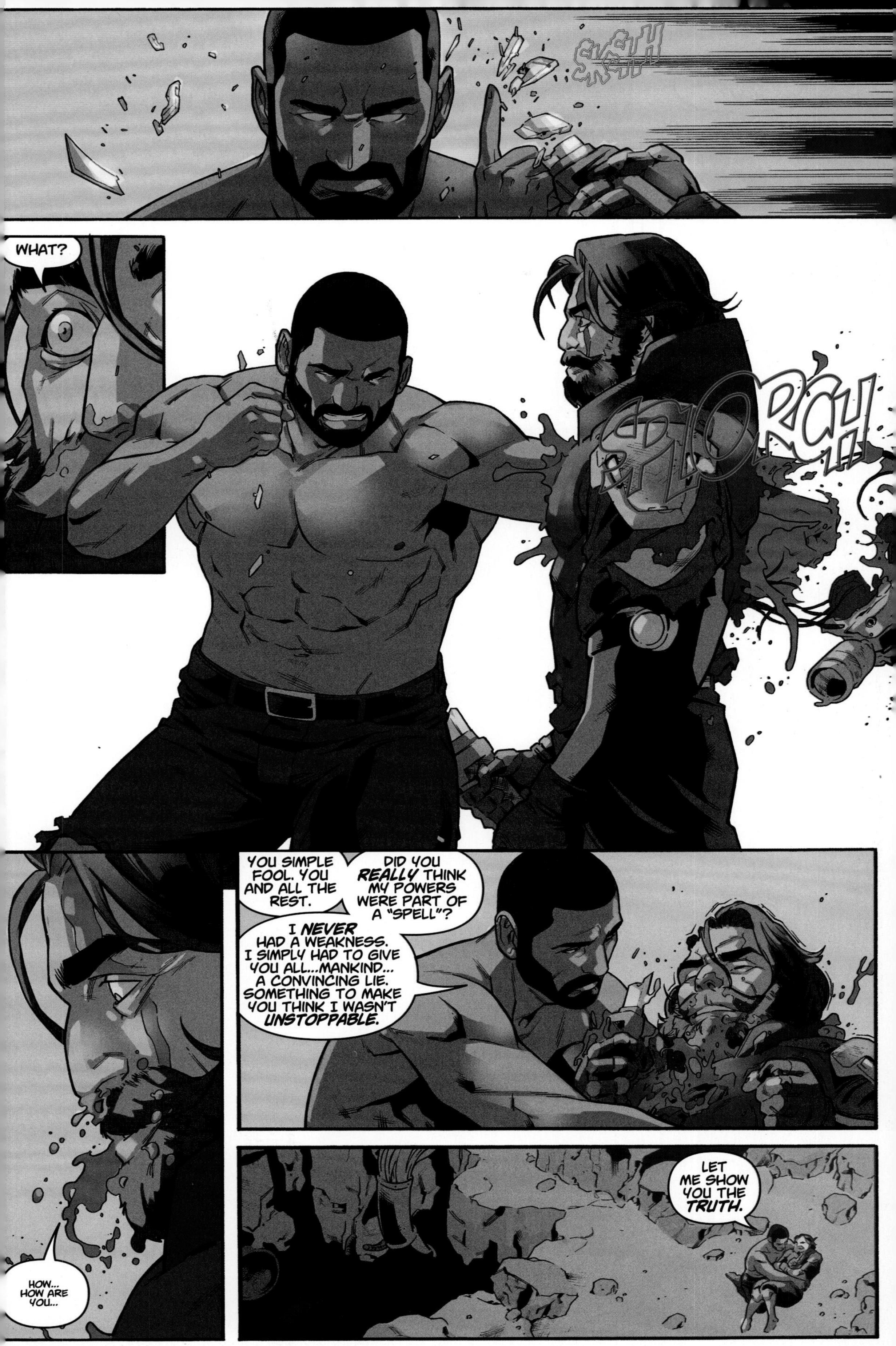
SKSH
WHAT?
SPLORCH
HOW... HOW ARE YOU...
YOU SIMPLE FOOL. YOU AND ALL THE REST.
DID YOU REALLY THINK MY POWERS WERE PART OF A "SPELL"?
I NEVER HAD A WEAKNESS. I SIMPLY HAD TO GIVE YOU ALL...MANKIND... A CONVINCING LIE. SOMETHING TO MAKE YOU THINK I WASN'T UNSTOPPABLE.
LET ME SHOW YOU THE TRUTH.

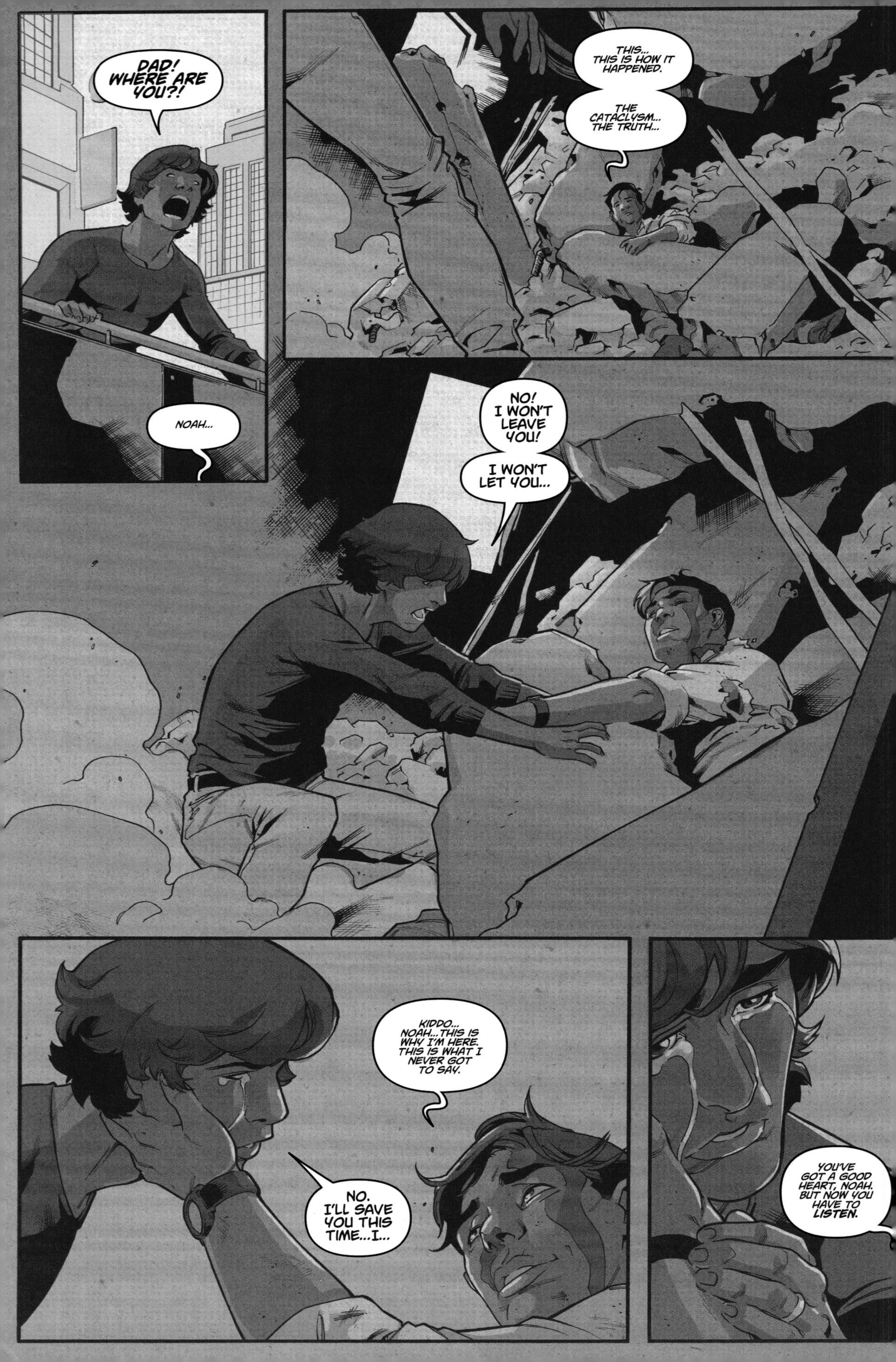
DAD! WHERE ARE YOU?!
NOAH...
THIS... THIS IS HOW IT HAPPENED.
THE CATACLYSM... THE TRUTH...
NO! I WON'T LEAVE YOU!
I WON'T LET YOU...
KIDDO... NOAH... THIS IS WHY I'M HERE. THIS IS WHAT I NEVER GOT TO SAY.
NO. I'LL SAVE YOU THIS TIME... I...
YOU'VE GOT A GOOD HEART, NOAH. BUT NOW YOU HAVE TO LISTEN.

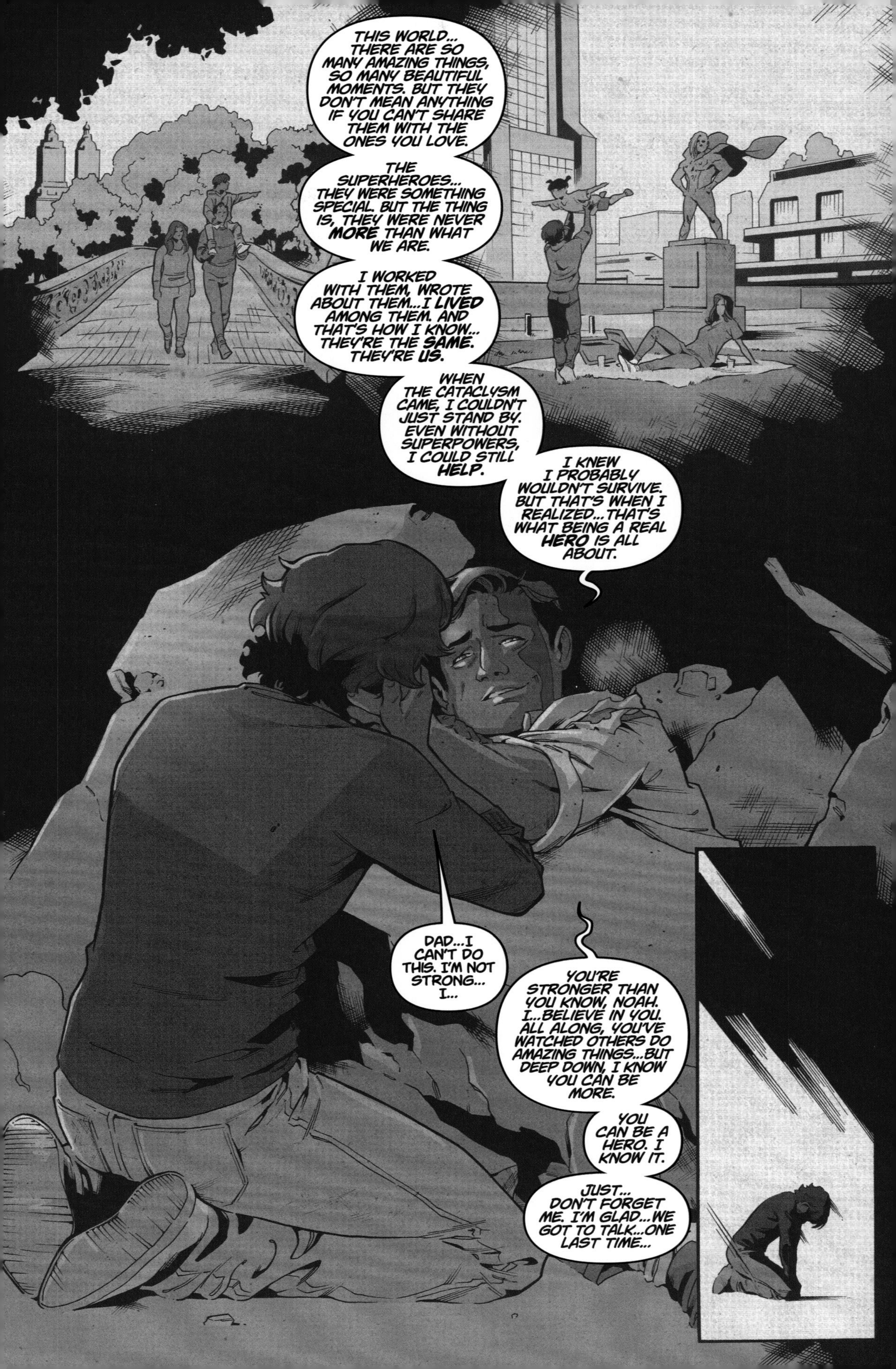
THIS WORLD... THERE ARE SO MANY AMAZING THINGS, SO MANY BEAUTIFUL MOMENTS. BUT THEY DON'T MEAN ANYTHING IF YOU CAN'T SHARE THEM WITH THE ONES YOU LOVE.
THE SUPERHEROES... THEY WERE SOMETHING SPECIAL. BUT THE THING IS, THEY WERE NEVER **MORE** THAN WHAT WE ARE.
I WORKED WITH THEM, WROTE ABOUT THEM...I **LIVED** AMONG THEM. AND THAT'S HOW I KNOW... THEY'RE THE **SAME**. THEY'RE **US**.
WHEN THE CATACLYSM CAME, I COULDN'T JUST STAND BY. EVEN WITHOUT SUPERPOWERS, I COULD STILL **HELP**.
I KNEW I PROBABLY WOULDN'T SURVIVE. BUT THAT'S WHEN I REALIZED...THAT'S WHAT BEING A REAL **HERO** IS ALL ABOUT.
DAD...I CAN'T DO THIS. I'M NOT STRONG... I...
YOU'RE STRONGER THAN YOU KNOW, NOAH. I...BELIEVE IN YOU. ALL ALONG, YOU'VE WATCHED OTHERS DO AMAZING THINGS...BUT DEEP DOWN, I KNOW YOU CAN BE MORE.
YOU CAN BE A HERO. I KNOW IT.
JUST... DON'T FORGET ME. I'M GLAD...WE GOT TO TALK...ONE LAST TIME...

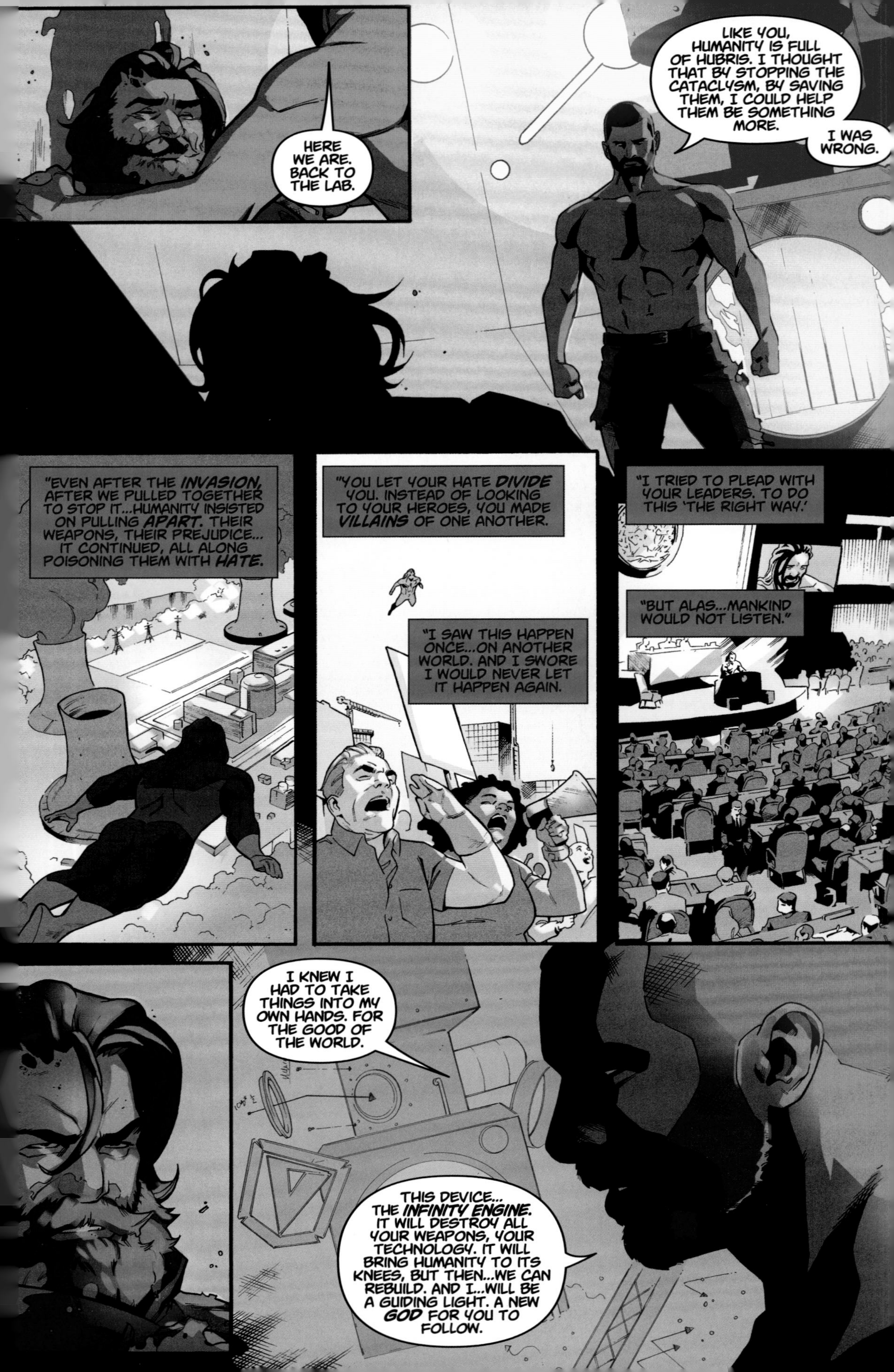
HERE WE ARE. BACK TO THE LAB.
LIKE YOU, HUMANITY IS FULL OF HUBRIS. I THOUGHT THAT BY STOPPING THE CATACLYSM, BY SAVING THEM, I COULD HELP THEM BE SOMETHING MORE.
I WAS WRONG.
"EVEN AFTER THE *INVASION*, AFTER WE PULLED TOGETHER TO STOP IT...HUMANITY INSISTED ON PULLING *APART*. THEIR WEAPONS, THEIR PREJUDICE... IT CONTINUED, ALL ALONG POISONING THEM WITH *HATE*.
"YOU LET YOUR HATE *DIVIDE* YOU. INSTEAD OF LOOKING TO YOUR HEROES, YOU MADE *VILLAINS* OF ONE ANOTHER.
"I SAW THIS HAPPEN ONCE...ON ANOTHER WORLD. AND I SWORE I WOULD NEVER LET IT HAPPEN AGAIN.
"I TRIED TO PLEAD WITH YOUR LEADERS. TO DO THIS 'THE RIGHT WAY.'
"BUT ALAS...MANKIND WOULD NOT LISTEN."
I KNEW I HAD TO TAKE THINGS INTO MY OWN HANDS. FOR THE GOOD OF THE WORLD.
THIS DEVICE... THE *INFINITY ENGINE*. IT WILL DESTROY ALL YOUR WEAPONS, YOUR TECHNOLOGY. IT WILL BRING HUMANITY TO ITS KNEES, BUT THEN...WE CAN REBUILD. AND I...WILL BE A GUIDING LIGHT. A NEW *GOD* FOR YOU TO FOLLOW.

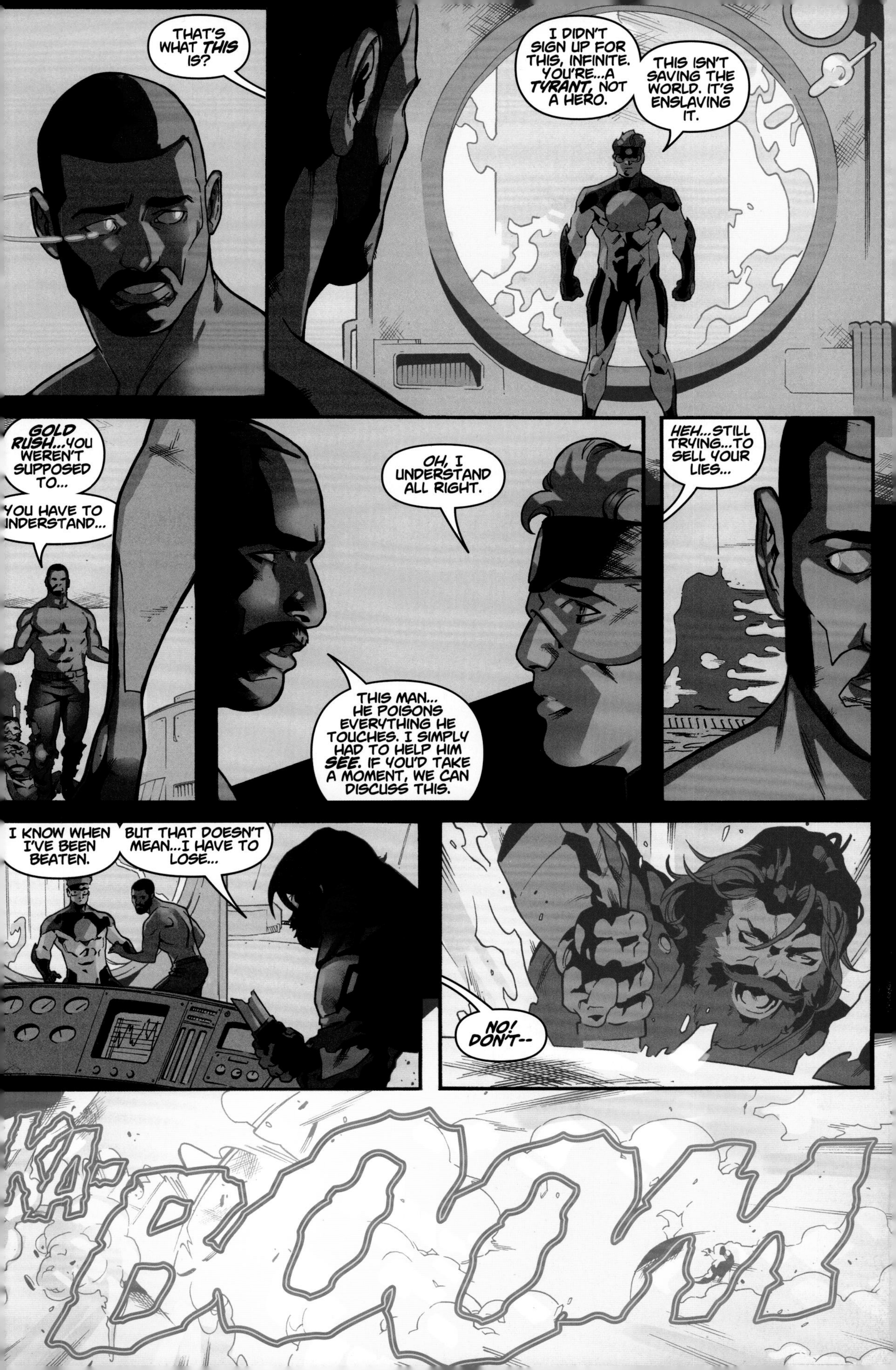
THAT'S WHAT *THIS* IS?
I DIDN'T SIGN UP FOR THIS, INFINITE. YOU'RE...A *TYRANT,* NOT A HERO.
THIS ISN'T SAVING THE WORLD. IT'S ENSLAVING IT.
GOLD RUSH...YOU WEREN'T SUPPOSED TO...
YOU HAVE TO UNDERSTAND...
OH, I UNDERSTAND ALL RIGHT.
THIS MAN... HE POISONS EVERYTHING HE TOUCHES. I SIMPLY HAD TO HELP HIM *SEE.* IF YOU'D TAKE A MOMENT, WE CAN DISCUSS THIS.
HEH...STILL TRYING...TO SELL YOUR LIES...
I KNOW WHEN I'VE BEEN BEATEN.
BUT THAT DOESN'T MEAN...I HAVE TO LOSE...
NO! DON'T--
KA-BOOM

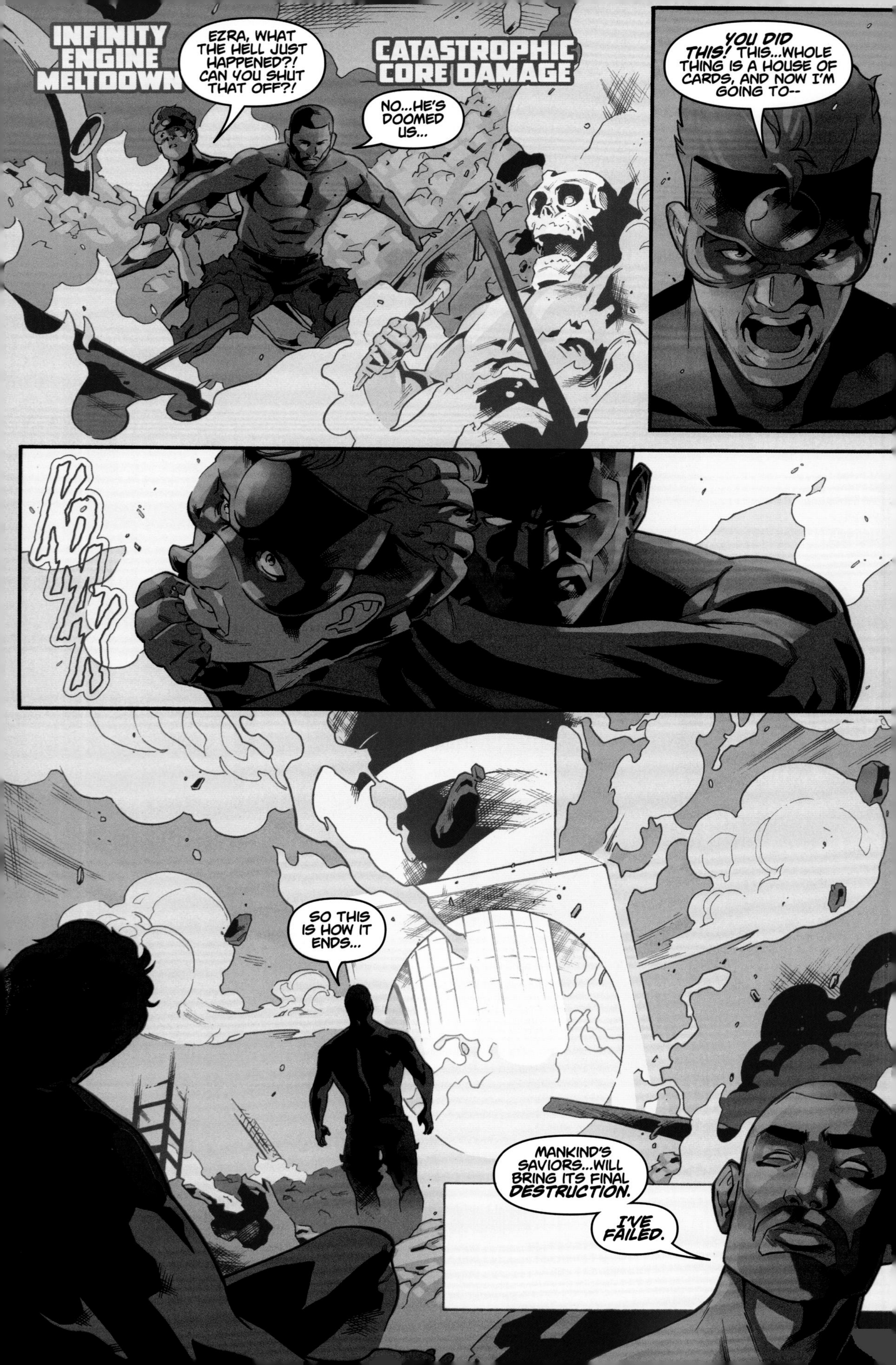
INFINITY ENGINE MELTDOWN
EZRA, WHAT THE HELL JUST HAPPENED?! CAN YOU SHUT THAT OFF?!
CATASTROPHIC CORE DAMAGE
NO...HE'S DOOMED US...
YOU DID THIS! THIS...WHOLE THING IS A HOUSE OF CARDS, AND NOW I'M GOING TO--
SO THIS IS HOW IT ENDS...
MANKIND'S SAVIORS...WILL BRING ITS FINAL DESTRUCTION.
I'VE FAILED.

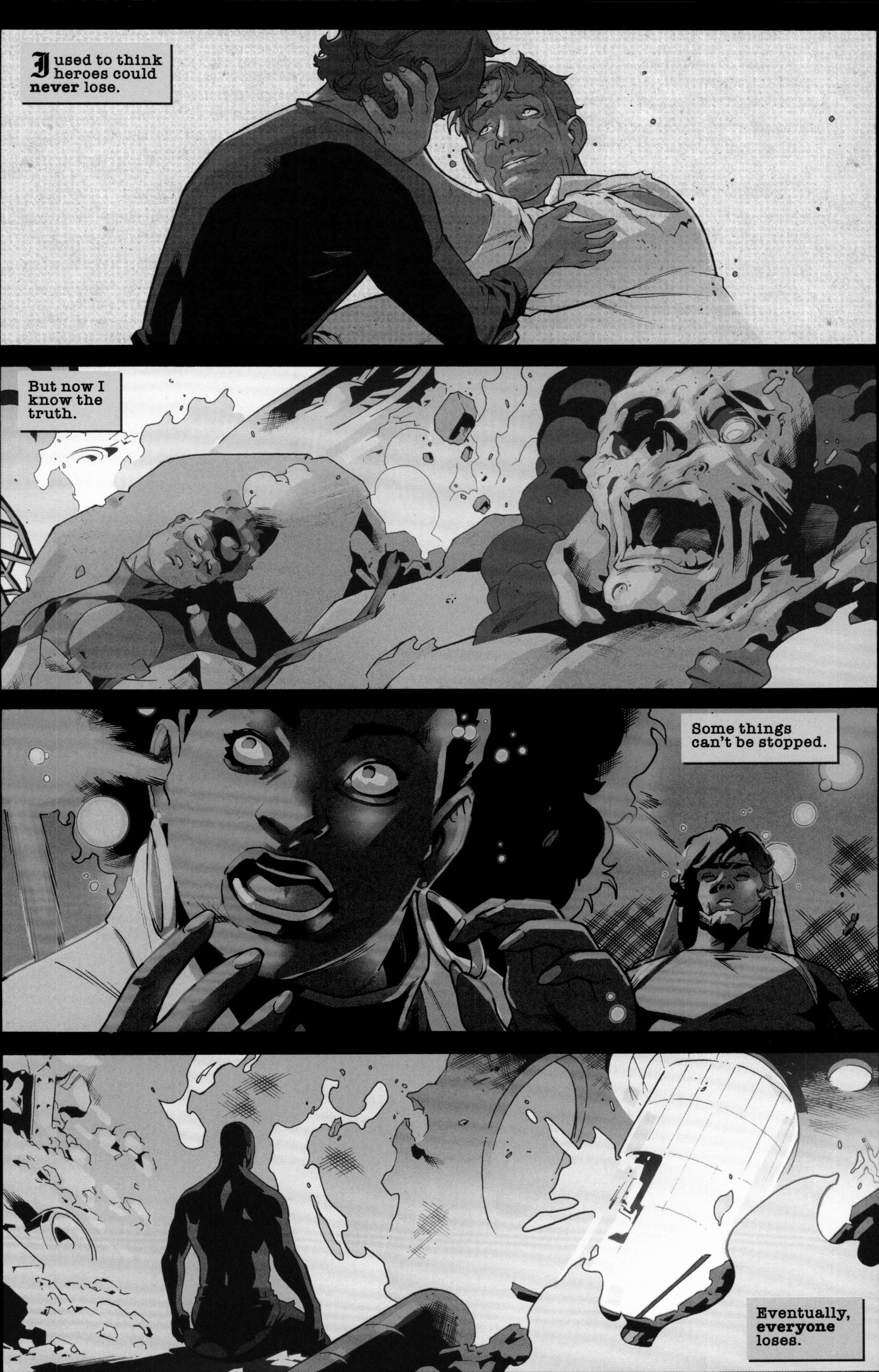
I used to think heroes could **never** lose.
But now I know the truth.
Some things can't be stopped.
Eventually, **everyone** loses.

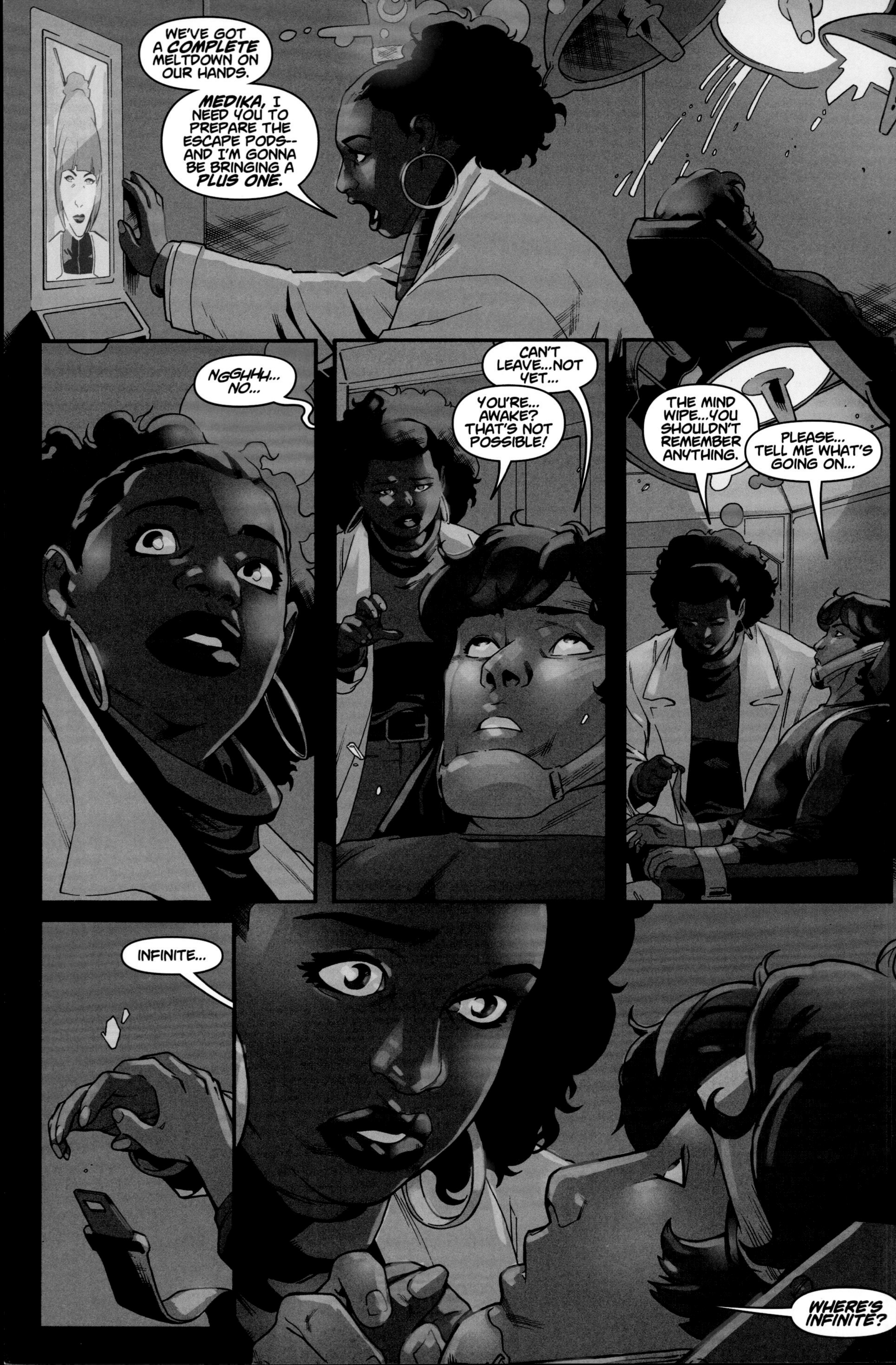
WE'VE GOT A COMPLETE MELTDOWN ON OUR HANDS.
MEDIKA, I NEED YOU TO PREPARE THE ESCAPE PODS-- AND I'M GONNA BE BRINGING A PLUS ONE.
NGGHHH... NO...
CAN'T LEAVE...NOT YET...
YOU'RE... AWAKE? THAT'S NOT POSSIBLE!
THE MIND WIPE...YOU SHOULDN'T REMEMBER ANYTHING.
PLEASE... TELL ME WHAT'S GOING ON...
INFINITE...
WHERE'S INFINITE?

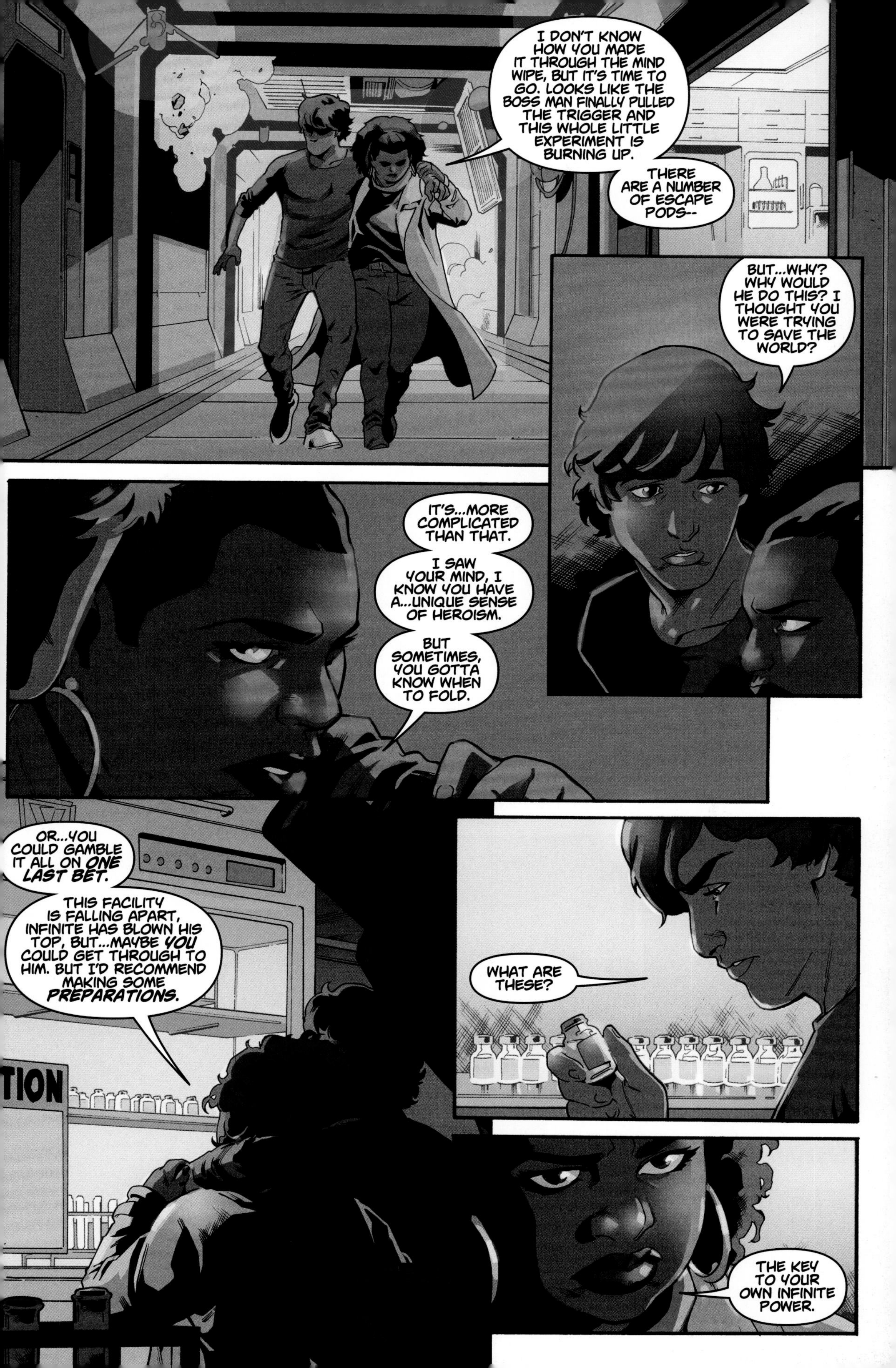
I DON'T KNOW HOW YOU MADE IT THROUGH THE MIND WIPE, BUT IT'S TIME TO GO. LOOKS LIKE THE BOSS MAN FINALLY PULLED THE TRIGGER AND THIS WHOLE LITTLE EXPERIMENT IS BURNING UP.
THERE ARE A NUMBER OF ESCAPE PODS--
BUT...WHY? WHY WOULD HE DO THIS? I THOUGHT YOU WERE TRYING TO SAVE THE WORLD?
IT'S...MORE COMPLICATED THAN THAT.
I SAW YOUR MIND, I KNOW YOU HAVE A...UNIQUE SENSE OF HEROISM.
BUT SOMETIMES, YOU GOTTA KNOW WHEN TO FOLD.
OR...YOU COULD GAMBLE IT ALL ON *ONE LAST BET*.
THIS FACILITY IS FALLING APART, INFINITE HAS BLOWN HIS TOP, BUT...MAYBE *YOU* COULD GET THROUGH TO HIM. BUT I'D RECOMMEND MAKING SOME *PREPARATIONS*.
WHAT ARE THESE?
THE KEY TO YOUR OWN INFINITE POWER.
TION

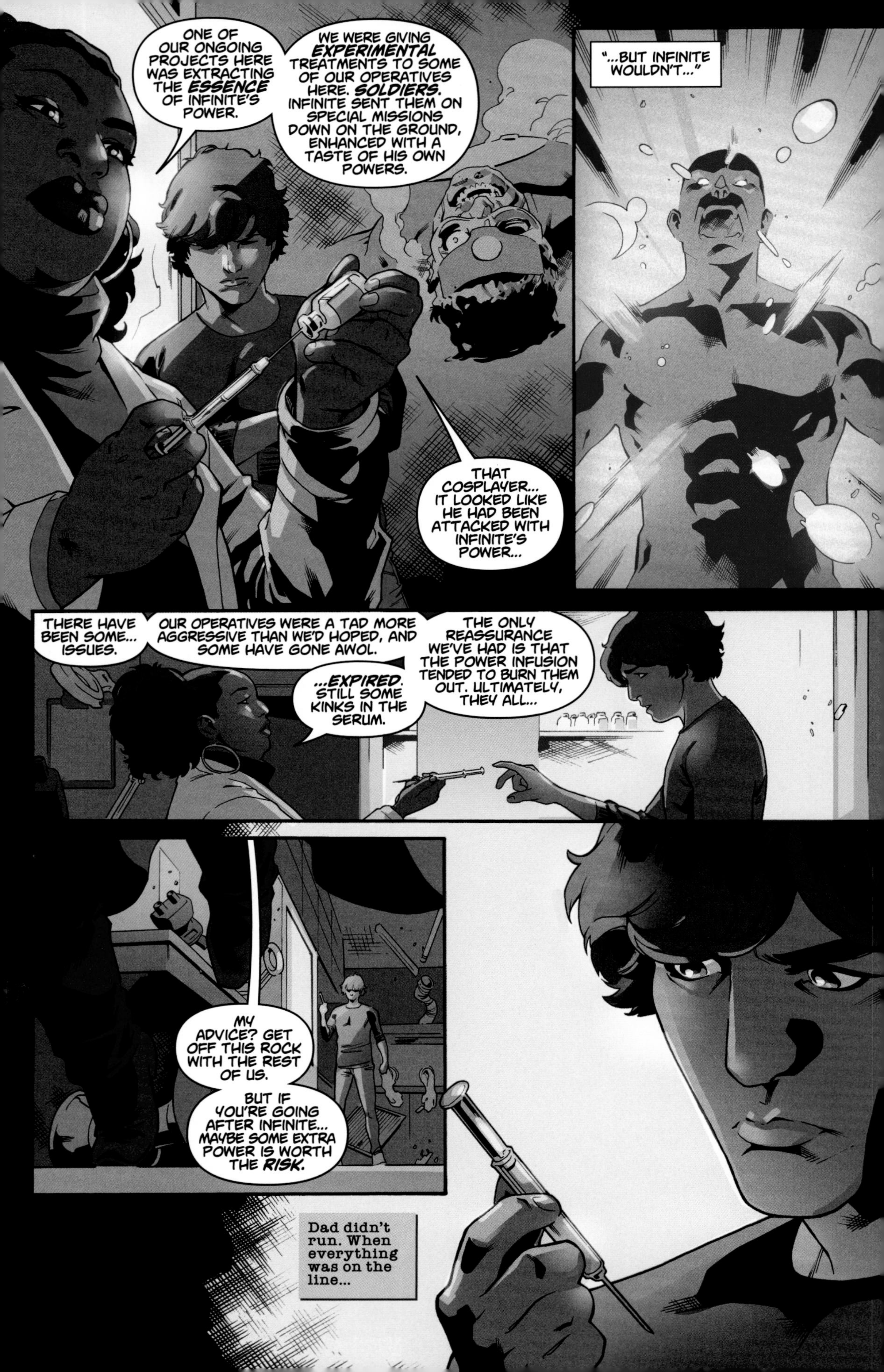
ONE OF OUR ONGOING PROJECTS HERE WAS EXTRACTING THE ESSENCE OF INFINITE'S POWER.
WE WERE GIVING EXPERIMENTAL TREATMENTS TO SOME OF OUR OPERATIVES HERE. SOLDIERS. INFINITE SENT THEM ON SPECIAL MISSIONS DOWN ON THE GROUND, ENHANCED WITH A TASTE OF HIS OWN POWERS.
THAT COSPLAYER... IT LOOKED LIKE HE HAD BEEN ATTACKED WITH INFINITE'S POWER...
"...BUT INFINITE WOULDN'T..."
THERE HAVE BEEN SOME... ISSUES.
OUR OPERATIVES WERE A TAD MORE AGGRESSIVE THAN WE'D HOPED, AND SOME HAVE GONE AWOL.
THE ONLY REASSURANCE WE'VE HAD IS THAT THE POWER INFUSION TENDED TO BURN THEM OUT. ULTIMATELY, THEY ALL...
...EXPIRED. STILL SOME KINKS IN THE SERUM.
MY ADVICE? GET OFF THIS ROCK WITH THE REST OF US.
BUT IF YOU'RE GOING AFTER INFINITE... MAYBE SOME EXTRA POWER IS WORTH THE RISK.
Dad didn't run. When everything was on the line...

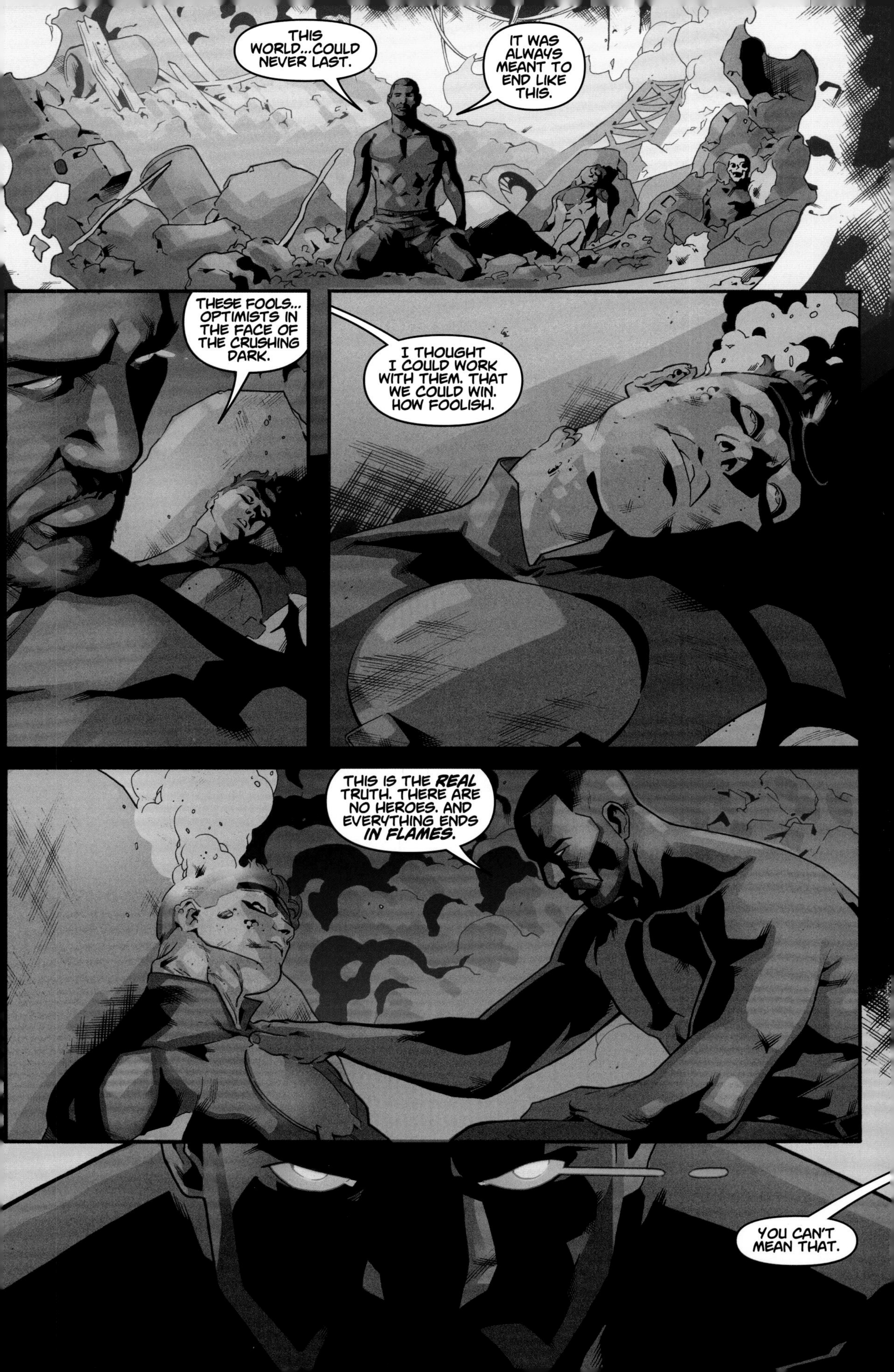
THIS WORLD...COULD NEVER LAST.
IT WAS ALWAYS MEANT TO END LIKE THIS.
THESE FOOLS... OPTIMISTS IN THE FACE OF THE CRUSHING DARK.
I THOUGHT I COULD WORK WITH THEM. THAT WE COULD WIN. HOW FOOLISH.
THIS IS THE *REAL* TRUTH. THERE ARE NO HEROES. AND EVERYTHING ENDS *IN FLAMES*.
YOU CAN'T MEAN THAT.

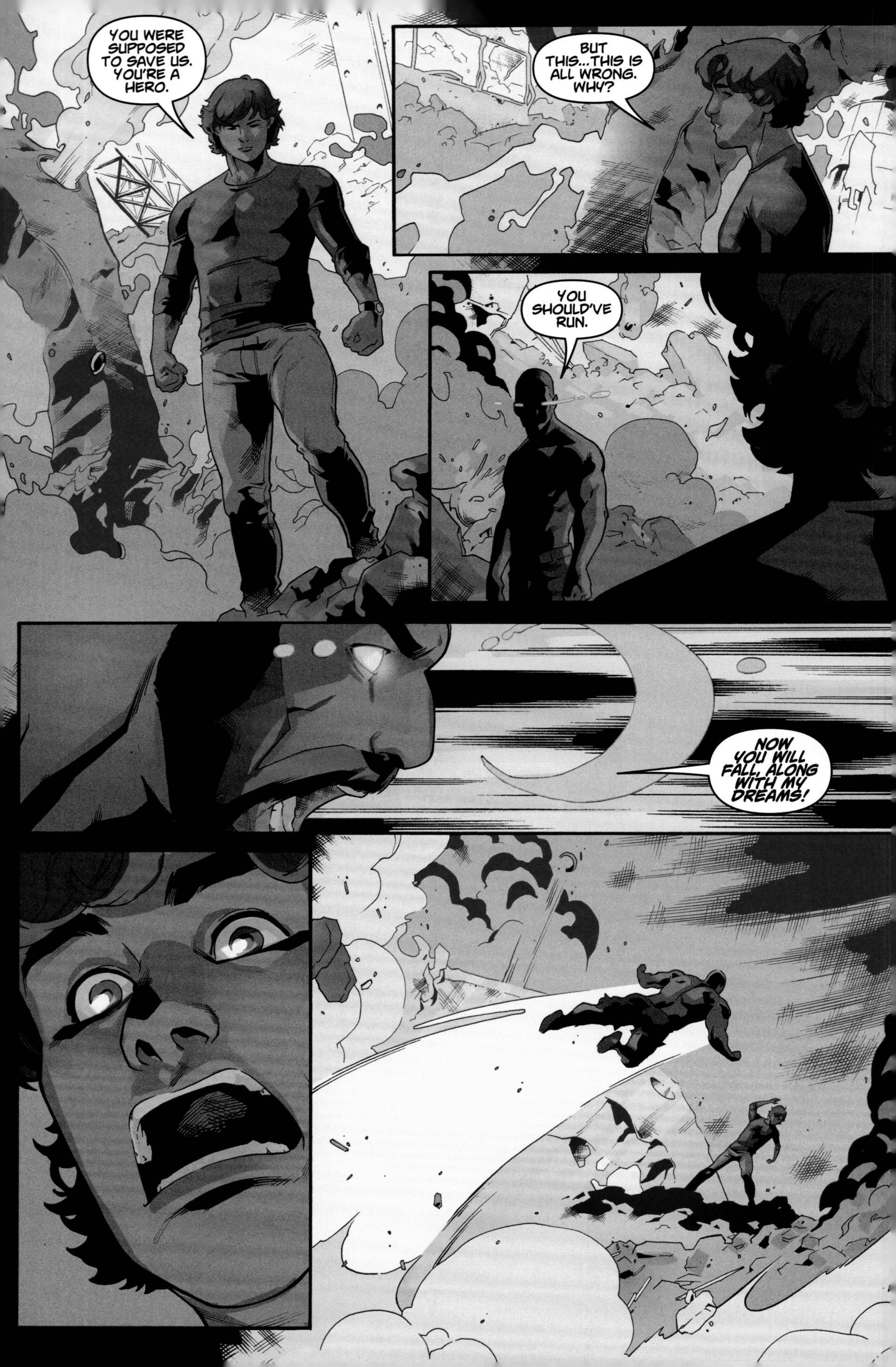
YOU WERE SUPPOSED TO SAVE US. YOU'RE A HERO.
BUT THIS...THIS IS ALL WRONG. WHY?
YOU SHOULD'VE RUN.
NOW YOU WILL FALL, ALONG WITH MY DREAMS!

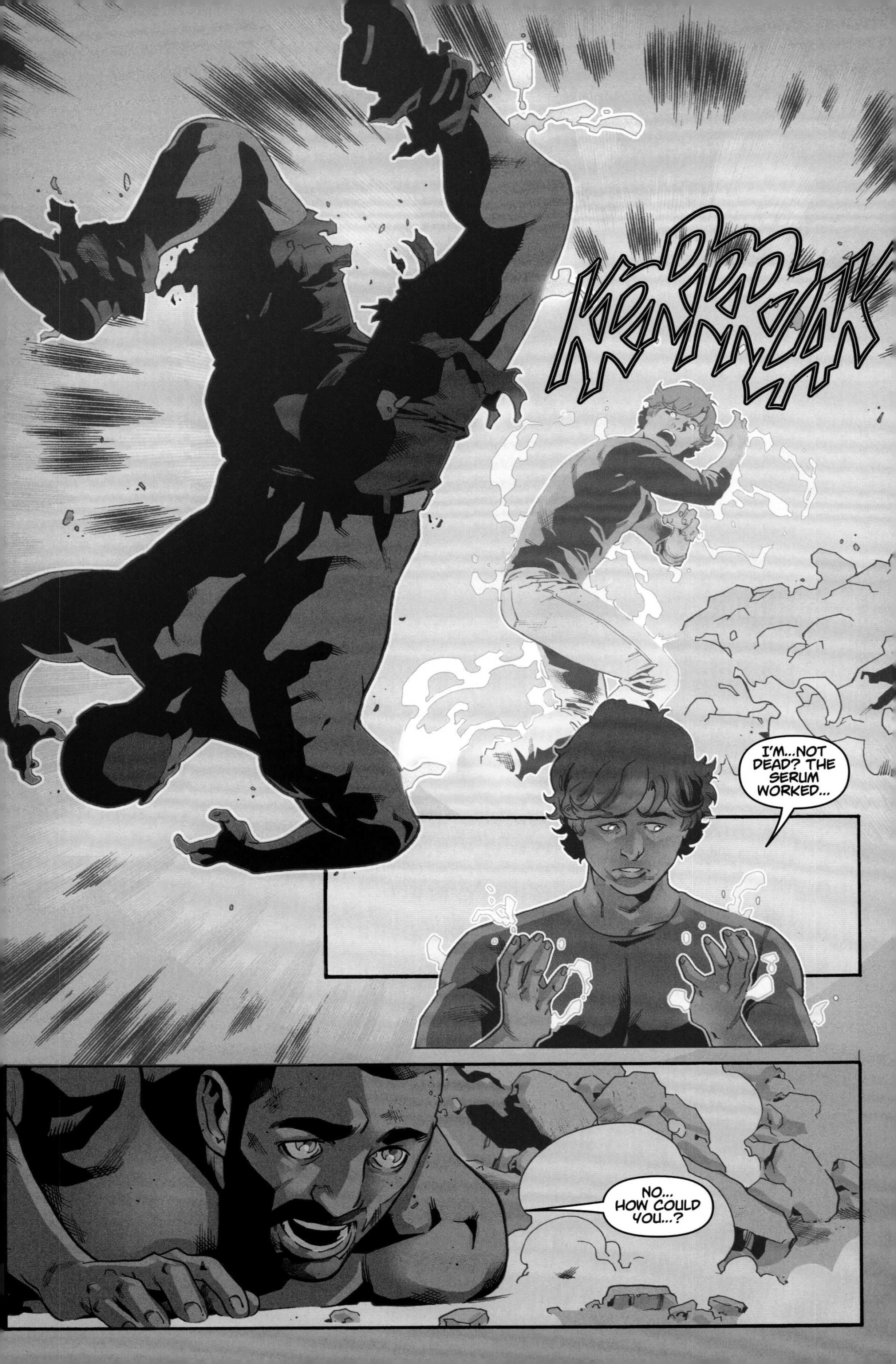
KRRRRRZAK
I'M...NOT DEAD? THE SERUM WORKED...
NO... HOW COULD YOU...?

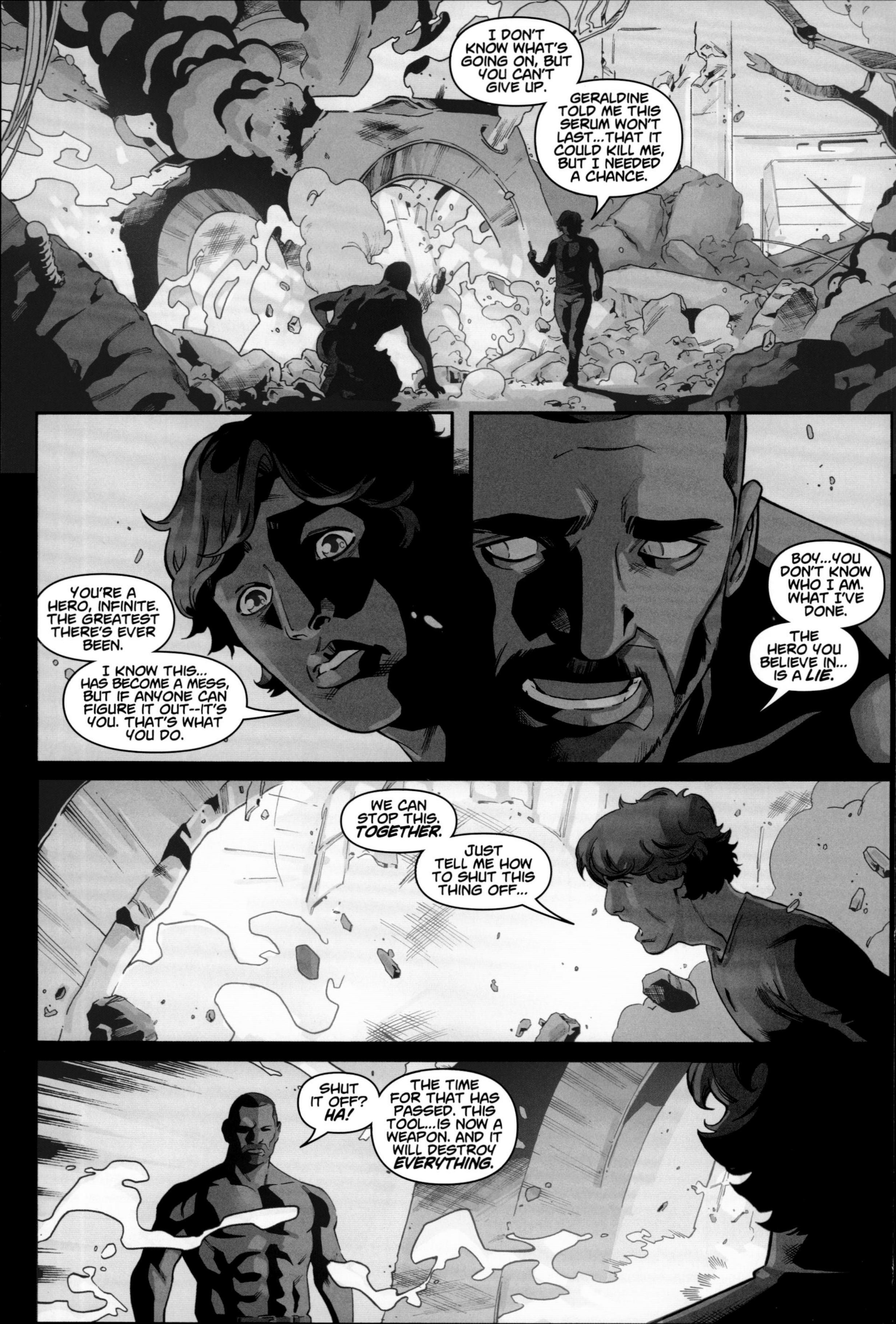

I DON'T KNOW WHAT'S GOING ON, BUT YOU CAN'T GIVE UP.
GERALDINE TOLD ME THIS SERUM WON'T LAST...THAT IT COULD KILL ME, BUT I NEEDED A CHANCE.
YOU'RE A HERO, INFINITE. THE GREATEST THERE'S EVER BEEN.
I KNOW THIS... HAS BECOME A MESS, BUT IF ANYONE CAN FIGURE IT OUT--IT'S YOU. THAT'S WHAT YOU DO.
BOY...YOU DON'T KNOW WHO I AM. WHAT I'VE DONE.
THE HERO YOU BELIEVE IN... IS A ***LIE.***
WE CAN STOP THIS. ***TOGETHER.***
JUST TELL ME HOW TO SHUT THIS THING OFF...
SHUT IT OFF? ***HA!***
THE TIME FOR THAT HAS PASSED. THIS TOOL...IS NOW A WEAPON. AND IT WILL DESTROY ***EVERYTHING.***

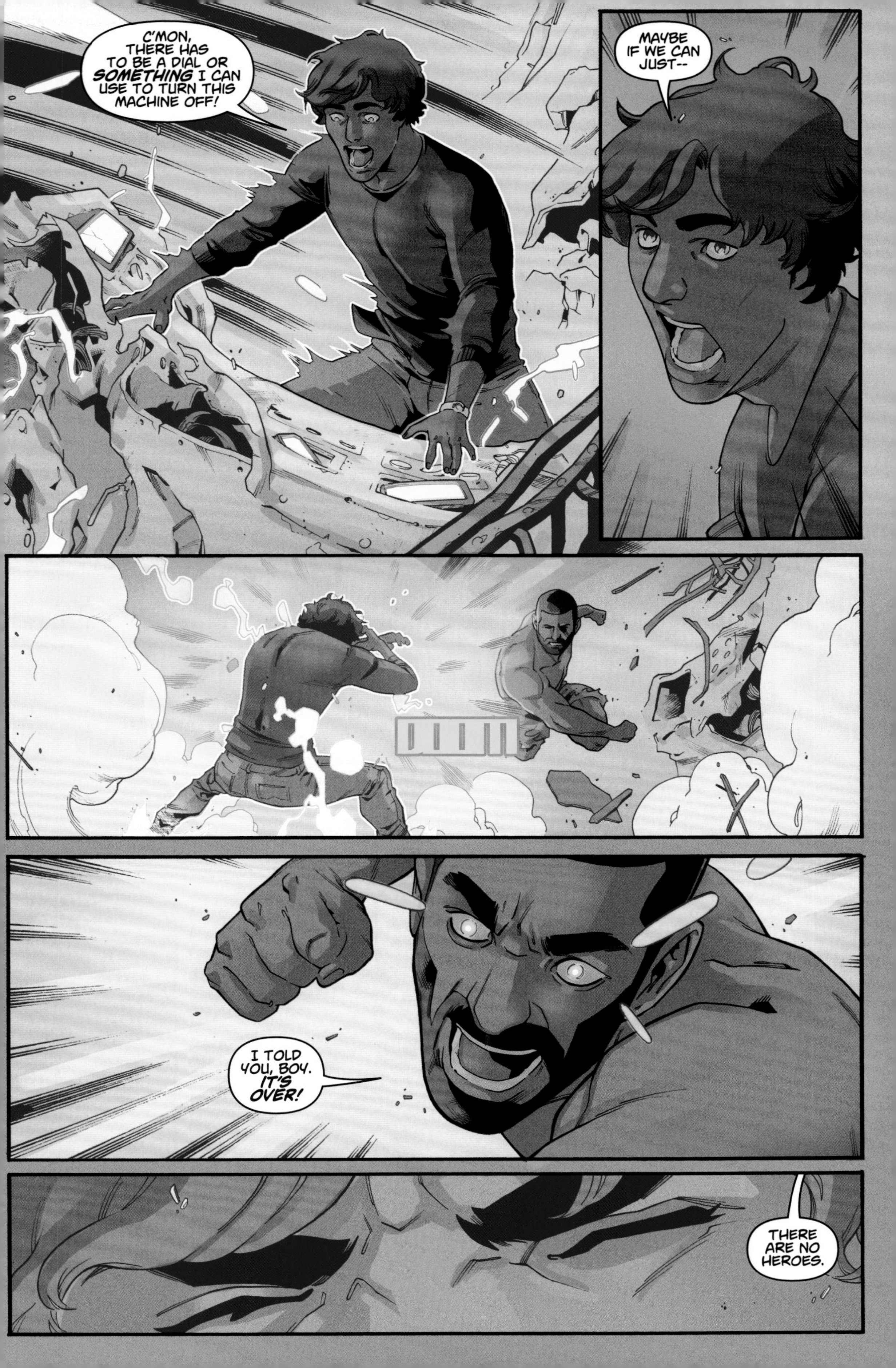
C'MON, THERE HAS TO BE A DIAL OR SOMETHING I CAN USE TO TURN THIS MACHINE OFF!
MAYBE IF WE CAN JUST--
DOOM
I TOLD YOU, BOY. IT'S OVER!
THERE ARE NO HEROES.

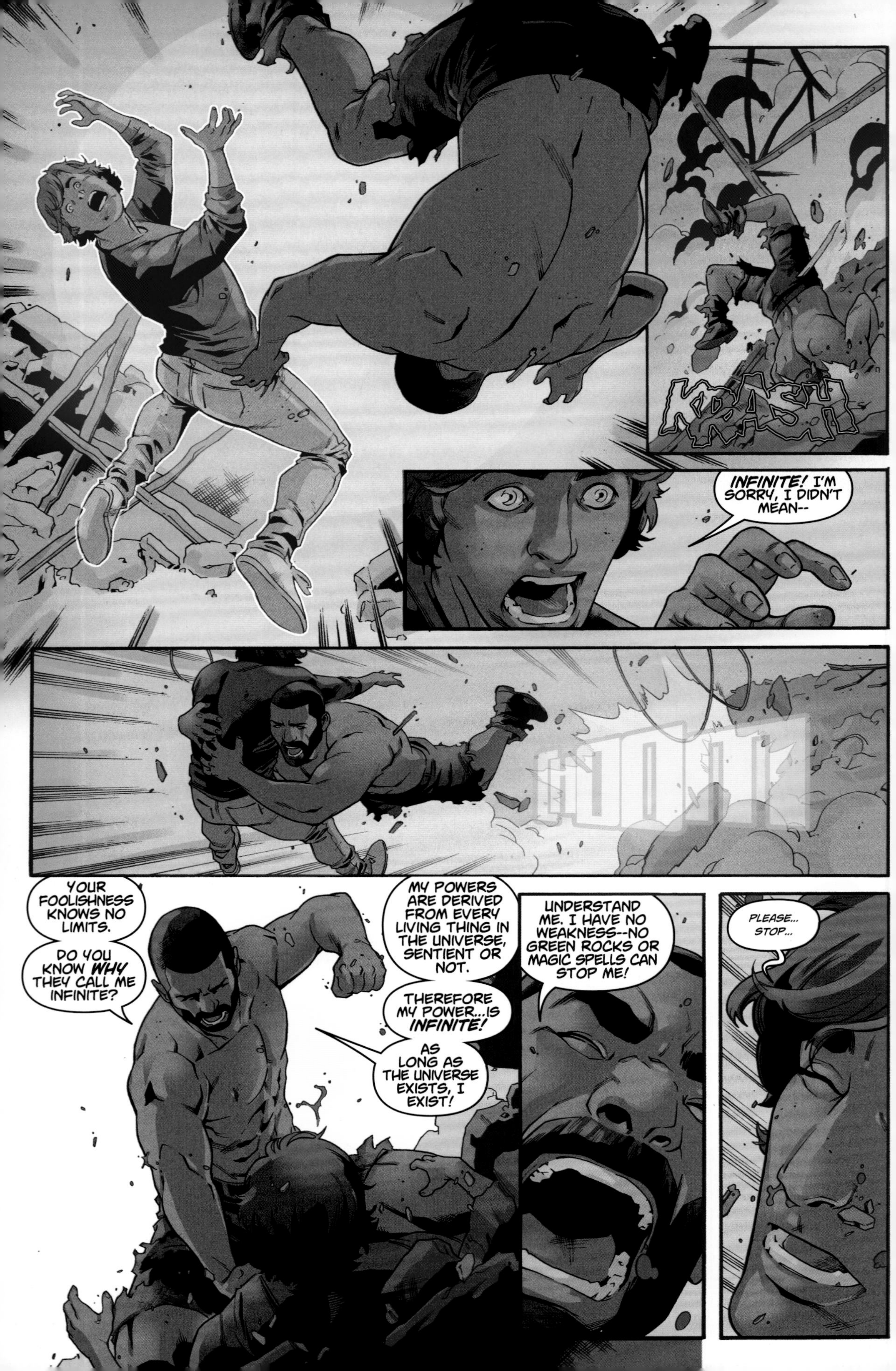
KRASH
INFINITE! I'M SORRY, I DIDN'T MEAN--
YOUR FOOLISHNESS KNOWS NO LIMITS.
DO YOU KNOW WHY THEY CALL ME INFINITE?
MY POWERS ARE DERIVED FROM EVERY LIVING THING IN THE UNIVERSE, SENTIENT OR NOT.
THEREFORE MY POWER...IS INFINITE!
AS LONG AS THE UNIVERSE EXISTS, I EXIST!
UNDERSTAND ME. I HAVE NO WEAKNESS--NO GREEN ROCKS OR MAGIC SPELLS CAN STOP ME!
PLEASE... STOP...

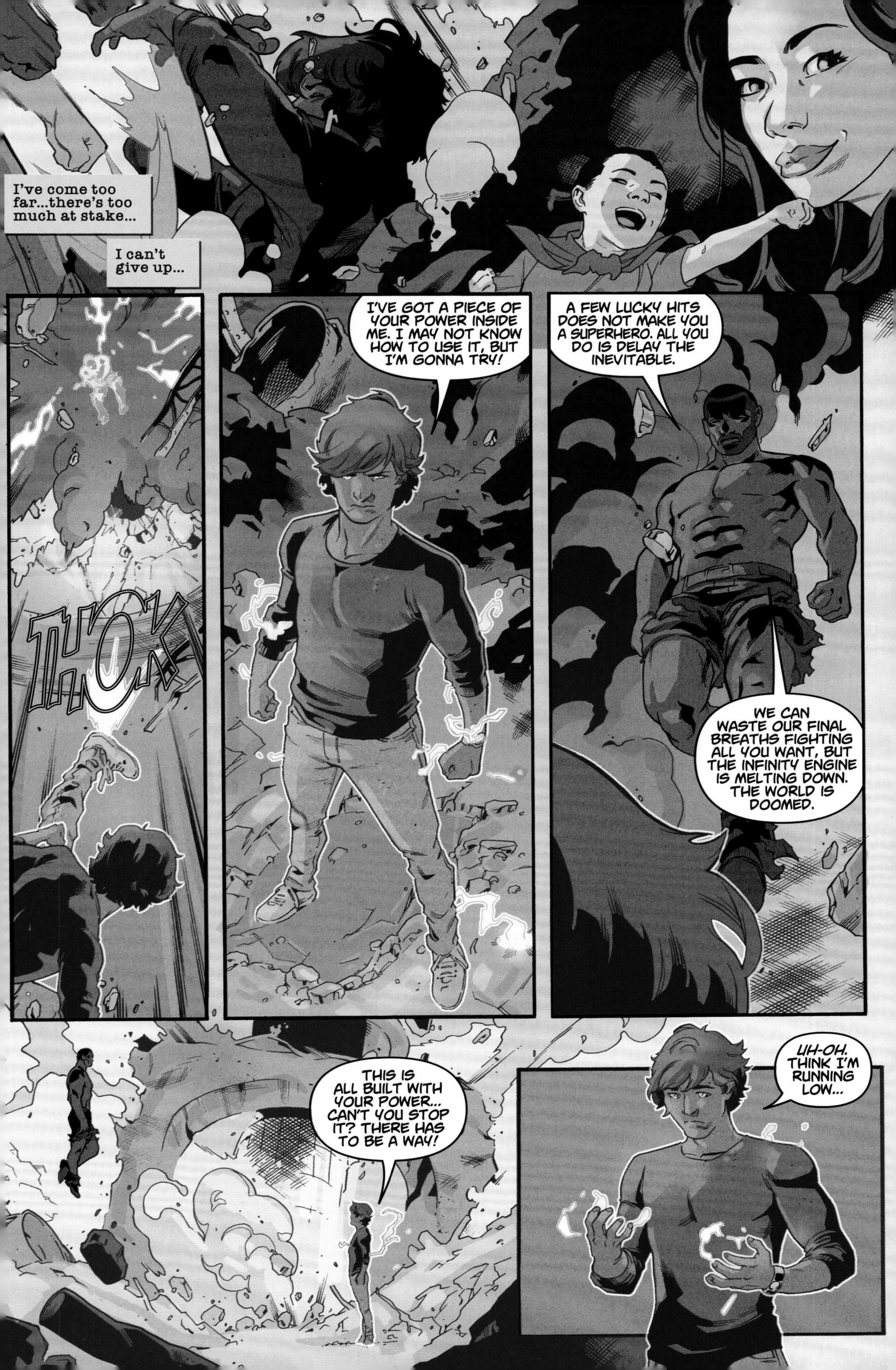
I've come too far...there's too much at stake...
I can't give up...
THOK
I'VE GOT A PIECE OF YOUR POWER INSIDE ME. I MAY NOT KNOW HOW TO USE IT, BUT I'M GONNA TRY!
A FEW LUCKY HITS DOES NOT MAKE YOU A SUPERHERO. ALL YOU DO IS DELAY THE INEVITABLE.
WE CAN WASTE OUR FINAL BREATHS FIGHTING ALL YOU WANT, BUT THE INFINITY ENGINE IS MELTING DOWN. THE WORLD IS DOOMED.
THIS IS ALL BUILT WITH YOUR POWER... CAN'T YOU STOP IT? THERE HAS TO BE A WAY!
UH-OH. THINK I'M RUNNING LOW...

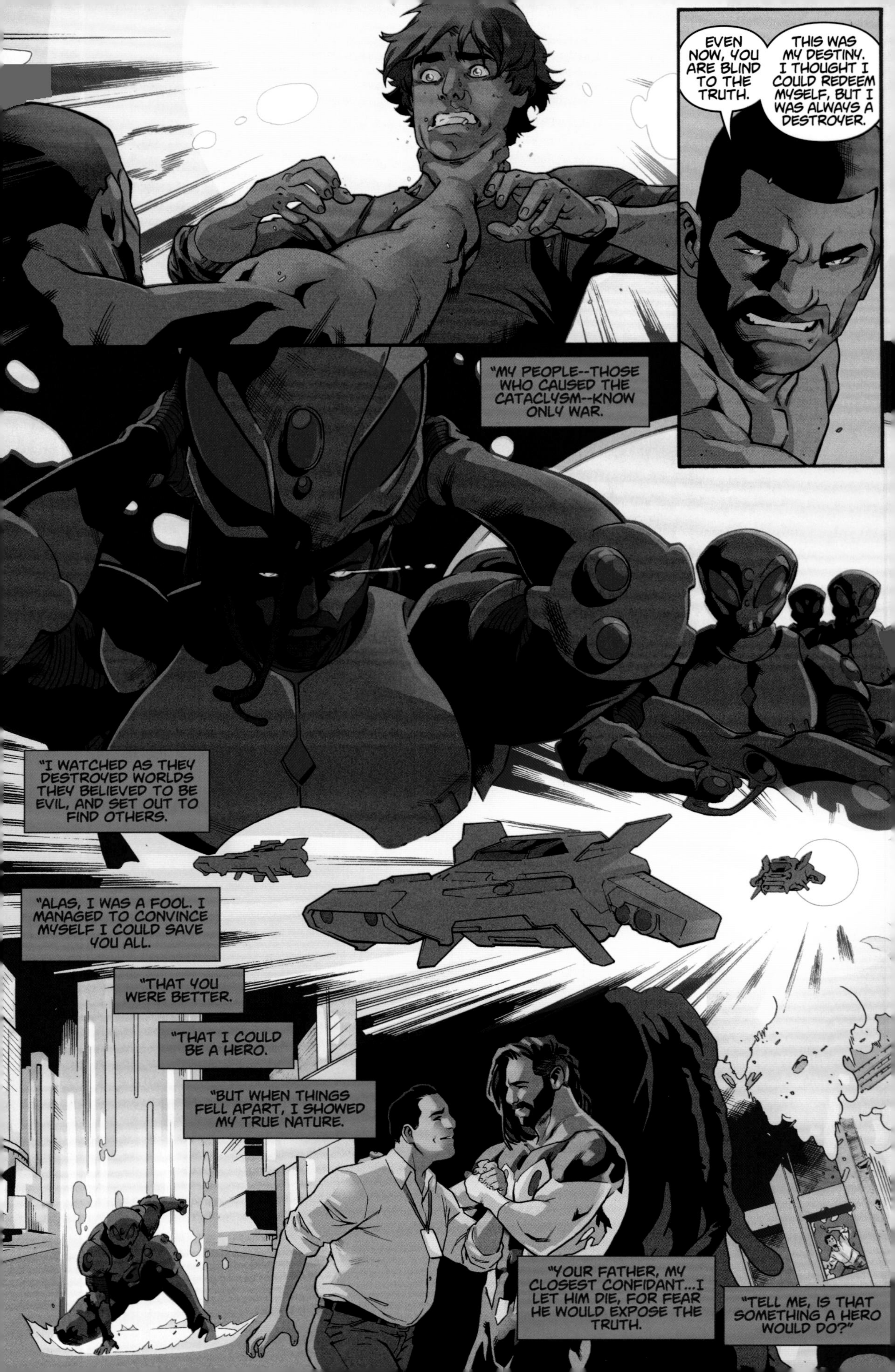

EVEN NOW, YOU ARE BLIND TO THE TRUTH.
THIS WAS MY DESTINY. I THOUGHT I COULD REDEEM MYSELF, BUT I WAS ALWAYS A DESTROYER.
"MY PEOPLE--THOSE WHO CAUSED THE CATACLYSM--KNOW ONLY WAR.
"I WATCHED AS THEY DESTROYED WORLDS THEY BELIEVED TO BE EVIL, AND SET OUT TO FIND OTHERS.
"ALAS, I WAS A FOOL. I MANAGED TO CONVINCE MYSELF I COULD SAVE YOU ALL.
"THAT YOU WERE BETTER.
"THAT I COULD BE A HERO.
"BUT WHEN THINGS FELL APART, I SHOWED MY TRUE NATURE.
"YOUR FATHER, MY CLOSEST CONFIDANT...I LET HIM DIE, FOR FEAR HE WOULD EXPOSE THE TRUTH.
"TELL ME, IS THAT SOMETHING A HERO WOULD DO?"

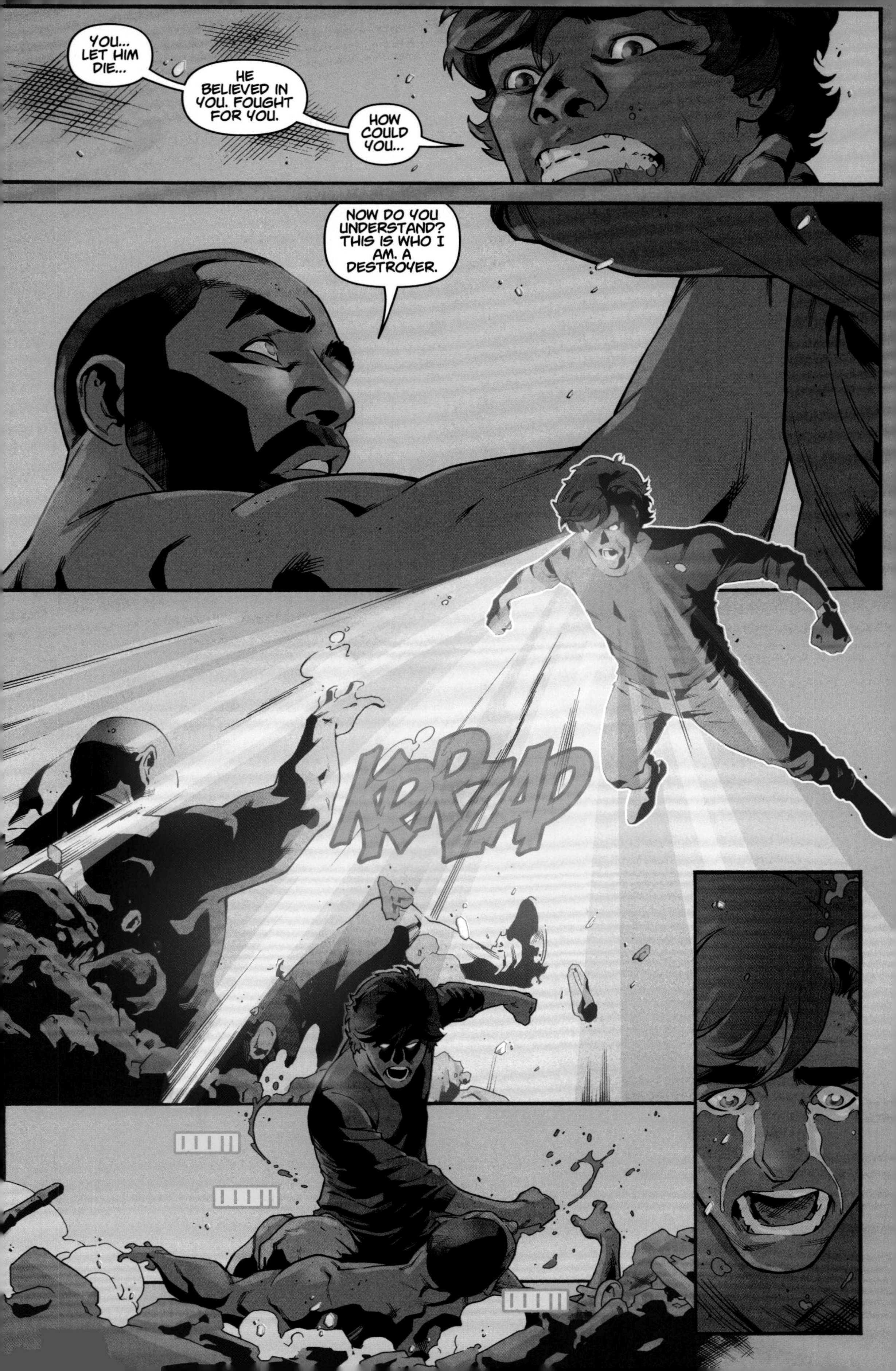
YOU... LET HIM DIE...
HE BELIEVED IN YOU. FOUGHT FOR YOU.
HOW COULD YOU...
NOW DO YOU UNDERSTAND? THIS IS WHO I AM. A DESTROYER.
KRRZAP

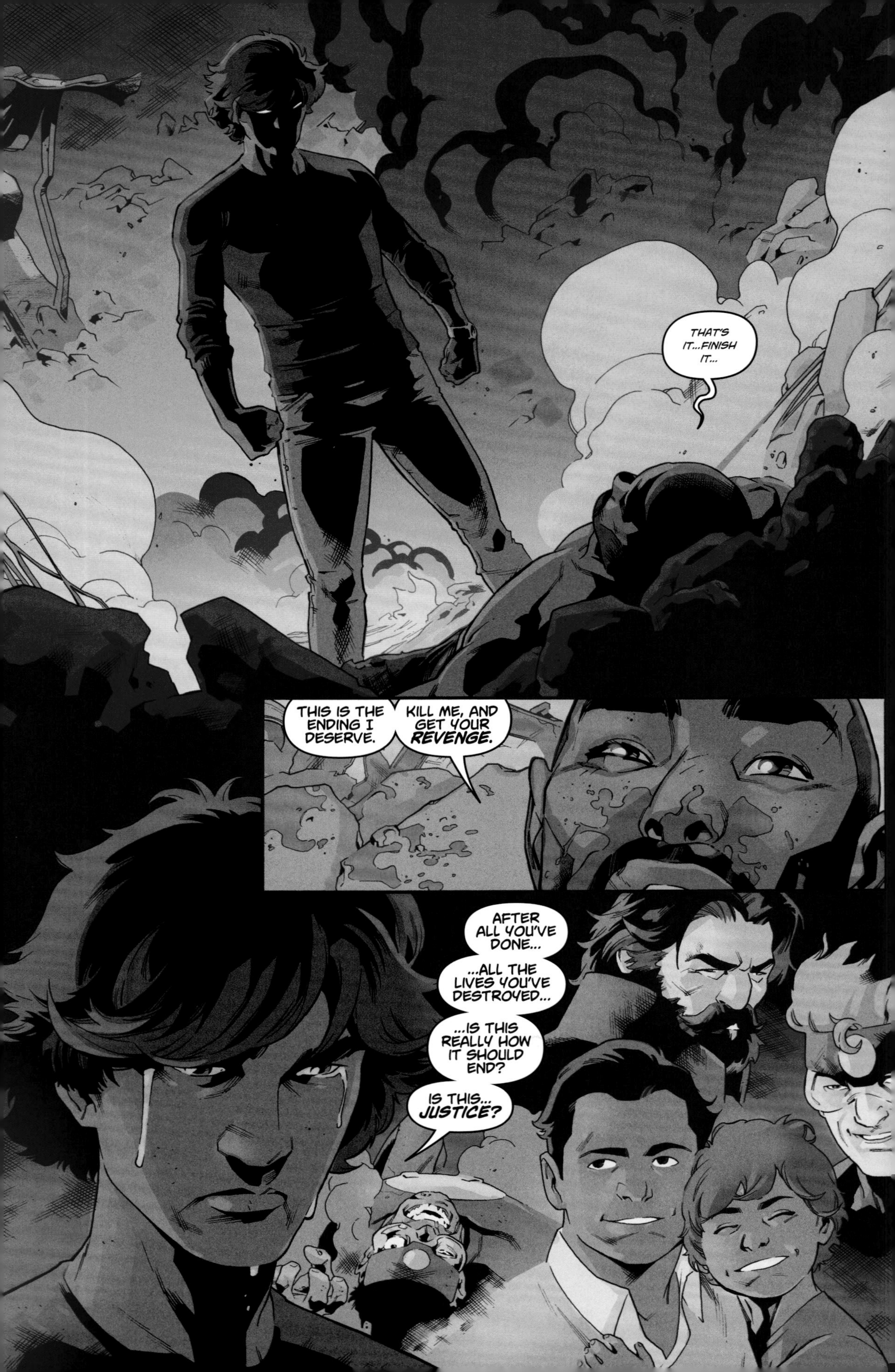
THAT'S IT...FINISH IT...
THIS IS THE ENDING I DESERVE.
KILL ME, AND GET YOUR REVENGE.
AFTER ALL YOU'VE DONE...
...ALL THE LIVES YOU'VE DESTROYED...
...IS THIS REALLY HOW IT SHOULD END?
IS THIS... JUSTICE?

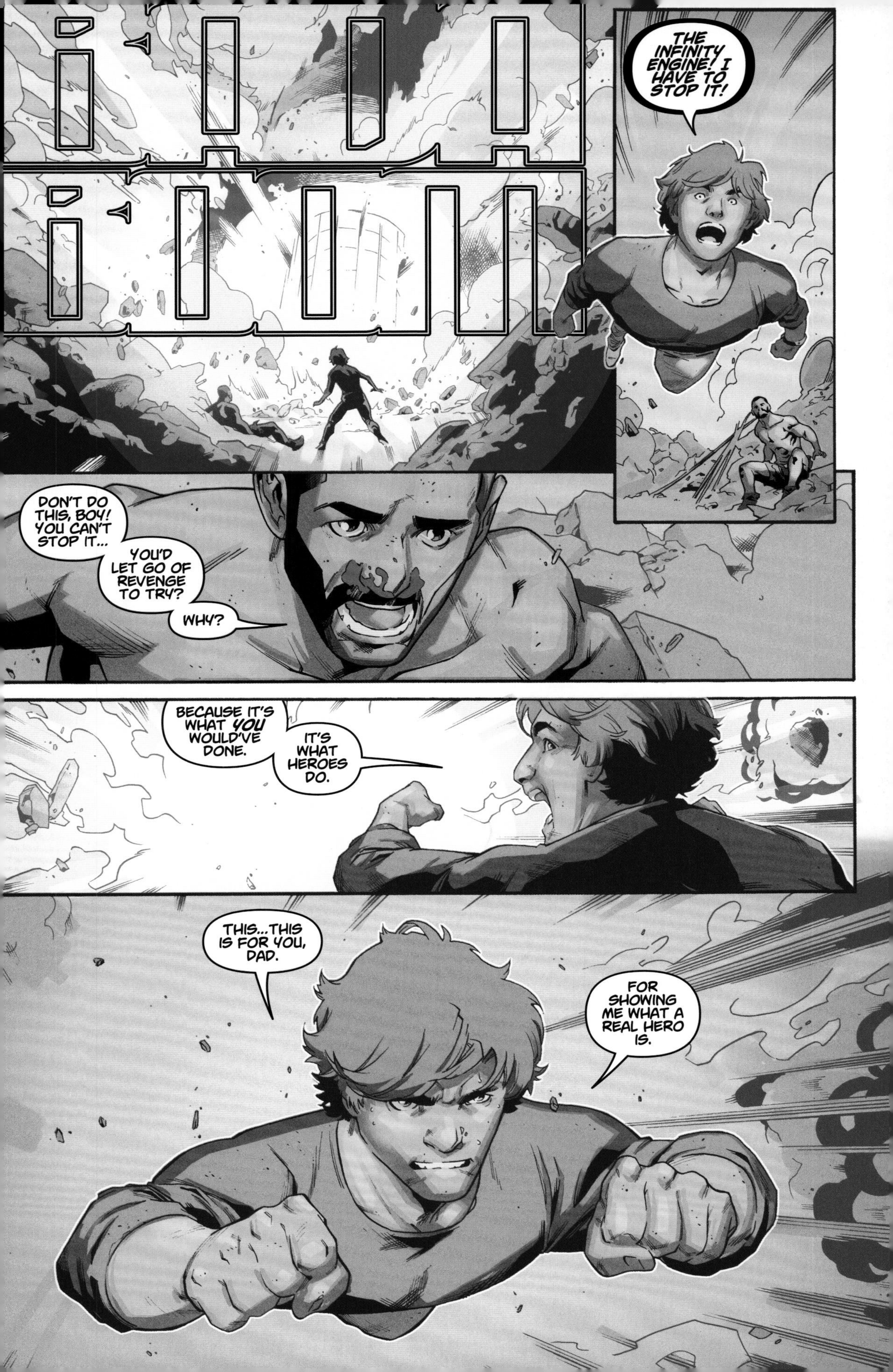
THE INFINITY ENGINE! I HAVE TO STOP IT!
DON'T DO THIS, BOY! YOU CAN'T STOP IT...
YOU'D LET GO OF REVENGE TO TRY?
WHY?
BECAUSE IT'S WHAT *YOU* WOULD'VE DONE.
IT'S WHAT HEROES DO.
THIS...THIS IS FOR YOU, DAD.
FOR SHOWING ME WHAT A REAL HERO IS.

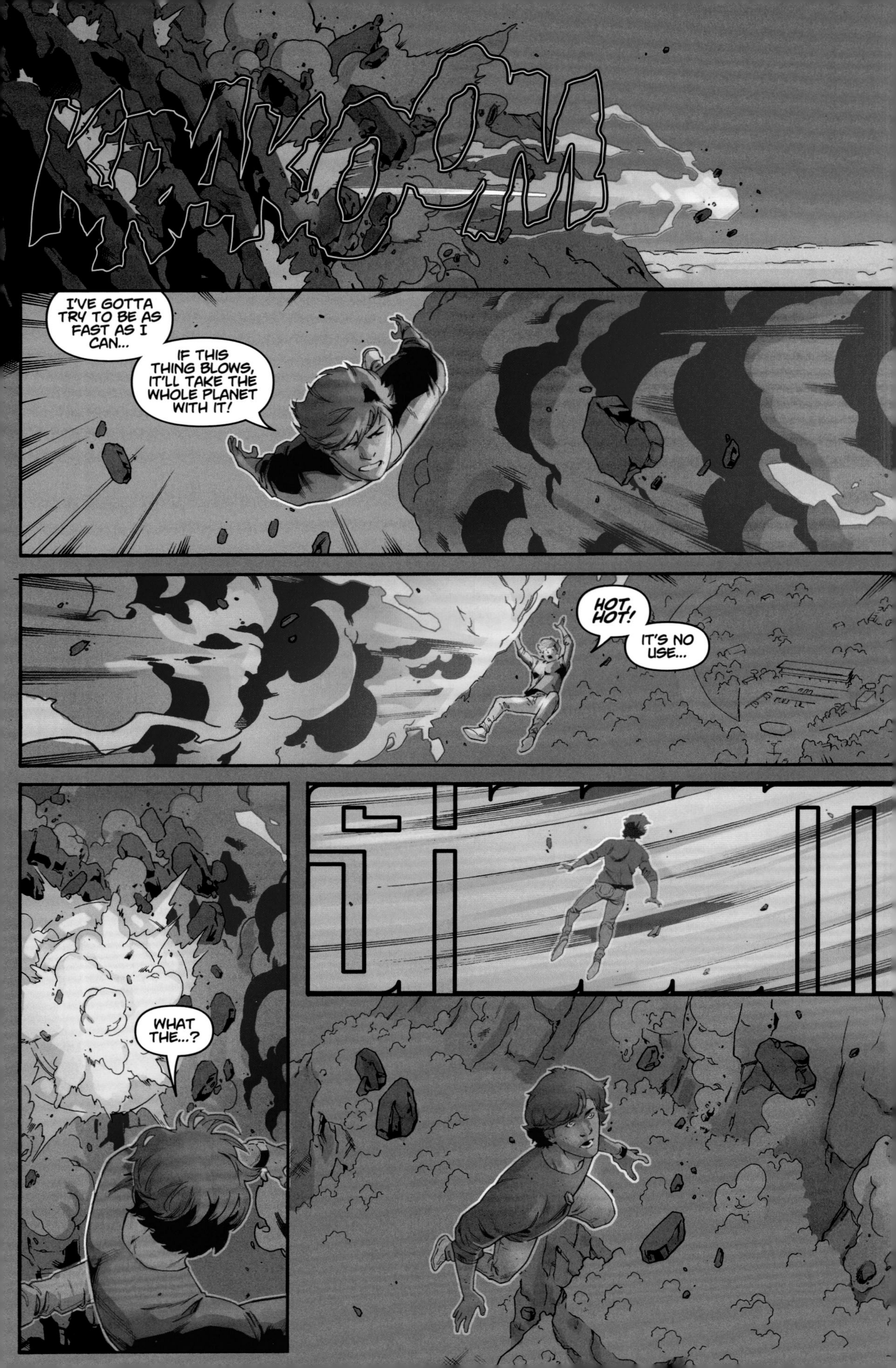
I'VE GOTTA TRY TO BE AS FAST AS I CAN...
IF THIS THING BLOWS, IT'LL TAKE THE WHOLE PLANET WITH IT!
HOT, HOT!
IT'S NO USE...
WHAT THE...?

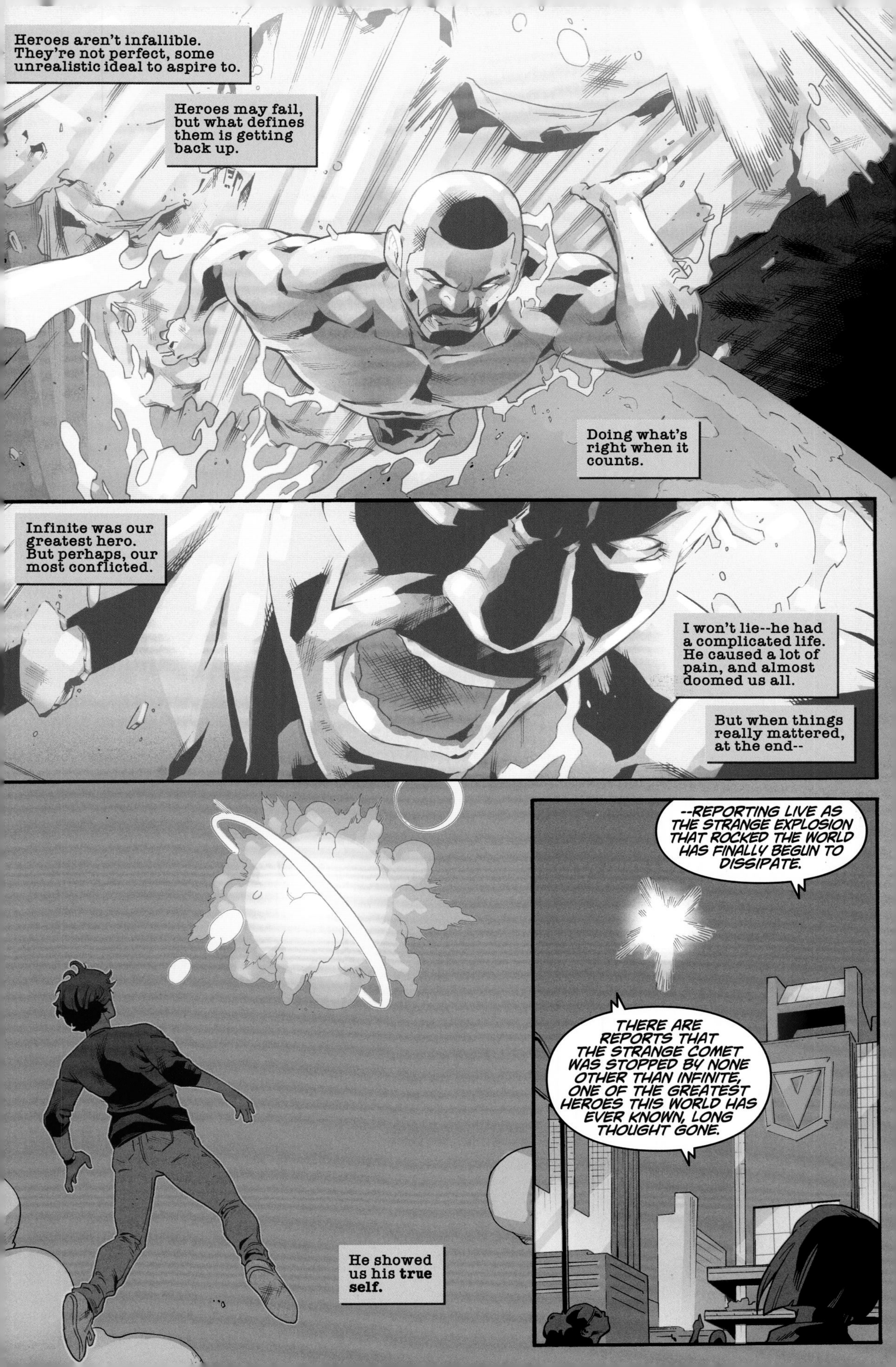

Heroes aren't infallible. They're not perfect, some unrealistic ideal to aspire to.
Heroes may fail, but what defines them is getting back up.
Doing what's right when it counts.
Infinite was our greatest hero. But perhaps, our most conflicted.
I won't lie--he had a complicated life. He caused a lot of pain, and almost doomed us all.
But when things really mattered, at the end--
He showed us his **true self.**
--REPORTING LIVE AS THE STRANGE EXPLOSION THAT ROCKED THE WORLD HAS FINALLY BEGUN TO DISSIPATE.
THERE ARE REPORTS THAT THE STRANGE COMET WAS STOPPED BY NONE OTHER THAN INFINITE, ONE OF THE GREATEST HEROES THIS WORLD HAS EVER KNOWN, LONG THOUGHT GONE.

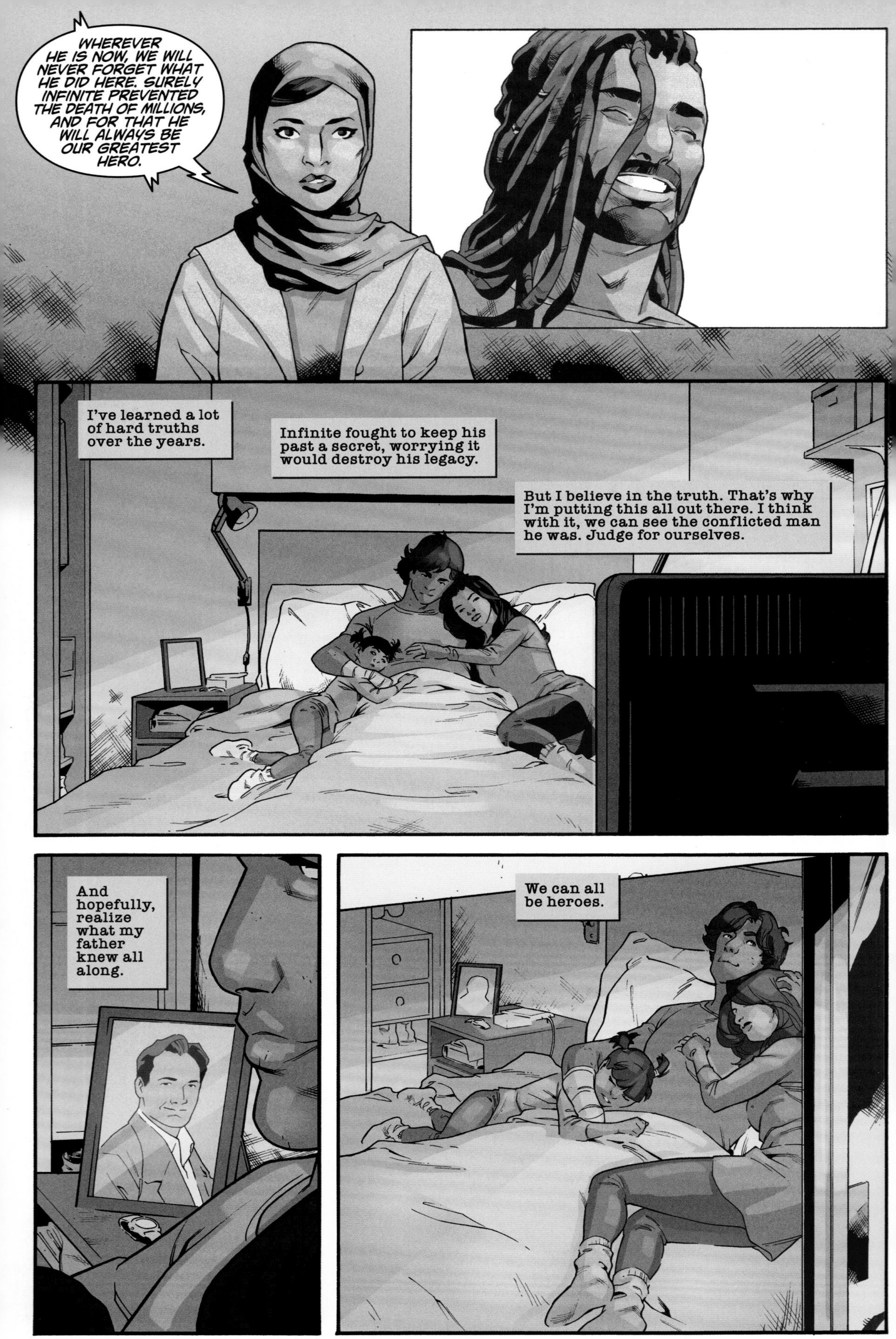

WHEREVER HE IS NOW, WE WILL NEVER FORGET WHAT HE DID HERE. SURELY INFINITE PREVENTED THE DEATH OF MILLIONS, AND FOR THAT HE WILL ALWAYS BE OUR GREATEST HERO.
I've learned a lot of hard truths over the years.
Infinite fought to keep his past a secret, worrying it would destroy his legacy.
But I believe in the truth. That's why I'm putting this all out there. I think with it, we can see the conflicted man he was. Judge for ourselves.
And hopefully, realize what my father knew all along.
We can all be heroes.

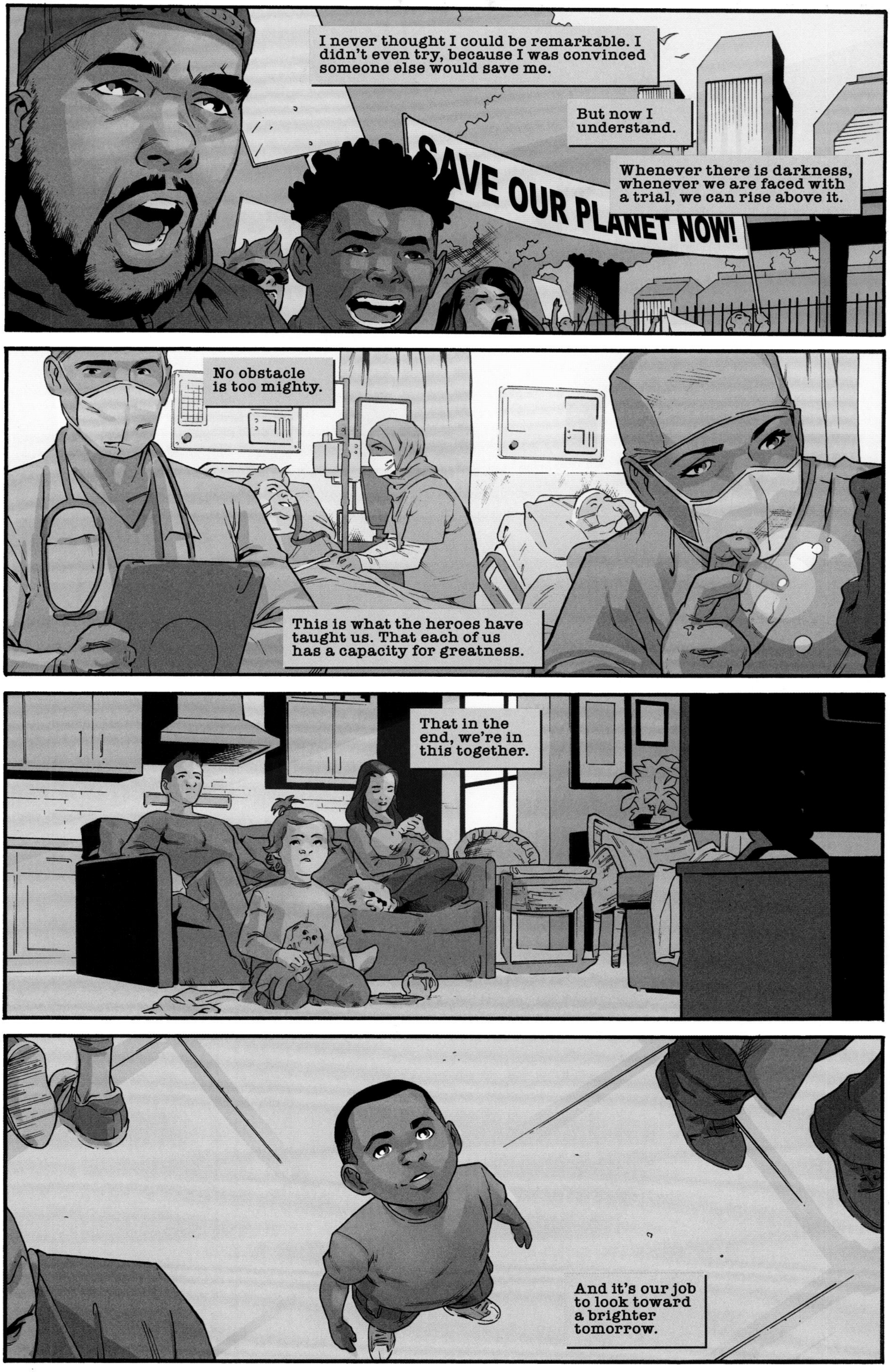
I never thought I could be remarkable. I didn't even try, because I was convinced someone else would save me.
But now I understand.
SAVE OUR PLANET NOW!
Whenever there is darkness, whenever we are faced with a trial, we can rise above it.
No obstacle is too mighty.
This is what the heroes have taught us. That each of us has a capacity for greatness.
That in the end, we're in this together.
And it's our job to look toward a brighter tomorrow.

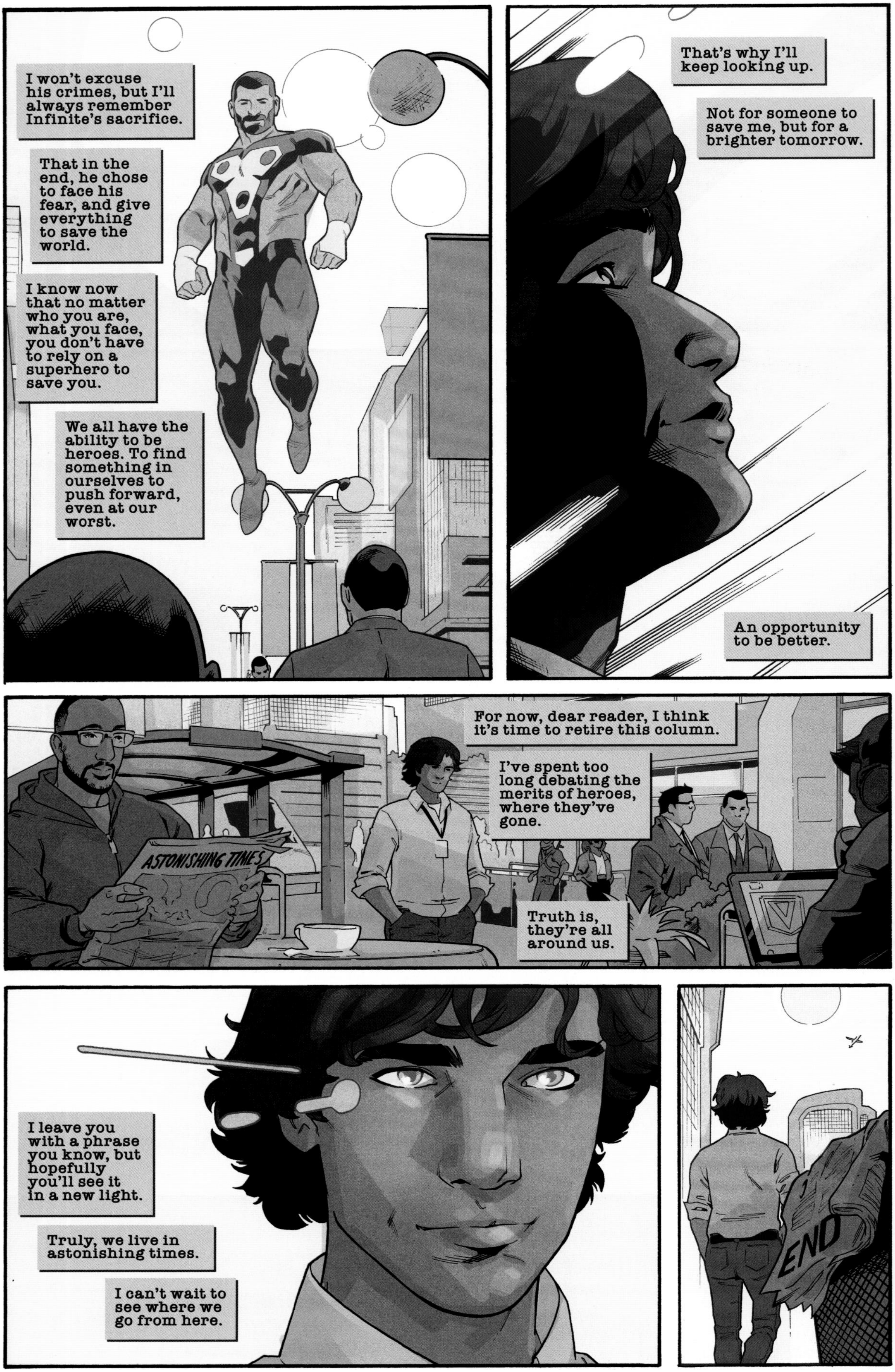
I won't excuse his crimes, but I'll always remember Infinite's sacrifice.
That in the end, he chose to face his fear, and give everything to save the world.
I know now that no matter who you are, what you face, you don't have to rely on a superhero to save you.
We all have the ability to be heroes. To find something in ourselves to push forward, even at our worst.
That's why I'll keep looking up.
Not for someone to save me, but for a brighter tomorrow.
An opportunity to be better.
ASTONISHING TIMES
For now, dear reader, I think it's time to retire this column.
I've spent too long debating the merits of heroes, where they've gone.
Truth is, they're all around us.
I leave you with a phrase you know, but hopefully you'll see it in a new light.
Truly, we live in astonishing times.
I can't wait to see where we go from here.
END

Astonishing Times #1 Cover Art by **RUAIRÍ COLEMAN** with **LAUREN AFFE**

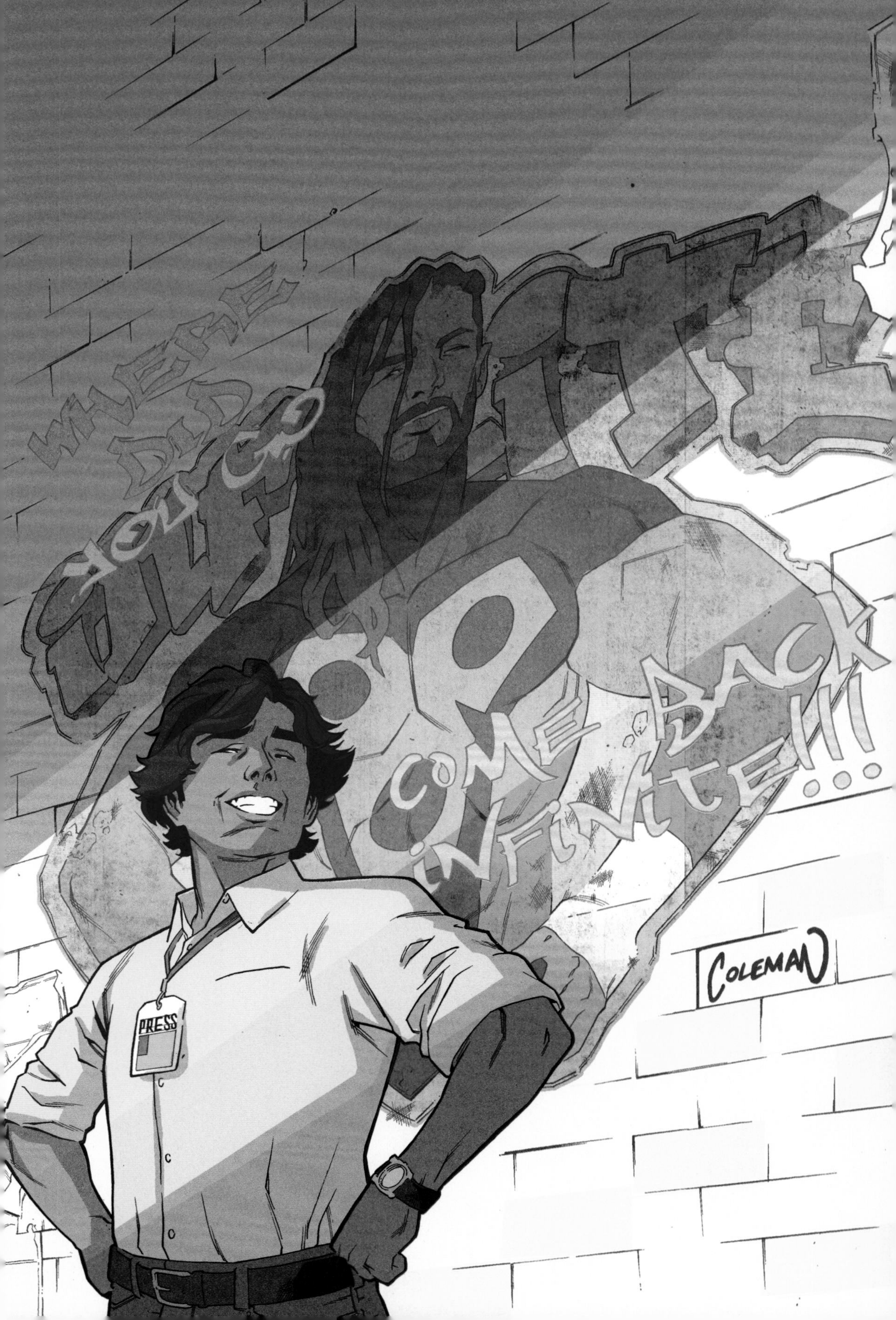
WHERE DID YOU GO
COME BACK INFINITE!!!...
PRESS
COLEMAN

Astonishing Times #2 Cover Art by **RUAIRÍ COLEMAN** with **LAUREN AFFE**

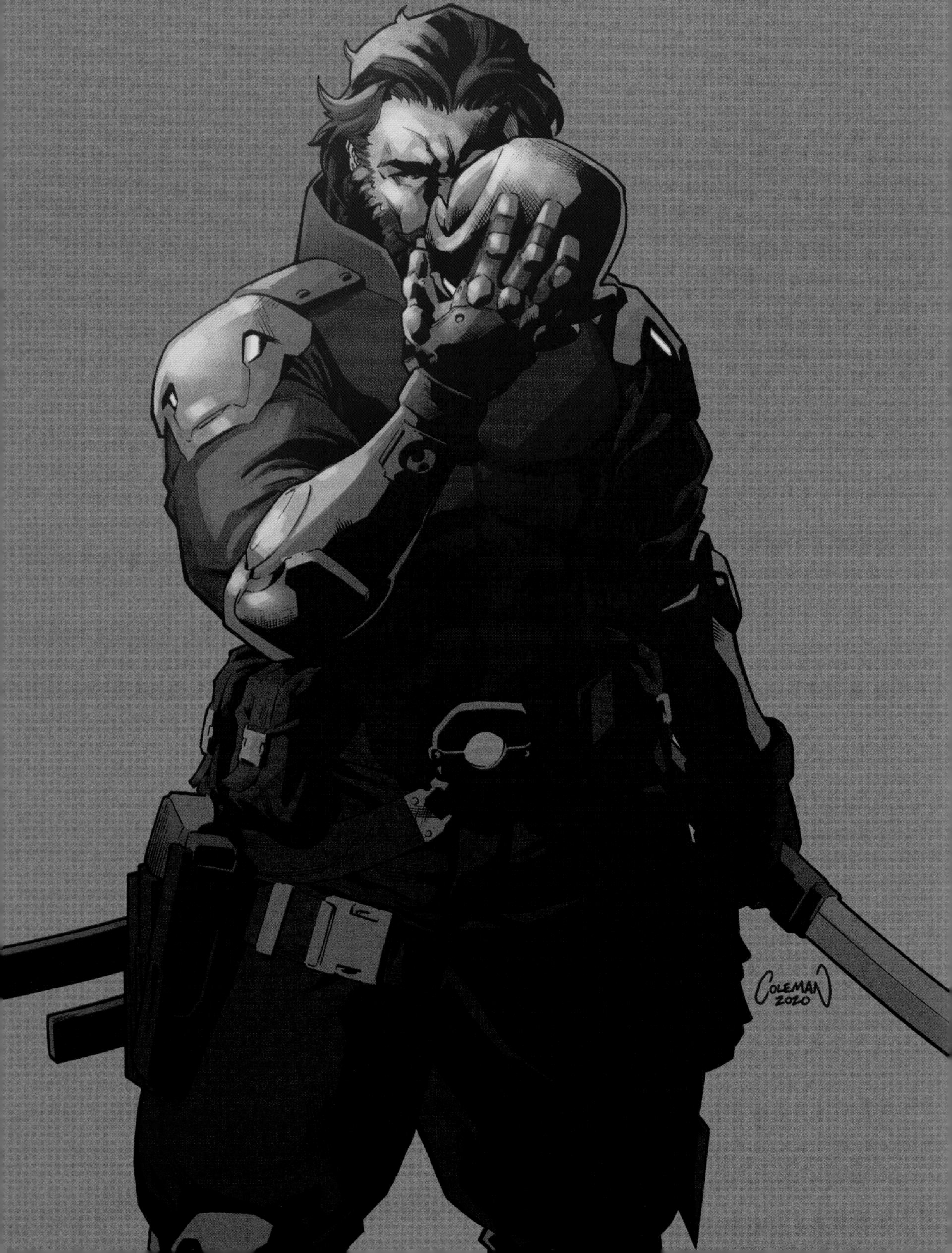

Astonishing Times #3 Cover Art by **RUAIRÍ COLEMAN** with **LAUREN AFFE**

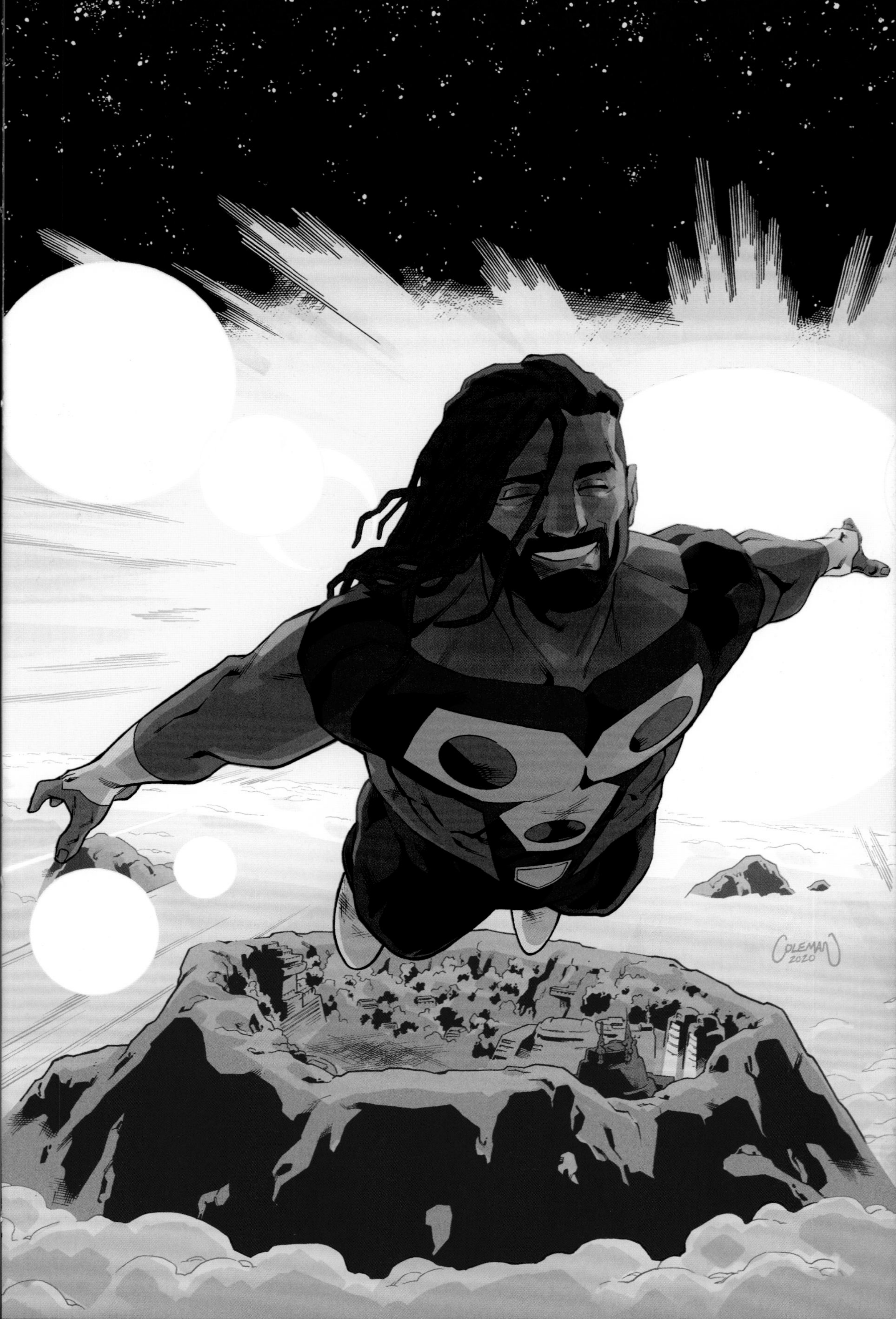
COLEMAN
2020

Astonishing Times #4 Cover Art by **RUAIRÍ COLEMAN** with **LAUREN AFFE**

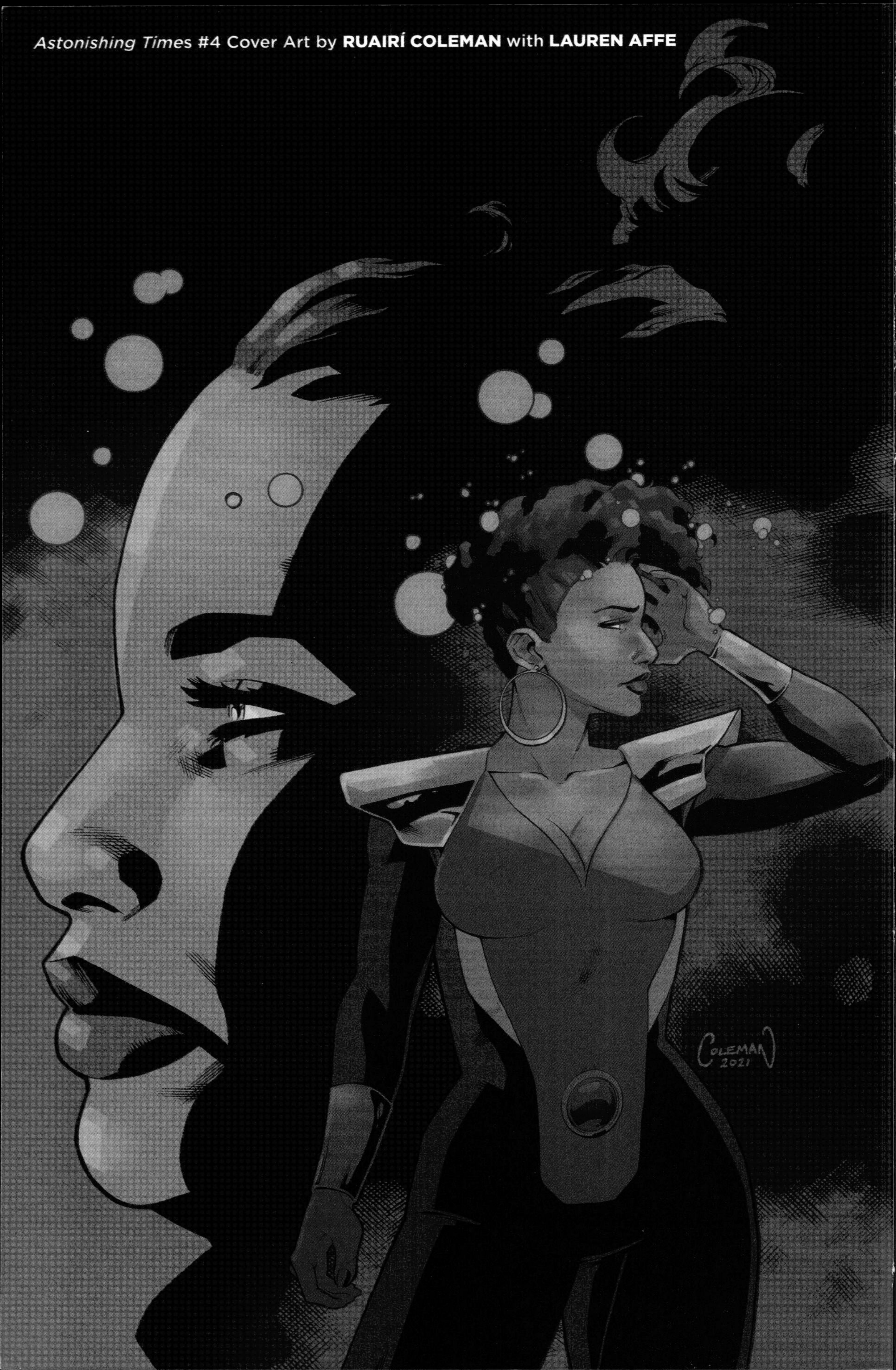
COLEMAN
2021

Astonishing Times #5 Cover Art by **RUAIRÍ COLEMAN** with **LAUREN AFFE**

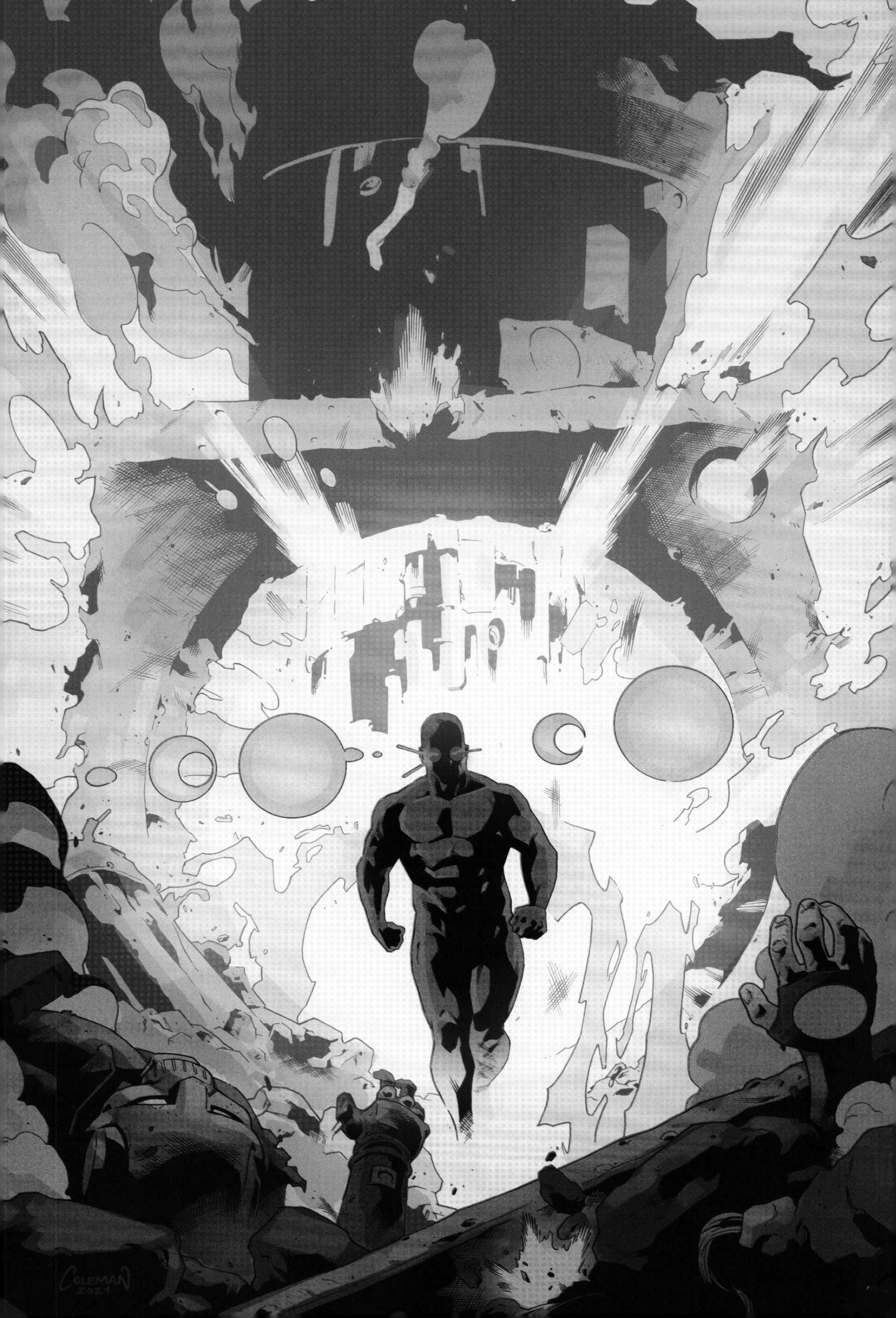
COLEMAN
2021

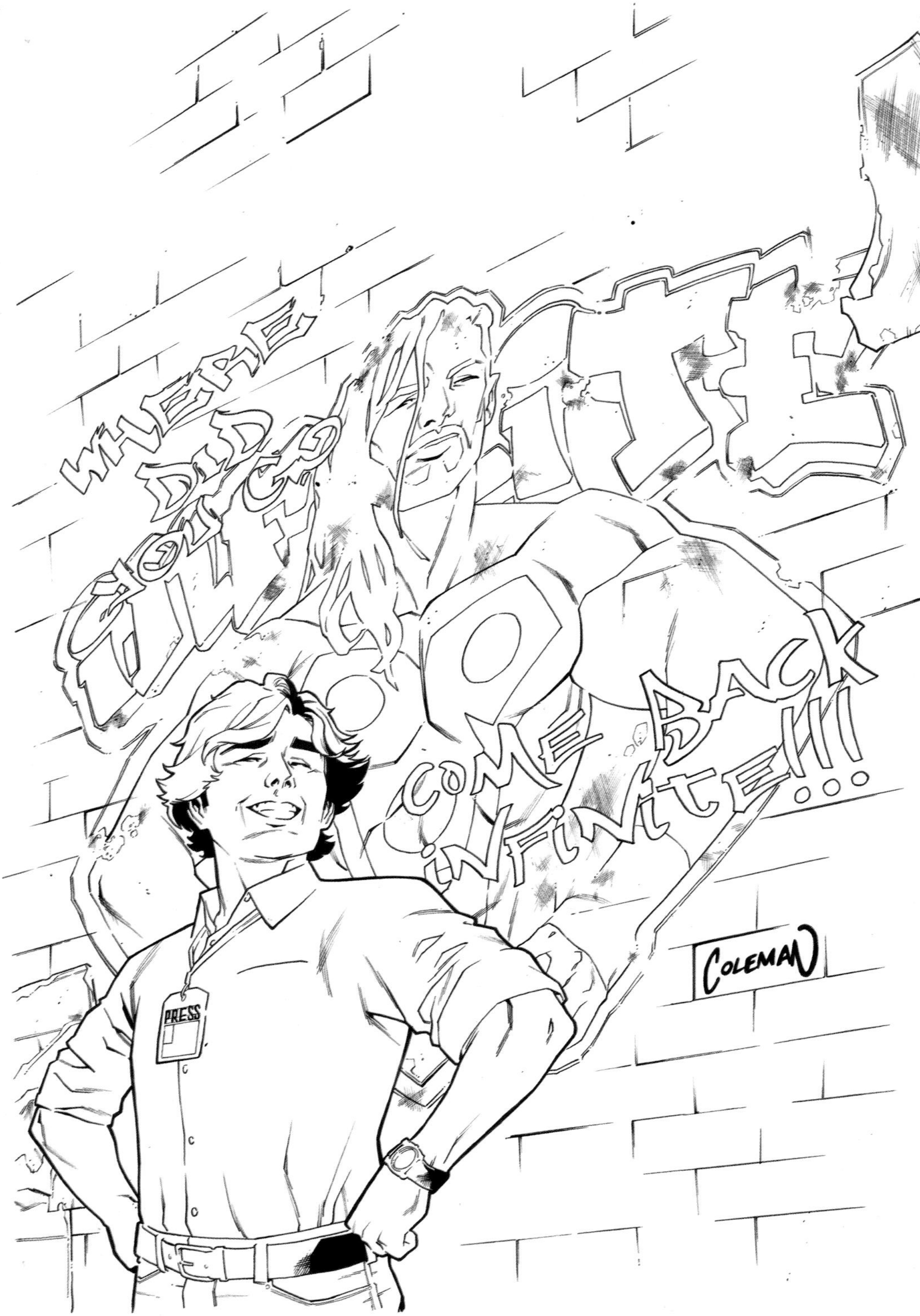
WHERE DID YOU GO
COME BACK INFINITE!!!
COLEMAN

ASTONISHING TIMES #1 COVER

COLEMAN

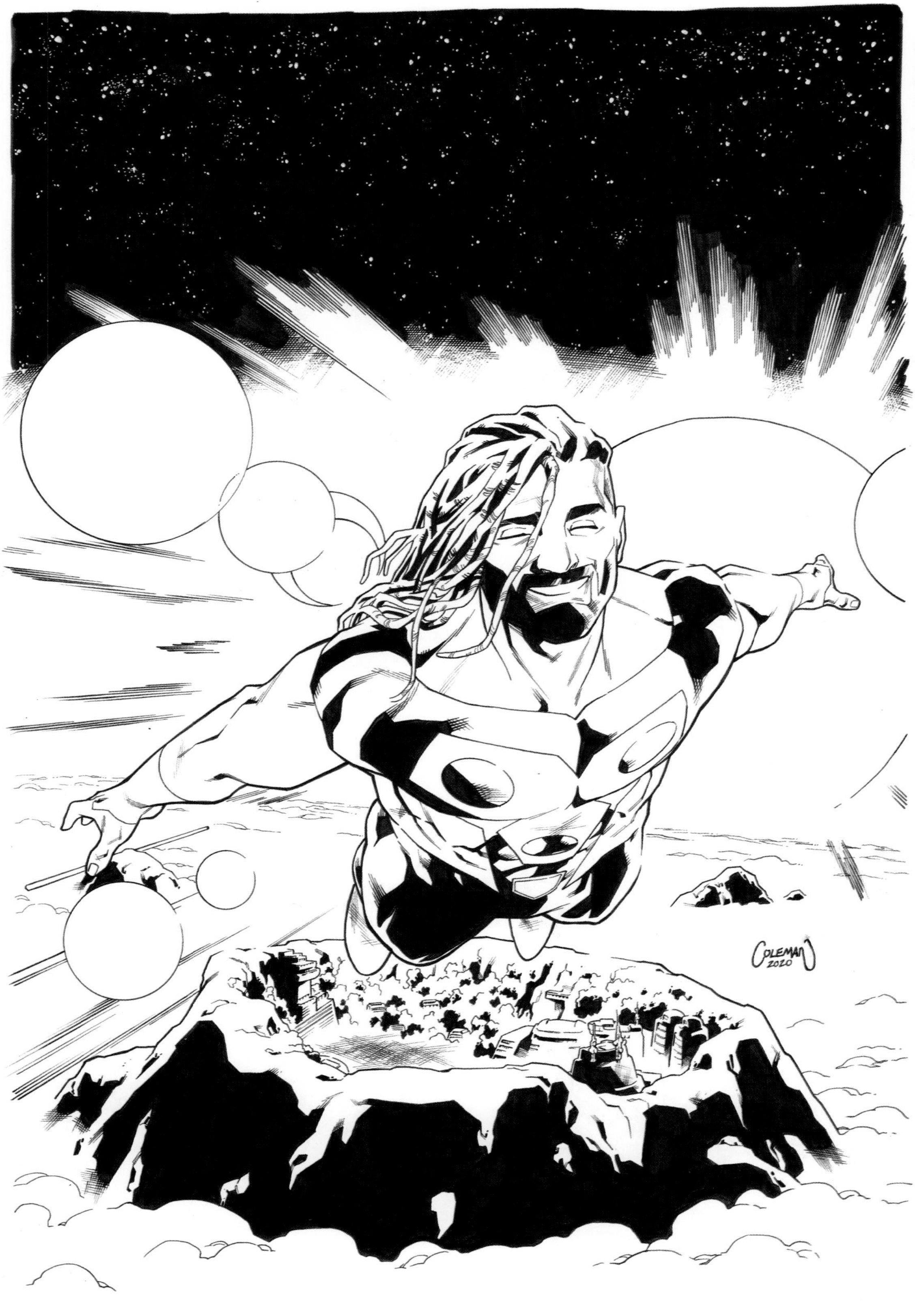
COLEMAN
2020

ASTONISHING TIMES #3 COVER COLEMAN

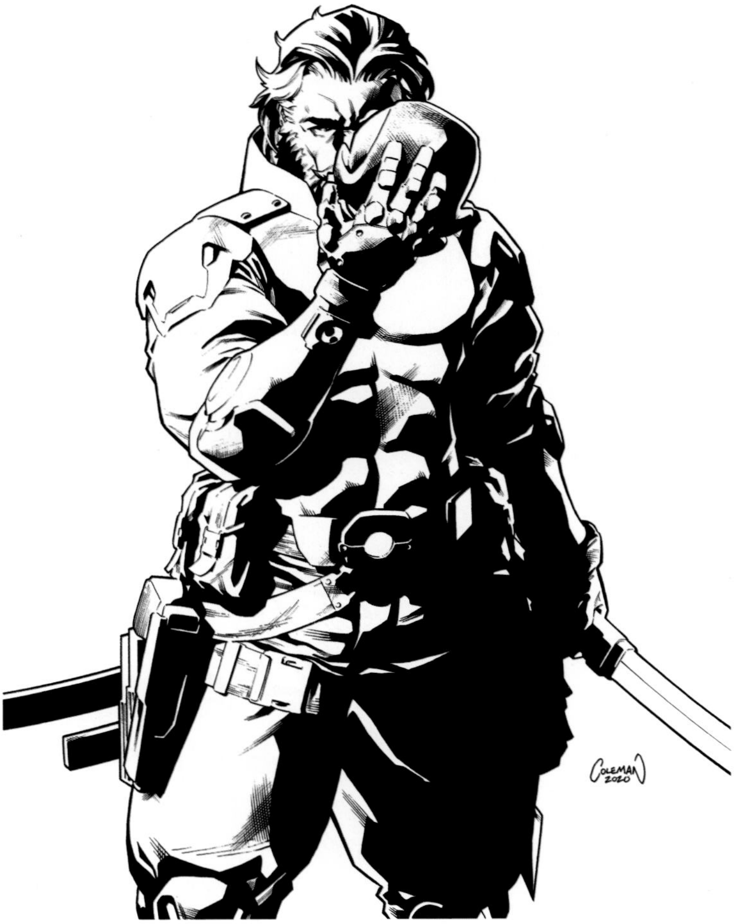
COLEMAN
2020

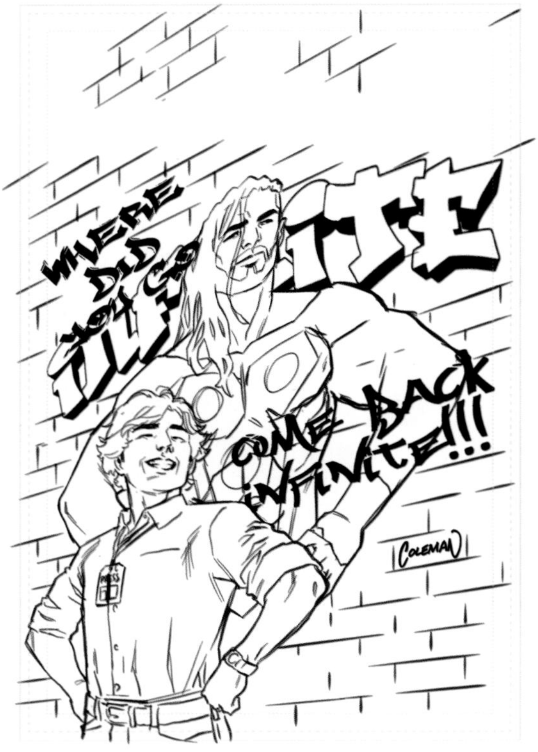
WHERE DID YOU GO
COME BACK INFINITE!!!
COLEMAN

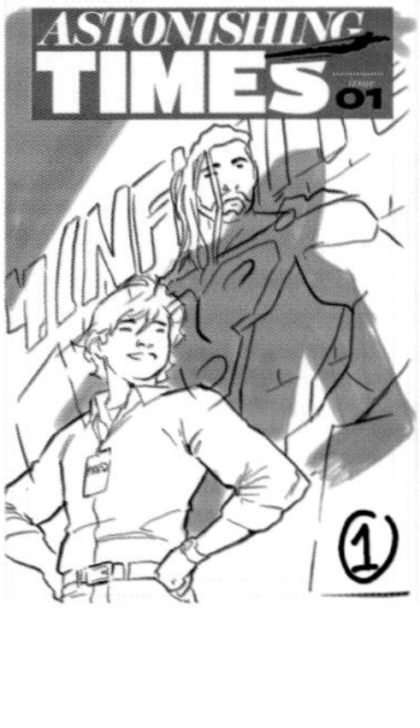
ASTONISHING
TIMES
01
1

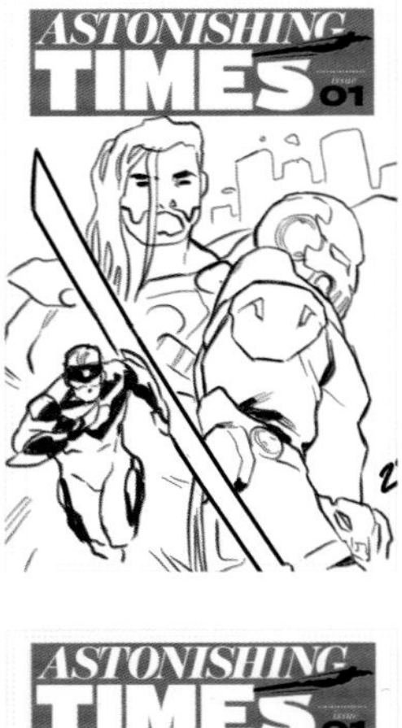
ASTONISHING
TIMES
01
2

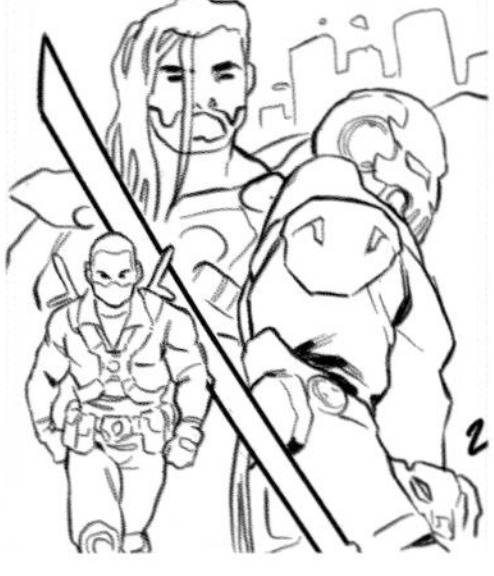
ASTONISHING
TIMES
01
2

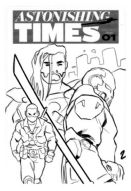

ASTONISHING TIMES #4 COVER U COLEMAN

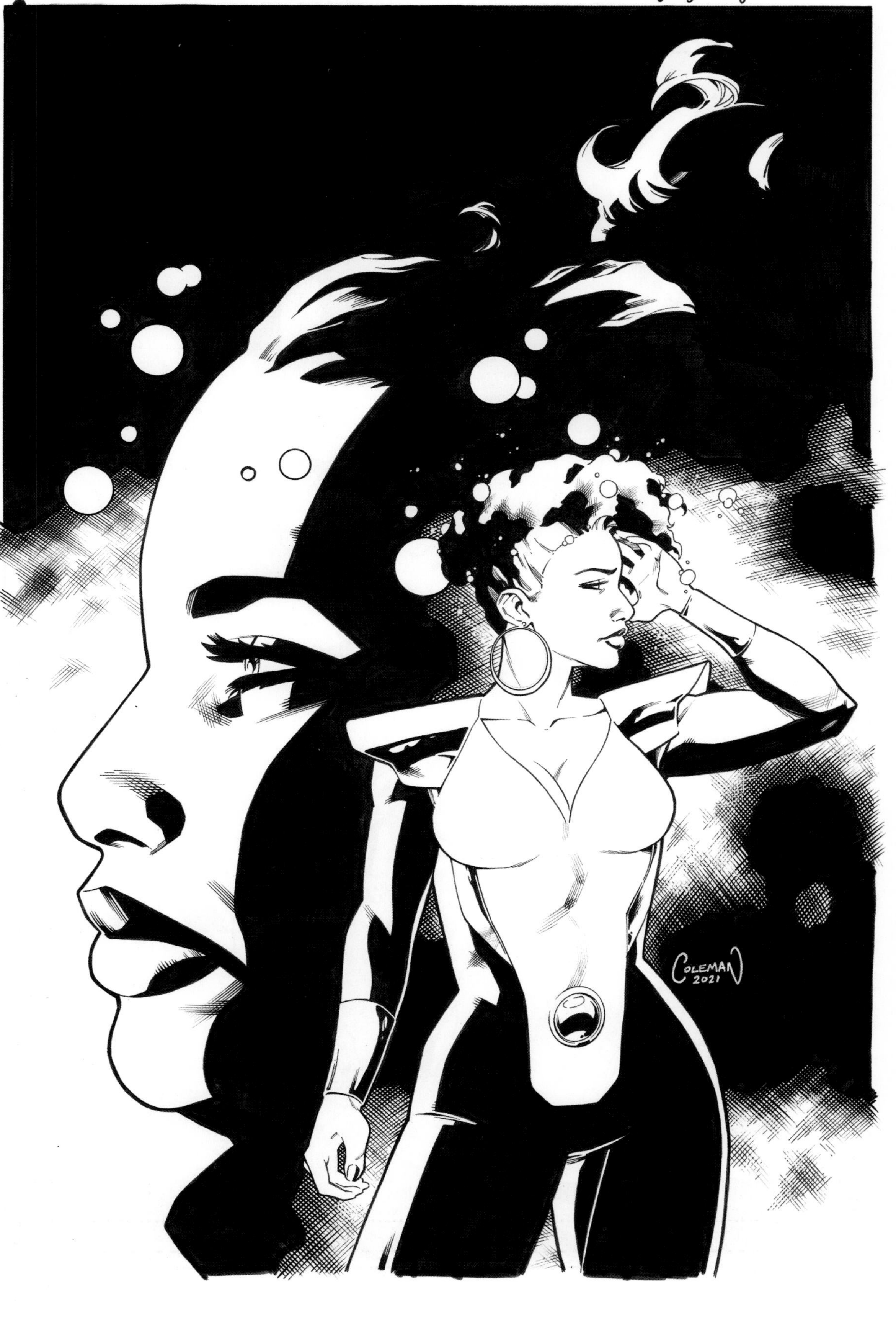
COLEMAN
2021

ASTONISHING TIMES #5 COVER COLEMAN

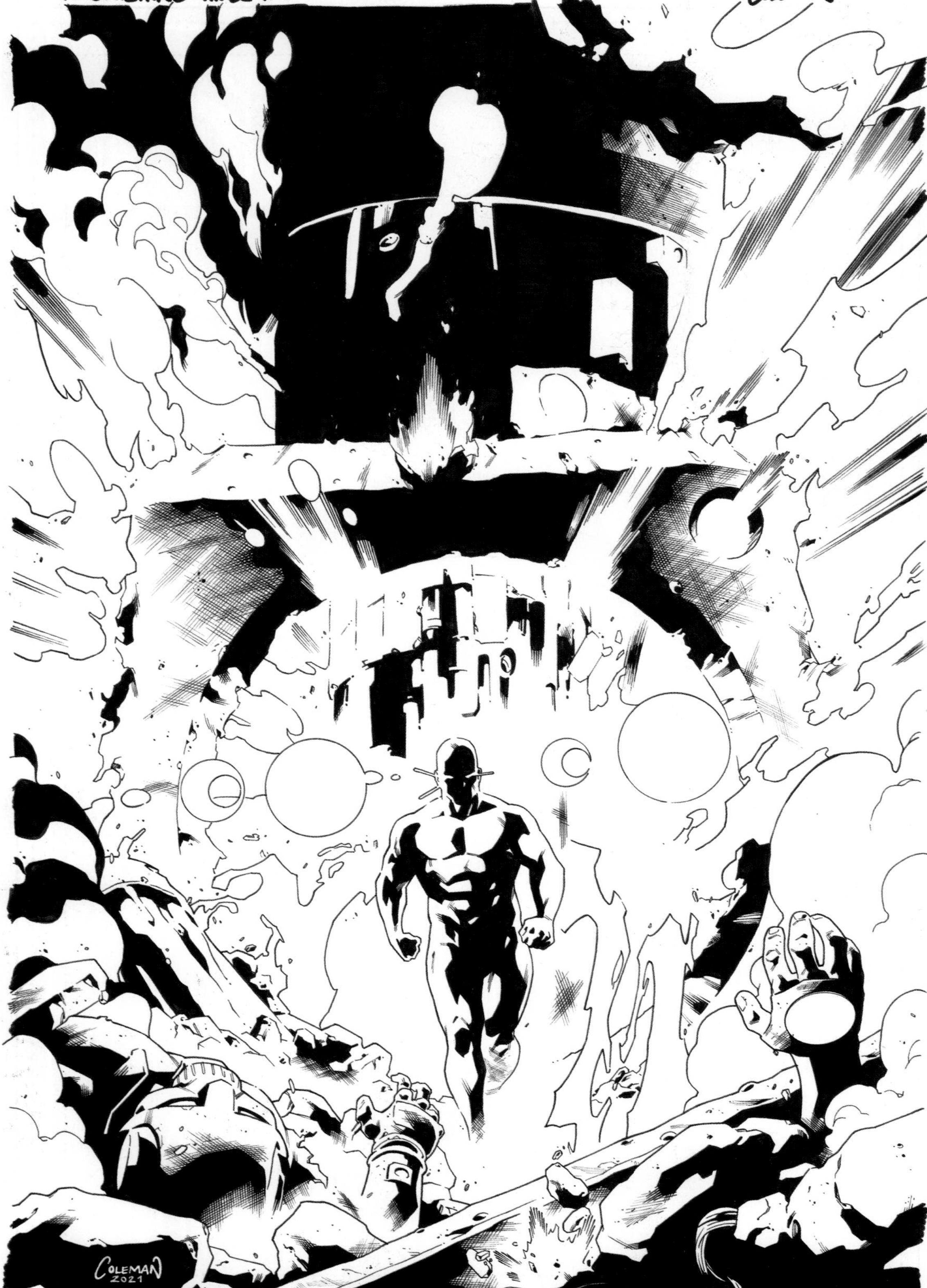
COLEMAN
2021